The Symbolisms in Buddhism

ALSO BY CHRISTINE H. HUYNH

Children's Picture Book Series
Bringing the Buddha's Teachings into Practice

My First Dharma Book

The Buddha in Me

The Great Ullambana Festival

The "I"s in Me

My Middle Path

Going on a Pilgrimage

Happy Birthday, Buddha!

The Four Noble Truths

The Symbolisms in Buddhism

As I Have Heard

Christine H. Huynh, M.D.
Illustrations by Katarina A. Lazic

Dharma Wisdom, LLC

The Symbolisms in Buddhism
Copyright © 2019 by Dharma Wisdom, LLC

All rights reserved.
Published in the United States of America by Dharma Wisdom, LLC. No part of this book may be reproduced or transmitted in any form or by any means, electronic or mechanical, including photocopying, recording, or by any information storage and retrieval system without the prior written permission of the author, except for the inclusion of brief quotations in critical reviews and certain other noncommercial uses permitted by copyright law. For permission requests or information, please contact the publisher.

Dharma Wisdom, LLC
Arlington, Texas
DharmaWisdomDW@gmail.com

Edited by Grace S. Pham, Rachel S. Storm, and Jonathan M. Wong

Illustrations by Katarina A. Lazic

Library of Congress Control Number: 2019912943

ISBN 978-1-951175-01-6

First Edition 2019

For my son Jonathan, a "gift from God," to further his understanding of Buddhism

For my family and friends, to share what I have learned in Buddhism

For everyone, to enjoy a translation of the innumerable sermons from the Venerable Thích Pháp Hòa on Buddhism

Contents

List of Illustrations		ix
Preface		xiii
Introduction		1
1	The Three Jewels	5
2	The Vesak Celebration	19
3	The Dharma Wheel	43
4	The Middle Way	57
5	Cause and Condition	61
6	Cause and Effect	67
7	Bodhisattvas and Buddhas	77
8	The Altar	85
9	The Ambience at the Temple	115
10	No Mud, No Lotus	123
11	Robes and Prayer Beads	129
12	The Five Aggregates	135

13	Planting the Positive Seeds	141
14	Impermanence	145
15	Crossing Over to the Other Shore	149
16	Pairs of Words and Opposites	155
17	Wisdom versus Knowledge	161
18	The Five Vehicles	169
19	The Practice	185
20	Significance of the Numbers	263
	The number 1	263
	The number 2	264
	The number 3	266
	The number 4	275
	The number 5	289
	The number 6	299
	The number 7	303
	The number 8	306
Conclusion		309
References		311
About the Author		351
About the Illustrator		353

Illustrations
by Katarina A. Lazic

1	The Three Jewels (The Triple Gems)	6
2	Queen Maya's dream	21
3	The udumbara flower	22
4	Birth in Lumbini Garden	23
5	The 7 steps at birth	26
6	Bathing of the baby Buddha	28
7	Enlightenment	30
8	The First Sermon	33
9	Nirvana	37
10	The important dates of the Buddha's life	40
11	The four pilgrimage sites	41
12	The 12 spoked Dharma Wheel set in motion	44
13	The 8 spoked Dharma Wheel	50

14	The three violins	59
15	Vaidurya, the Medicine Buddha	80
16	Maitreya, the Happy Buddha	82
17	The Kshitigarbha Bodhisattva, the Buddha, and the Avalokiteshvara Bodhisattva	86
18	The Samantabhadra Bodhisattva, the Buddha, and the Manjushri Bodhisattva	86
19	The Great Mahasthamaprapta Bodhisattva, the Amitabha Buddha, and the Great Avalokiteshvara Bodhisattva	87
20	The Buddha	89
21	The Buddha's swastika and the Nazi's emblem	90
22	The four mudras (hand seals): meditation, touching the earth, emotional support, and teaching transmission	92
23	The Thousand-hand Avalokiteshvara	94
24	The three faces of Avalokiteshvara	95
25	The Great Avalokiteshvara Bodhisattva	96
26	The Avalokiteshvara Bodhisattva	97
27	The Kshitigarbha Bodhisattva	99
28	The Manjushri Bodhisattva	101
29	The Samantabhadra Bodhisattva	103
30	The Great Mahasthamaprapta Bodhisattva	104
31	The Amitabha Buddha	106
32	The altar	109
33	The sequences in the prostration ritual	113
34	The drum meditation instrument	117
35	The ambience at the temple: the curved roof, lion statues, wavering flags, and lotus pond	118

36	Symbolic objects at the temple: the drum, bell, elephant, and flag	120
37	The eight lotus petals	125
38	The Kasaya robe and rice paddy of Magadha	130
39	The practitioner's farmland	143
40	The Prajna Paramita Mantra	151
41	Crossing over to the other shore	154
42	The one shoe Bodhidharma	159
43	The four stages of life	182
44	The five objects of reverence: the Buddha statue and Kasaya robe, Bodhi tree, lotus flower, stupa, and Dharma Wheel	187
45	The kerosene lamp's analogy to the illumination of the mind	212
46	The four postures: the bell, peacock, pine tree, and archery bow	215
47	The three poisons	220
48	The mudra of the three mountains	232

Preface

The Symbolisms in Buddhism is based on the teachings of the Venerable Thích Pháp Hòa, transcribed from his numerous sermons on YouTube that are delivered in Vietnamese. What started out as a mother's gift for her son, organizing and summarizing the notes of this teacher's sermons into a few hours of reading, transformed into an enthusiasm to share this writing with others. The philosophies taught by the Buddha are deep and require our diligence to study in order to understand. The purpose of this book is to delve into the heart of the Buddha's teachings, discuss the many symbolisms associated with his philosophies, and demonstrate how they can be applied to our everyday practice. The writing style of this book was intended to mirror the structure of the original lectures in terms of how the information is conveyed, with detailed definitions and consistent use of a numbering system to facilitate learning. There is an inundated amount of information condensed in each chapter, which can be difficult to absorb, so it is recommended to reread each chapter so the philosophies can be thoroughly understood. Every effort was made to scrupulously recount each one hour to one and a half hour sermon into an English translation to accurately reflect each sermon's message and meaning. I extend much gratitude and appreciation to many of the teacher's followers and supporters who have spent countless hours videotaping, editing, and uploading his myriad of talks onto YouTube, as this book would not be made possible without their access.

This book is organized into chapters covering the key topics that comprise the core philosophy of Buddhism. The first two chapters go into great depth to define who the Buddha is and the significance of the events in his life. It is important to understand the life history of a teacher who revealed the philosophies of truth, which have become well-known as the practice of Buddhism. The Three Jewels are introduced as the Buddha, the Dharma, and the Sangha; they are the three foundations of faith that a practitioner takes refuge in. The Vesak Celebration describes the three important events of the Buddha's life consisting of his birth, Enlightenment, and Nirvana. The terminologies of "Enlightenment" and "Nirvana" are defined in detail as they will be applied in the practice outlined in subsequent chapters. The next few chapters discuss the main doctrines of study in Buddhism, which are the Four Noble Truths, the Noble Eightfold Path, the Thirty-Seven Paths to Enlightenment, the Middle Path, Cause and Condition, and Cause and Effect. These doctrines reveal the true nature of our life as well as the virtuous path to follow in order to transform our karma. The Buddha teaches that the presence of forms and phenomena are contingent upon sufficient favorable conditions, and their absence occurs when these conditions are no longer present. Karma explains the reasons why we have blessings and sufferings in life; therefore, it is important to regulate our thoughts, speech, and actions as they are the factors that culminate into our resulting karma. Chapters seven through eleven describe the environment at a Buddhist temple and the symbolisms of the objects and statues of the Bodhisattvas and Buddha at the altar. Symbols represent the teachings and the vows that practitioners should commit to practice. Chapters twelve through sixteen define the Five Aggregates that make up the state of our existence, and how we should mindfully recognize them in our practice and daily interactions. Here, the important philosophies of impermanence, non-self, non-reality, and interbeing are explained in relation to their corresponding symbolic objects. Chapters seventeen and eighteen define the differences between wisdom and knowledge and the steps to practice the Five Vehicles to attain wisdom, foster compassion, and generate blessings. The chapter on the Five Vehicles explains in great detail the philosophies and practice in order to achieve the enlightened and virtuous mind. Chapter nineteen, "The Practice," describes at great length on how to apply the Dharma teachings to our life. This is an important chapter to review and reread to thoroughly understand the foundations of practice. The last chapter summarizes and lists the teachings and philosophies in a numerology that is commonly used throughout Buddhist studies, as this was how the Buddha's teachings were orally transmitted to facilitate memorization. This is where we can reflect back and review the teachings so as to apply them to our daily practice. Again, it is important to emphasize that both the contents and writing style throughout this book were written to capture what was heard from the sermons. Hence the subtitle, *As I Have Heard*.

The Venerable Thích Pháp Hòa is much adored by many Vietnamese Buddhist practitioners, both young and old, as his encouragement for us to lead a virtuous life is manifested in his outward charisma and demeanor, which attract many followers to study and practice the Dharma teachings. His Dharma name, "Pháp Hòa," translates to applying the Dharma teachings to live harmoniously and amicably, which is well-fitting for his character. He is referred to as "Thầy," which means teacher in Vietnamese. Thầy is a gifted, dynamic speaker whose sermons and lectures bring enlightenment to the mind, joy and laughter to the heart, and warmth to the soul. He takes the unintelligible Sutras and transmutes them into captivating and easily comprehensible discourses. For these reasons, this first series of *As I Have Heard* was written so that it may be available for those who do not understand Vietnamese nor have the time to listen to the innumerable hours of Thầy's sermons. May every reader receive awakening from this reading and, henceforth, apply the Dharma teachings into his or her daily practice.

Written from the heart,
Christine H. Huynh, M.D.

The Venerable Thích Pháp Hòa is the Abbott at Truc Lam Monastery and Westlock Meditation Center in Canada.

The Talented Wisdom with radiant acumen is worthy of praise
Take refuge and commit to the precepts in their entirety
Bind in the Five Precepts and gaze toward the right path
Train in the refuge of the Three Jewels to cease all delusions
Intake mindfully and pay homage to the Buddha are the perfect blessed conditions
Practice generosity and diligence to avoid the nadir
Follow the benevolent path expeditiously upon its realization
Reliance on the Three Jewels is where your true home resides.

> (a translation of a poem written by the monastic teacher for Thầy upon his vow of the Five Precepts)

Body, speech, and mind, all in peaceful harmony
Together flowing with each strike of the bell
Listen, listen, and be awakened to the bell's sound of
    compassion
To cross the shore from distress to liberation.

Deep prayers for the bell to resonate the Dharma teachings
For everyone to hear even in the distant darkness
For anyone who is lost can stop to reflect clearly
And be awakened to see the Right Path of Enlightenment.

Introduction

For young children and new visitors entering the temple for the first time, there is much curiosity in the splendor of the altar with the grandeur of the statues, the fragrant incense smoke permeating the rising air, and the unintelligible words of the Sanskrit mantras. Understanding is the essence of Buddhist practice. The Buddha placed Right View or Understanding as the first factor in the Noble Eightfold Path, as it is an important prerequisite to attain before developing the other seven factors. And in order to appreciate the teachings of the Buddha, we have to understand the meanings of the names and nomenclatures, representations of figures and statues, and the objects and rituals in Buddhist practice. Understanding is the cornerstone of everything we do in life, as misunderstanding leads to irrational thoughts, unkind words, and broken relationships. Life and religious philosophy are intertwined. In life there is religion; in religion there is life. Our life events and difficulties propel us to seek religion, and we must then apply the teachings to understand and lessen our difficulties in life. It has been mentioned that Buddhism is pessimistic, as the teachings are centered on the topics of suffering, impermanence, and the retributions of our vice. The truth is that Buddhism reveals the true nature of the universe and our life, so we can be awakened to understand the natural course of human nature. Subsequently, we can practice the teachings that the Buddha has laid out for our mental well-being. It is no different than a physician who concentrates upon the different types of physical illnesses and provides a medical treatment for each of them. Phenomena are persons, objects, and occurrences that manifest as means to aid us in our practice. Buddhism uses all phenomena as symbols to relay a message and serve as a point for teaching. The lotus flower provides an important teaching that something good can arise from a difficult passage, as there is beauty in the lotus that grows from the mud. Forms are physical objects that are visible. Forms can serve as the initial attraction to draw us in to develop a feeling toward and commit to the Dharma practice. For it was the Buddha's radiant beauty and character that attracted Ananda, the Buddha's personal attendant, to leave home and follow the Buddha to become an ordained monastic. Despite the beauty of physical forms, they constantly change as this is the true nature of all physical properties of objects. This doctrine is called impermanence. We see the teaching of impermanence in the flower as we enjoy its transient beauty until it decomposes. It is important for us to recognize that phenomena are vehicles for us to learn and not for us to cling to or become attached. Just as a raft is used to cross to the other shore, the raft is not carried with us, but is left behind once we have successfully crossed over. Recognizing the temporary nature of all phenomena, as well as the suffering we experience from their loss, the Buddha reminds and forewarns us to enjoy them when they are present, but to gently let go when the conditions no longer support their continued presence. This is akin to a physician who knows the mechanisms and causes of physical illnesses such as diabetes, and can prevent us from developing this disease by educating us to exercise and eat healthy. Buddhism uses the presence of phenomena to serve as symbols that reveal the true nature of the universe for us to learn and practice. With deep understanding as the foundation, we can develop insight into the symbolisms and teachings of the Dharma to weather through life's rising and falling journeys.

Chapter 1

The Three Jewels

In the Buddhist world, the Three Jewels that we cherish are not pearls, gold, or diamonds. The commonly revered Three Jewels are the Buddha, the Dharma, and the Sangha. They are referred to as Jewels because they are rare and treasured by all Buddhist practitioners. The jewels on earth (e.g., gemstones) have an inherent characteristic of being shiny and bright. The Three Jewels also have radiance, but they can illuminate our mind to help us manage difficulties and guide us in the right path of our life. The Three Jewels were first formed when the Buddha set the Dharma Wheel in motion and gave his First Sermon to a group of five ascetic friends after his Enlightenment. Although both the Three Jewels and the jewels of the earth are cherished, only the Three Jewels possess the wisdom to recognize what is precious in life versus what is temporarily treasured. The Buddha exhibits compassion, the Dharma contains wisdom, and the Sangha embodies harmonious strength.

6 *The Symbolisms in Buddhism*

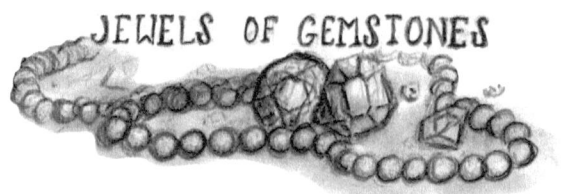

The Three Jewels (The Triple Gems)

The word Buddha is derived from the Sanskrit word "Bodhi," which means full awakening, enlightenment, and understanding the true nature of things. The Buddha is also referred to as Shakyamuni, a name from his paternal lineage of the Shakya clan in northeast India; he is the sage of the Shakya clan. "Muni" means one who has the capability of living with compassion, patience, harmony, and purity. "Muni" embodies the characteristic of a Saint who has great heroism, great strength, and great compassion. Heroism here does not mean to dominate others, but to be humble and use compassion to relinquish past hatred as well as the wants of the future, and not be fixated with anything in the present moment in order to live with a good-natured and an imperturbable mind. The Buddha is a great hero because he can let go of the extraordinary things that an ordinary person would not relinquish, such as leaving the riches and comforts of the royal life he grew up in to live the life of a mendicant. The Buddha has great strength because he has realized the difficulties of life, found the path to develop peace and harmony, and spent forty-five years of his life teaching this awakening to everyone. The Buddha has great compassion because his teachings can bring happiness and lessen suffering to others. He has compassion for all living beings despite their birth forms, whether they are from live births, egg-laying animals, birth in the soil of the earth, or birth through metamorphosis. The Buddha's given name at birth is Siddhartha Gautama. The last name Gautama was taken from his father's last name, as this is the usual tradition. The word Siddhartha means one who is accomplished and has lived a meaningful life. Accomplished here does not mean having attained a high level of degree or a high position in the workplace, but having fulfilled the role of a human being who knows how to treat others righteously. Siddhartha was a Prince who left a luxurious life at the age of twenty-nine to pursue a spiritual one. His renunciation is significant because it indicates that worldly treasures are only temporary. Because of his great compassion for people, Prince Siddhartha sacrificed what he temporarily possessed to find a path to happiness and liberation to share with others. He left behind his wealth and possessions, his family, wife (Princess Yasodhara) and son (Rahula), and his royal status and kingdom. It was after his Enlightenment at the age of thirty-five that he was referred to as the Buddha. The Buddha has qualities of self-enlightenment, shares this enlightenment with others, and attains the supreme enlightenment through services that are wholeheartedly carried out to completion. He has the true, perfect, and great Enlightenment. As such, the Buddha possesses ten merits that have earned him the title of "The World-Honored One":

1) A true nature with an unwavering mind and is liberated from the coming and going
2) Deserving to be revered and receive offerings
3) True noble insight and understanding
4) Perfect in wisdom and action
5) Ability to skillfully transcend all difficulties
6) Deep understanding to provide the path to resolve the problems of the world
7) The supreme noble practitioner
8) Ability to subdue and transform sentient beings
9) The teacher of heaven and earth
10) The Enlightened One

These merits yield the virtuous qualities of compassion that the Buddha has for all sentient beings. The Buddha is a teacher who has shown us the path to enlightenment and wisdom. He is the teacher for all teachers. He is the king of all phenomena and paths because he can see their true nature and is able to manage, resolve, and overcome them all. His main purpose of coming to this world is to reveal, show, and awaken us to the truths of the universe so we can accept and internalize them in order to overcome difficulties with more ease. The Buddha modeled the life that we need to emulate so we can recognize the "Muni" in others and treat everyone with love and respect. The Jewels of the Buddha are represented and seen in the Buddha statue, the Buddha and Bodhisattva, and our innate Buddha-nature.

"Dharma" is a Sanskrit word which means the teachings of the truth and encompasses all phenomena of the universe. Dharma is the Buddha's teachings that provide the Way, a clear path for us to follow in all aspects of life. The Dharma is a clear, bright light that illuminates a place of darkness in order to guide and relieve us from the delusions and difficulties of our life. The Dharma light radiates through its four constituents:

1) The Dharma teaching
2) The noble truth
3) The mindfulness practice
4) The benevolent and favorable outcome resulting from the practice

The Dharma teaches us how to promote happiness and minimize adversity through mindfulness practice and realization of the true nature of things. For example, the teaching of impermanence reminds us of the constant changes in life. We acknowledge that impermanence is a true principle, especially in light of our declining health as our body ages.

Therefore, we act with awareness to nourish our body and, in return, we cultivate a healthier body that is less prone to sickness. Another example is the teaching of the third precept that teaches us to build and maintain faithful relationships in a marriage to create happiness in the family. The truth is that if we engage in activities with our spouse and children, this will promote closeness and happiness within the family. If we engage in extramarital relationships, we ruin the happiness of our family and others. This teaching can also be applied to business relationships and friendships. When we mindfully keep our word in contracts with our colleagues and fulfill our promises with our friends, we develop trust and strengthen the relationship. The Buddha teaches us the infallible truth and encourages us to apply what we learn into actual practice to yield a benevolent outcome.

The Dharma teachings, which are available for everyone to learn, is comparable to rainfall. Rainwater does not discriminate either, as it spreads on the ground for all foliage to absorb. What and how much a person comprehends depend on each person's capability and potential. Just like a practitioner, the amount of rainwater that is absorbed by the plant or tree depends on its potential to take up water. Not everyone can comprehend the Dharma at the same level; there are superior, intermediate, and inferior practitioners. Some of us have the inherent capacity to hear and understand the Dharma, and there are those who are not yet at the level to comprehend the deep aspects of the Dharma teachings. The outpouring of the Dharma has been described as the Dharma rain, which results in the springing up of new transformed life and virtuous deeds.

The Dharma is food and medicine for our mind. There are several benefits derived from listening to the Dharma. It provides the teaching and understanding that we have not yet heard or understood. It resolves doubts and provides right view, clarity, and wisdom. And it provides a stable guide to take us to a state of peace and enlightenment. One should believe, reflect, cherish, and put the Dharma into practice. We may have our own path, but without proper guidance, we may not achieve the ultimate goal, given our potential. The Dharma is like a raft that helps us cross to the other shore in life. It is like an updated GPS, correctly guiding us down the proper path of life and preventing us from getting lost at a certain road junction or new road. Just as physicians are always needed to treat chronic physical ailments, the Dharma will continue to exist as long as life is present. The Buddha's son, Rahula, once asked what treasures from the Buddha's Princehood possessions would be bequeathed to him. The Buddha replied that the Dharma is the only treasure to give that is priceless and permanent. When the Buddha reached Nirvana (a term that refers to his passing), he stated that the greatest gift he was leaving behind in the world is the Dharma. When we have disappointments and are not able to receive the affirmation and approval that we seek from our friends or colleagues, the one thing we can confidently rely on as our rock and foundation is the Dharma. It is permanent even through the changes in time. The Dharma is supreme, deep, and miraculous. It is so precious that we are even able to encounter it in our lifetime. The Jewels of the Dharma are represented and seen in the Dharma Sutras, the Mahayana Sutras, and the four qualities that we develop from the practice of the teachings (loving-kindness, compassion, sympathetic joy, and forgiveness).

In the Buddha's lifetime, the Dharma was not recorded in written form. It was not until after the Buddha's passing that an assembly of the Buddha's great disciples convened to gather the sermons and organize them into a memorizable format. The format included poetic verses and a numbering system to facilitate recollection and recitation of the teachings. Most discourses were recalled by the Buddha's personal attendant, Ananda, who was gifted with a magnificent memory and had attended all the Buddha's discourses. The remainder of the discourses delivered prior to Ananda's service were recounted by the Buddha for him, as this was the agreement based on Ananda's request to hear all the Buddha's teachings. The teachings were passed on by oral tradition since no written form was available at the time. The Dharma was well-preserved for four hundred years after the Buddha's passing by repetition and recitation of the teachings carried out in groups to ensure their accuracy as heard from the Buddha. Thus, the tradition of collective chanting of the Sutras is still maintained at the temple to this day by the Sangha and individual practitioners. The Dharma teachings were later transcribed in the first century B.C.E.

The written text connecting the discourses of the Buddha is called a Sutra. It contains scriptures that serve as a guide towards the highest and right path toward happiness. There are several purposes of a Sutra. It connects each Dharma teaching like a garland of flowers and gives our life happiness and a bright future. It reveals the true nature of life and the universe and directs us to a noble, straight path. It acts as a strong water current and delivers us from the crevices of life's hindrances and afflictions. The Sutra has powerful insights that shine upon the practitioner to reveal the infallible truth. It entices the practitioner to study and practice by serving as an aid and convenience to transmit the teachings. It provides the rules of moral conduct, directs us to the right path, and increases our blessings. Each written discourse has six descriptions to validate that the sermons took place and were preached by the Buddha. The first two are contained in the four introductory words, "Thus have I heard," present in each written discourse. The phrase "Thus have I heard" conveys that the scriptures were recorded exactly the way they were heard from the Buddha. The word "I" specifically refers to Ananda, who served as a witness at each sermon. The next four characteristic descriptions of the written discourses confirm the Buddha as the speaker of the sermon, indicate the time period, describe the location, and recount the number and identity of the members and attendants present. The Buddha's sermons always consisted of gentle, loving, and truthful speech. The Sutras were written in either Pali or Sanskrit, as they were the languages of the time. The current translation into modern language was either done by phonetic or meaning; there are five instances where the words are untranslatable. Certain words have multiple meanings and translating them would compromise their actual definitions. An example of this is the Pali and Sanskrit word "Bodhi," which means enlightenment, awakening, and wisdom. It is, therefore, translated phonetically into "Buddha." The names of Buddhas and Bodhisattvas and words with holy connotations are difficult to translate, as doing so would cause them to lose their sacred meanings. There are words that cannot be translated because the objects are nonexistent in certain places, such as the name of the fruit "kiwi." Lastly, there are mystical words that are better left as is, such as the Sanskrit word "Prajna," which means great wisdom. Although the exact translation from Pali and Sanskrit to English is difficult, we are very fortunate that the spiritual patriarchs dedicated their time to undertake this feat.

The Sangha consists of the monastics and a community of practitioners who study and practice the Dharma. The abbot or abbess is the principal authority of the temple, whose role is to settle in the temple as his or her home and to safeguard and preserve the Sutras. Bhikkus and Bhikkunis are male and female monastics who have been ordained. They are at least twenty years of age and have finished five years of training. They commit to avoid any malevolent acts, avert all afflictions, and live as a mendicant. A mendicant seeks the Dharma teachings from the divine realm above and transmits them to the lay person when the right conditions are created from almsgiving. Novice monks and nuns, Samanera and Samaneri, have the responsibility to eliminate malevolence, perform benevolence, diligently study and practice, and pursue purity and serenity. Bhikkus, Bhikkunis, Samanera, and Samaneri are collectively called Sramana, the monastics. They are to eliminate malevolent acts, foster benevolent and virtuous acts, and practice diligently. The foundation of practice for the monastics is to develop purity and tranquility of the mind and pledge the great vow to provide compassion for others. In Vietnamese, we refer to a venerable male monastic as "Thầy," which means teacher. The word "Thầy" is pronounced phonetically similar to the Sanskrit word "Tathagata," a term that references the Buddha in the Sutras. Tathagata means one who sees the true nature of things and has a steady mind at peace with the coming and going of life. The monastics serve as teachers to preach and explain the Dharma and guide the community in the practice. They are joyous in their commitment to reside, concentrate, and practice the true teachings. The Jewels of the Sangha are represented and seen in the monastics, the Buddha's historical disciples, and our collective practitioners together in harmony.

The Buddha is the Enlightened teacher. The Dharma is the teaching of the true right path. The Sangha is the group of practitioners living in harmony.

The monastics' renunciation of the ordinary life consists of leaving their family to enter into their Sangha family, relinquishing the afflictions of the world, and forgoing the three realms of cravings, forms, and non-forms. The monastics also give up all their possessions and rely on only two sources for their sustenance: material charity and the Dharma teachings. The monastics receive material charity from the community to nourish their bodies and are endowed with the spiritual teachings to nourish their minds. The community makes offerings to provide and nourish the monastics with donations of shelter, food, clothing, and medicine. In return, the monastics provide the community the opportunity to learn the Dharma. The monastics' generosity to the community is their renunciation and commitment of their life to study the Dharma, and share and preach the Dharma to the community. The three requirements upon entering the monastic life are:

1) To live in the house of compassion, the temple
2) To wear the wardrobe of patience, the Kasaya robe
3) To sit on a pedestal that is ingrained in the dharma teaching of Conditioned Genesis and non-reality

The temple is a home filled with compassion that welcomes everyone with love and kindness. The monastics' Kasaya robe embodies patience and harmony. The Dharma is deep and supreme, allowing us to see the true essence of life and understand that the existence of forms is not real, as they are based on the presence or absence of sufficient conditions. The monastics' renunciation is an act of great generosity since it is a rare occurrence that very few can accomplish.

The two most obvious identifying characteristics of the monastics are their fully shaved head, lacking any thread of hair, and their simple robe. Their shaved head reminds them to be rounded and fulfilled like a circle and perform all services to completion. The ritual of the monastics shaving off their hair represents the act of eliminating sorrow, hardship, and affliction. Our hair becomes disheveled after a night of sleep or on a windy day, and we have to wash, blow dry, comb, and style it every day. Our hair represents hardship and difficulties that affect us physically and mentally. The Buddha points out that shaving our head and putting on a robe do not necessarily constitute a practitioner who is deeply committed to practicing the path of enlightenment. This is only a symbolic form and ritual portraying the practice of simplicity and release of attachments. While we may not have met the sufficient conditions to be ordained physically, we can practice diligently to be ordained in spirit. The Buddha describes the four types of person who are ordained:

1) The person who is ordained in the physical body but not in the mind
2) The person who is not ordained in the physical body but is ordained in the mind
3) The person who is neither ordained in the physical body nor the mind
4) The person who is ordained in the physical body and the mind

The ordination of the physical body involves leaving the family home. However, it is more important to work on leaving the house of afflictions, which can be attained by practicing to be ordained in the mind. This can be extended to everything we do in life. Physicians wearing a white coat only represent that they can treat people for their physical ailments. They are not true physicians until they put their heart and mind into healing patients. We need to be both present in physical form and practice with the mind and heart.

The Three Jewels range from the external physical form of the worldly life to the ordained world that we take refuge in. There are three categories of the Three Jewels:

1) The Three Jewels of the worldly life: the Buddha is in the Buddha statue, the Dharma is in the Sutra, and the Sangha is in the group of monastics and practitioners.
2) The Three Jewels of the ordained life: the Buddha is in the Buddhas and Bodhisattvas, the Dharma is in the Mahayana Sutras, and the Sangha is the Buddha's historical disciples.
3) The Three Jewels present in everyone: the Buddha is in our inherent Buddha-nature, the Dharma is in the four true qualities of loving-kindness, compassion, sympathetic joy, and forgiveness, and the Sangha is the collective practitioners in harmony.

The Three Jewels guide us to reflect inward to find our own enlightenment, truth, and peace. They collectively provide the radiant wisdom for us to take refuge in and depend on to live a fulfilling life.

Chapter 2

The Vesak Celebration

Vesak is the name of the lunar month in India that corresponds to April-May of our calendar. The annual Vesak celebration commemorates the three important life events of the Buddha: his birth, Enlightenment, and Nirvana. In the past, it was difficult for people to convene frequently, so all three important events were commemorated simultaneously in a single occasion. Their important dates on the lunar calendar are:

1) His birth on April 8
2) His Enlightenment on December 8
3) His Nirvana on February 15

Another date that we should remember is Prince Siddhartha's renunciation along the Anoma River on February 8. As we remember to celebrate and wish our friend a happy birthday or Valentine's Day, we should also remember to wish our friend a "Happy Buddha's Day" or "Happy Vesak Day" to commemorate the three important events in the Buddha's life. Vesak is a celebration to honor the teacher who has taught us the path and way to live in order to attain happiness.

Vesak is a celebration of the Buddha's birth, Enlightenment, and Nirvana.

The Buddha was born around 624 B.C.E. in the garden of Lumbini, situated in what is now the mid-southwest of Nepal that borders India. His birth was preceded by a dream conceived by Queen Maya, his mother, who saw a white elephant enter her right side. The white elephant possessed six tusks and a lotus flower wrapped around its trunk. The elephant symbolizes the enormous strength and greatness it takes to bring the Dharma teachings that will help us overcome all difficulties. The white color of the elephant exemplifies the cleansing of all our karma. The six tusks represent the six practices in the Vehicle of the Bodhisattva (generosity, morality, patience, diligence, concentration, and wisdom) that will help liberate us from life's afflictions. The lotus flower symbolizes purity, indicating what the Buddha and his teachings represent. Queen Maya represents compassion, as she can carry the six practices of the Vehicle of the Bodhisattva that will help us cross the shore to liberation. Queen Maya's dream was prophesied as a divine message that she is bearing a prodigious child who will bring the true teachings to help liberate humankind. Another auspicious event prior to the Buddha's birth was the blossoming of the udumbara flower, which signals the arrival of a great enlightened being. The udumbara flower is of a celestial nature and is said to only bloom once every 3,000 years. The significance of the Buddha's birth is that he came into this world in a human body so as to be at the same level as us in order to reveal the Noble Truths. It is because of the cause of the world's suffering and under the right conditions that the Buddha appeared among the impurities of living beings to provide his great service. His birth is a special event that provides an extraordinary joy for all sentient beings, as he will go on to reveal the path to a happy life.

Queen Maya's dream

22 *The Symbolisms in Buddhism*

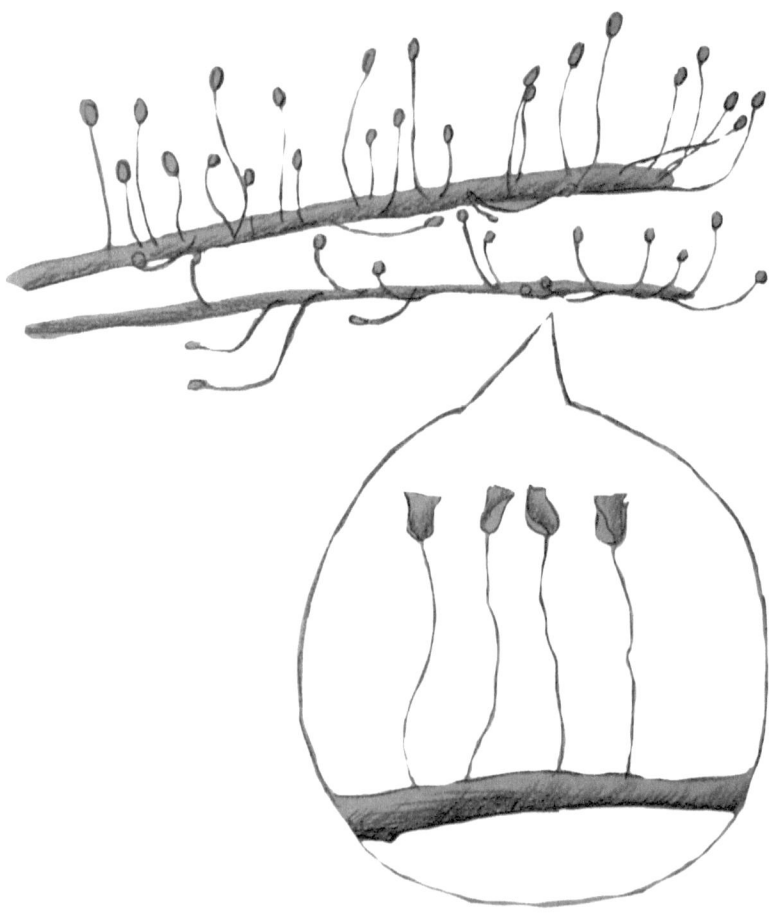

The udumbara flower

Birth in Lumbini Garden

The sequence of events immediately following the Buddha's birth heralded an auspicious sign that the Buddha had arrived to teach us the truth and path to liberation. The events may be considered as supernatural, but they are accepted in the history of Buddhism to represent the arrival of an Enlightened teacher. At birth, the baby Buddha faced north, took seven steps on the lotus in the pond, and scanned in four directions. Two streams of water (cold and warm) sprayed from the sky to bathe the Buddha. The lotuses bloomed and supported each step, illustrating that we should do everything wholeheartedly so that happiness will arise with each action. The seven steps signify several true phenomena:

1) There are seven elements comprising this universe, just as there are seven musical notes that make up the melody of a song. The seven elements are earth, water, wind, fire, view, consciousness, and emptiness (space). Here, we examine the example of a bell: its composition consists of earth, water, wind, and fire. The person who makes the bell needs to envision and distinguish how he or she wants to shape and mold the bell; this is view and consciousness. In a bell and every object, there is dead space and emptiness.
2) There are Seven Elements of practice to attain Enlightenment: mindfulness, determination of the right path, diligence, serenity, joy, concentration, and non-attachment.
3) There are seven past Buddhas, with Shakyamuni Buddha being the seventh.
4) There are seven disciples of the Buddha: layman, laywoman, samanera (novice monk), samaneri (novice nun), siksamana (novice nun observing the precepts),

bhikku (male monastic), and bhikkuni (female monastic).

5) There are seven cherished jewels characteristic of a practitioner: faith, morality, repentance with self, repentance with others, deep listening, release of attachments, and wisdom.

6) There are seven directions consisting of the four cardinal directions of north, south, east, and west as well as three eras of past, present, and future; these indicate that the Buddha will have influence throughout the world. His Enlightenment not only will prevail in one hemisphere or time period, but it will span all places and time frames.

The Buddha's first step on the lotus signifies the initiation of the vow and commitment to bring light and liberation to the people of this world. The remainder of six steps are to overcome the Six Paths of existence in the cycles of rebirth of life. As the Buddha takes his first few steps, he raised his right hand upwards pointing to the sky, declaring that "I am the World-Honored One" who will attain enlightenment to see the truth and true nature of all phenomena. The Buddha is not proclaiming his self-importance with this statement. There is a deeper meaning in reference to the word "I," as Buddhism teaches the concept of non-self. Here, the word "I" equates to liberation and the Buddha-nature that is most revered and present in every one of us. He then pointed his left hand downward, signifying that there is no other time than now, the present moment. In essence, do not worry about the past because it has already passed. Don't worry about the future, as the time has not yet arrived. Remember, the future is made of the present moment, so be mindful, take care, and enjoy the present moment. Each of the baby Buddha's first few steps

The 7 steps at birth

symbolizes the daily rebirth in life; each day is a new day, and we have a fresh start and new awakening each morning to live peacefully without regrets over mistakes made in the past.

One of the rituals celebrating the Buddha's birth is the bathing of the baby Buddha, which symbolizes the process of cleansing the mind. The ceremony is fully adorned with a variety of decorative flowers surrounding a small tub of water that the baby Buddha stands in. A ladle is used to scoop and pour the water over the baby Buddha, washing him from the shoulders downward. The flowers represent morality. The still water embodies concentration. And the Buddha is depicted as the awakened, purified mind. The combination of morality and concentration leads to wisdom, which are the three goals to achieve through our practice. The Buddha's birth models a renewal of each thought, speech, and action which we can improve through practice, meditation, and mindfulness.

Prince Siddhartha went through eight characteristic stages in life to attain enlightenment to become the Buddha:

1) The first stage is to abide in a heavenly realm in preparation for descent into the world.
2) The second stage consists of the remarkable event of Prince Siddhartha's conception. It was said that he entered the right side of his mother, Queen Maya, and remained for a ten-month pregnancy, rather than the typical nine months and ten days.
3) The third stage is Prince Siddhartha's birth after an extended pregnancy. He emerged into the world from Queen Maya's right side in Lumbini Garden. The specific birthplace chosen to bring enlightenment was in the country of India, a place stricken by poverty and inequality with multiple levels of the caste system at the time.

Bathing of the baby Buddha

4) The fourth stage is Prince Siddhartha's renunciation of the worldly life along the river Anoma, after viewing a series of the Four Sights during his first trip outside of the palace with his attendant Channa. He saw the three traits of life's suffering consisting of old age, sickness, and death, and questioned Channa to confirm each state he witnessed. This confirmation reminds us not to forget the inevitable nature of life that everyone is subjected to, despite his or her hierarchy in life. The last sight Prince Siddhartha saw was an ascetic, of whom he questioned about his purpose. The ascetic's answer, to find the solution to end the vicious cycle of life's suffering, stimulated Prince Siddhartha to do the same.
5) The fifth stage is overcoming the seductions of evil spirits and not succumbing to life's diversion during his meditation toward enlightenment.
6) The sixth stage is the attainment of Enlightenment under the Bodhi tree.
7) The seventh stage is setting the Dharma Wheel in motion to share his teachings with others.
8) The eighth stage is the attainment of Nirvana.

These stages are important highlights of events leading to Prince Siddhartha's Enlightenment.

Enlightenment is the awareness and acknowledgment of the true nature of all things in the universe. Prince Siddhartha's renunciation of the royal life is an important and significant event in the pursuit of his Enlightenment that culminated under the Bodhi tree, after six years of his dedicated training and practice. The sacred Bodhi tree still stands in Bodhgaya, India today. It is the last of the seven places where Prince Siddhartha sat in meditation for forty-nine days to attain

Enlightenment

enlightenment. The Bodhi tree is actually a pippala tree (a sacred fig), but is so named because it was the tree where Prince Siddhartha attained the fruit of enlightenment. The exact meaning of enlightenment is indescribable, as we have to experience it to really know it, such as tasting a lemon to truly know that its juicy, sour taste is different from that of vinegar. The Buddha attained self-enlightenment and the ultimate complete enlightenment. He came to this world in the same flesh and body as us to help us see that we, too, can achieve enlightenment.

The Buddha's Enlightenment was a momentous time when he came to the realization of several fundamental principles:

1) The Four Noble Truths and the Noble Eightfold Path
2) The Middle Path
3) The doctrine of Cause and Condition
4) The doctrine of Cause and Effect

After his Enlightenment, the Buddha shared these principles with the five ascetic friends in his First Sermon at Deer Park in Sarnath, India. The Four Noble Truths reveal that:

1) There is suffering in life.
2) The cause of suffering is our craving to want for more.
3) There is a solution for the suffering.
4) The Noble Eightfold Path is the guide for treatment and a way to live a happy life.

The Middle Path teaches the importance of living in moderation and avoiding both extremes. The Buddha saw that all events have a Cause and Condition, and that the true nature of things is not real, as they perish or come into existence due to a combination of favorable or unfavorable conditions. He also saw that every event has a Cause and Effect and that each action results in consequences or rewards. These principles are evident, but the Buddha's Enlightenment serves to reveal and awaken us so we can live mindfully in order to manage our life's events and prevent the untoward consequences of our actions.

From this realization, the Buddha describes two types of truths: the relative truth and the absolute truth. The relative truth is a life event that is used to reveal the absolute truth of the universe. It is a manifestation or an expression of the absolute truth for us to understand and see more clearly in order for us to live a happy and virtuous life. For example, a wedding ceremony and the exchange of wedding rings are the relative truth. These rituals reveal a deeper meaning in the absolute truth to signify the love and commitment required in a marriage and the role each person needs to fulfill in a relationship. The relative truth can demonstrate a traditional custom for a younger person to bow and greet an elderly person. This portrays the teaching of respect in the absolute truth. When the Buddha asked Ananda to smell his hands after holding a fish, Ananda commented that his hands have a foul smell of the fish. This is the relative truth. The Buddha points out the absolute truth that we, too, would gravitate to do bad things when we choose to associate with friends who do bad things. Another example of the relative truth is when a shepherd told the Buddha that there are eleven ways to guard and herd buffaloes, as one has to understand their characters. Likewise, the Buddha points out the absolute truth to his disciples that there are eleven ways to tame the mind. The

The First Sermon

Buddha sees the relative truth in life and uses it to teach the absolute truth of life. The relative truth symbolizes the absolute truth. We can then use the understanding of the absolute truth to embrace the events in our life in order to live in harmony. And this is the wonderful truth.

The Buddha affirms that everyone has an innate Buddha-nature to realize enlightenment. During the time period of the Buddha's life around 6th century B.C.E., the caste system in India categorized people into different classes based on their birth in a family's social status. The Buddha explains the differences in our misfortunes and blessings are due to the retributions or rewards from our karma. He brought the idea of equality and nondiscrimination to every person and class of persons. We are all the same in that we shed salty tears when experiencing suffering and our blood manifest a red hue. The Buddha's declaration that everyone has a Buddha-nature nullified the caste system and, therefore, gave everyone hope that each person can practice and cultivate his or her innate Buddha-nature to realize liberation and enlightenment. This Buddha-nature is our true mind that is always clear and bright. We frequently forget this since our Buddha-nature is often clouded by our slanted and false views and biases. There are seven qualities we can cultivate to bring out our Buddha-nature to reinforce this enlightenment:

1) Mindfulness
2) Right determination
3) Right effort
4) Serenity
5) Joy
6) Concentration
7) Equanimity

These Seven Enlightenment Factors are the branches that comprise the Bodhi tree. They are also part of the Thirty-Seven Paths of practice to Enlightenment. Each factor is interrelated to one another. Mindfulness is the key and heart of the practice, as it leads to right thought to make the appropriate determination in choosing the Dharma Vehicle well suited for us to practice. Once we identify a goal, we work diligently toward our chosen path to give us serenity and joy. Because we work in a clear and serene state of mind, we develop concentration and wisdom to act righteously. We develop a clear understanding of the nature of all phenomena, know when to let things go, and not suffer from the attachment of things. Equanimity is the ability to withstand any situation with a calm composure and is often equated with nondiscrimination or the release of attachments and difficulties. The time when we develop awareness and enlightenment can be experienced in different ways. We can develop enlightenment through listening to the Dharma study or guidance from the monastic teacher. Sometimes, it takes a distressing experience for us to realize our initial enlightenment. An example is when we hear the sound of sirens rushing toward the hospital, which makes us then realize that life is fragile. We further realize the teaching of impermanence upon witnessing the tragedy of a death from a car accident or the sudden news of a terminal illness. There are different levels of enlightenment. We start out with the absence of enlightenment and progress to partial enlightenment where we fluctuate between enlightenment and delusion, depending on the diligence of our practice. As we advance in our practice and training, we arrive to a complete and perfect enlightenment and can achieve a collective enlightenment with the Sangha. The Buddha's Enlightenment is bestowed upon us so we understand that each one of us has a Buddha-nature and can attain enlightenment to follow the path to happiness and peace.

Nirvana is a state where the mind is at peace despite the changing events of life. There may be a misconception that Nirvana is a heavenly place to go after we pass away. However, Nirvana is not a physical destination. It is a state of sublime and true, inner peace. Nirvana is a Sanskrit word which means "the absence of," such as the absence of form or a disturbed mental state. In regards to the absence of form, Nirvana has been equated to the Buddha's passing, which occurred around 544 BCE in the Sala Forest at Kusinara, India. Nirvana is also interpreted as the elimination of afflictions and liberation from the cycles of birth and death. Here, the cycles of birth and death not only refer to our life but also to the fluctuations of our mental state between happiness and sorrow. Contrary to our mental state, the Buddha is in a constant state of Nirvana with purity and serenity.

Nirvana is attained when there is an absence of the negatives. "Nir" means "no." "Vana" means "negative." The negatives are the ten roots of our afflictions consisting of:

1) Greed
2) Anger
3) Delusion
4) Pride
5) Skepticism
6) Wrong view
7) One-sided view
8) Wrong view of self
9) Attachment to our view
10) Attachment to misperceptions of how the precepts should be practiced (Precepts are a set of rules that guide us toward virtuous deeds.)

Nirvana

The three most common negatives targeted in our practice are greed, hatred, and delusion. When there is an absence of greed, there is the presence of Nirvana. When we no longer have hatred is the time we enter Nirvana. When we no longer have delusion is when we experience Nirvana. When we can live with the fluctuations of life's circumstances without emotional, roller coaster-like reactions is when we are in Nirvana. If we can cultivate the positive acts of generosity, loving-kindness, and wisdom despite adversities, we are in Nirvana. Generosity is the antidote for greed. Loving-kindness is an antidote for hatred, and wisdom is the antidote for delusion. When we can overcome the ten negative roots of our afflictions is when we achieve Nirvana.

Nirvana has four qualities:

1) Permanence
2) Inner peace and joy
3) Liberation
4) Purity

The first quality, permanence, is a condition that is constant and lasting. Although we can experience Nirvana, we have difficulty maintaining the permanence of Nirvana that the Buddha possesses. Our state of Nirvana fluctuates. For example, when we are at the temple, we have peace, happiness, and joy because there is no one to bother us. But once we leave the meditation hall and realize that our slippers have disappeared, we get frustrated and lose this peace. This is when we cease to remain in Nirvana. Our happiness and peace are unstable because they fluctuate based on our emotional state and ownership of things. The Buddha is always able to live in peace. Even in difficult situations, the Buddha can handle and face all afflictions without any reactive emotions. The Buddha's Nirvana is permanent, as his peace is stable and his emotions cannot be stirred by any changes or disturbances. The second quality of Nirvana is inner peace and joy. When we practice equanimity and release the negative feelings against a person that has caused us sadness, we can experience this true inner joy. It is natural that we enjoy doing things that we like and are discontent when we have to do things we dislike. For example, if we are asked to carry a box of rocks, we would not be happy as we see no value in the rocks. However, if we are asked to carry a box of gold, we would be more willing, as gold is more valuable to us. The Buddha teaches that we should be mindful and have joy in everything we do in the present moment, whether it is pleasant or unpleasant. When we are able to achieve this, we experience Nirvana. The third quality of Nirvana is liberation. Liberation is not equivalent to freedom. Freedom refers to the state of the physical body, while liberation refers to the state of the mind. We can be imprisoned in jail and wish for physical freedom, but can still feel liberated mentally. Liberation is when we are free from the feelings of anguish and discontent caused by difficulties or hardships. Liberation exists when we are not bound by suffering. It is experienced when we are free from external and internal negative emotional reactions. For example, when we stay at the temple for lunch and realize that the food is all vegetarian, we can either choose to enjoy the vegetarian dishes or be discontent. When we decide to have a positive attitude and not allow the absence of meat in one meal to ruin our day, we achieve liberation and are free from attachment. Freedom from attachment doesn't mean that we do not care or ignore our circumstances and feelings. We attain liberation when we are able to open our heart and receive things easily, without negative emotions. The last quality of Nirvana is purity. Purity is freedom from contamination and

THE LUNAR CALENDAR

JANUARY

FEBRUARY

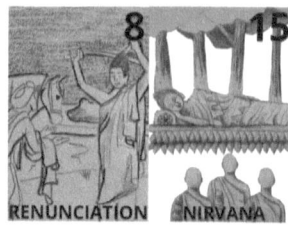

MARCH

APRIL 8

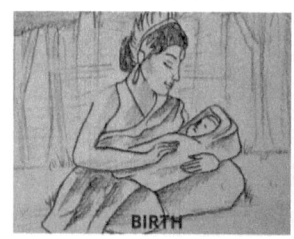

MAY

JUNE

JULY

AUGUST

SEPTEMBER

DECEMBER 8

OCTOBER

NOVEMBER

The important dates of the Buddha's life

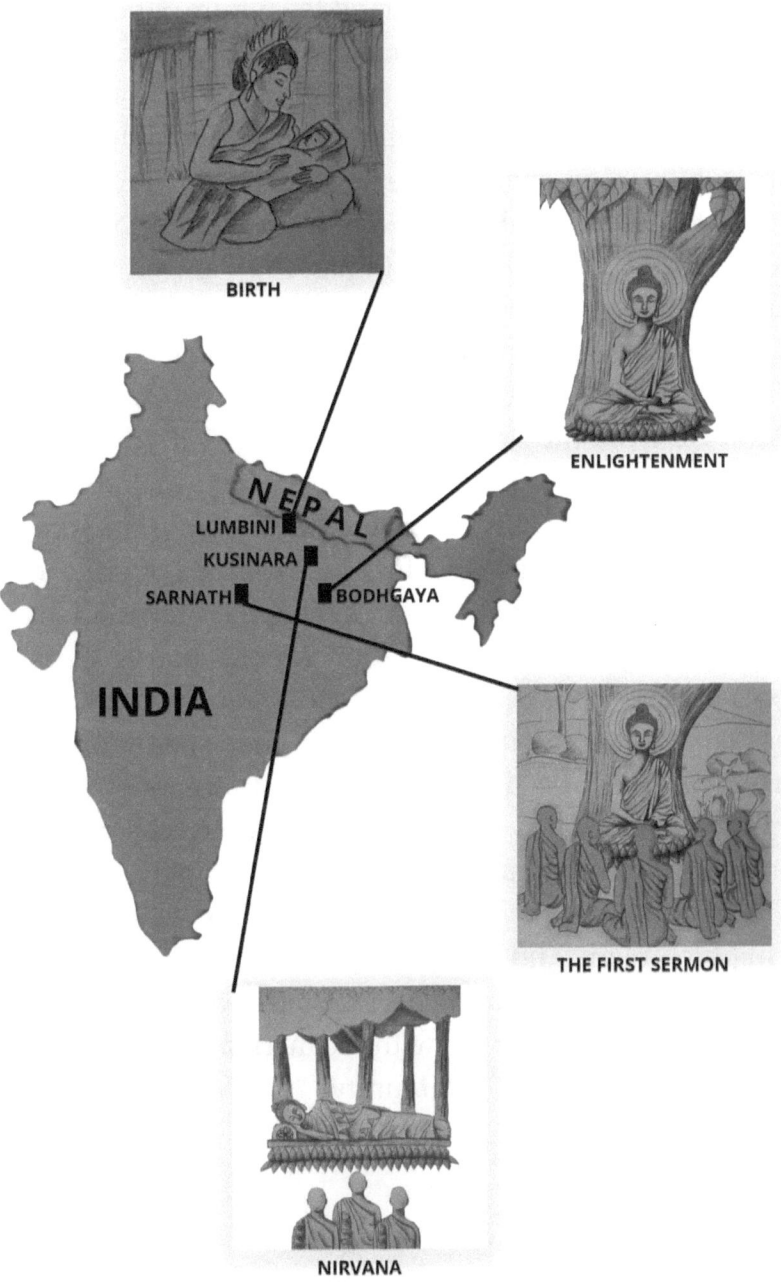

The four pilgrimage sites

attachment. When we understand the nature of things, we can be free from attachments in our thoughts, speech, and actions and achieve a sense of calmness. When we have the qualities of inner peace and joy, liberation, and purity of the mind that are stable and permanent, we have reached Nirvana.

The Buddha's life is closely connected with nature. He was born in the garden of Lumbini, renounced the worldly life alongside the river Anoma, and practiced for six years in the forest. He subsequently attained enlightenment under the Bodhi tree in Bodhgaya and preached his First Sermon at Deer Park. He wore the Kasaya robe designed with the pattern of the rice paddy of Magadha and passed away in the Sala Forest at Kusinara. Ironically, he passed away from an accidental ingestion of poisoned mushrooms from an offering of rice porridge. It is said that we will have great merits if we go on a pilgrimage to visit the four sacred places (Lumbini, Bodhgaya, Deer Park in Sarnath, and Kusinara) marked by the important timeline in the Buddha's life. These are the sites where we will be deeply touched and experience intense emotions with tears of joy. The Buddha lived a meaningful and purposeful life and served as an exemplary role model. Therefore, it is fitting that the life events of his birth, Enlightenment, and Nirvana are honored and celebrated perpetually. If we follow in his footsteps, we, too, can celebrate toward the end of our life with the merits, work, and services we contributed to our community.

Chapter 3

The Dharma Wheel

When the Buddha gave his First Sermon, he "turned the wheel in motion," propelling his teachings to be preached and spread throughout the world. The wheel he set in motion is the Dharma Wheel. The symbol of a hand supporting the wheel represents the hand spinning and maintaining the wheel in motion. The wheel is round and can be easily rolled. Wherever the Dharma Wheel rolls, it can stamp out suffering and afflictions. One of the distinct thirty-two auspicious features of the Buddha is the presence of the Dharma Wheel, decorated with a thousand flowers, on the sole of the Buddha's feet. This represents the eventual spread of his Dharma to all nations and people.

The Dharma Wheel is sometimes seen with twelve spokes. The twelve spokes should not be mistaken to represent the twelve factors of the doctrine of Cause and Condition. The twelve spokes symbolize spinning each of the four factors of the Four Noble Truths in motion three times. The first turning

The 12 spoked Dharma Wheel set in motion

of the wheel represents the Buddha's declaration of the Four Noble Truths. The second turning of the wheel attests that the Buddha has realized and experienced the causes of life's suffering and, through this awakening, has overcome suffering and achieved the practice of the Noble Eightfold Path. The third turning of the wheel encourages us that we, too, can overcome life's suffering and attain enlightenment by studying the Four Noble Truths and practicing the Noble Eightfold Path. We have to experience suffering, acknowledge it, and practice to overcome it before we become awakened and enlightened.

The Four Noble Truths is a core principle in Buddhism that every practitioner should grasp. It states that:

1) There is suffering in our life.
2) Our extreme craving is the reason for our suffering.
3) There is a way to end our suffering.
4) The Noble Eightfold Path is the way.

Here, the four steps parallel that of a physician who makes a diagnosis of an illness, explains the cause of the illness, expresses that there is a cure for the illness, and provides a treatment for the illness. The Buddha's approach to the treatment of an illness, consisting of examination, listening, questioning, and treatment, is similar to that of a physician. Buddhism treats mental illnesses, and the physician treats physical illnesses. Young people who are healthy do not visit the doctor until they develop uncomfortable physical symptoms that accompany advanced age, and then the physician reveals the development of elevated blood pressure, high sugar, and cholesterol. Similarly, people who are in their prime and enjoying their life often do not seek religious studies until they experience emotional and mental sufferings. Just as a physician gives a diagnosis and causes of hypertension or diabetes, the Buddha defines the diagnoses and causes of suffering. The Buddha not only points out suffering and its causes, but he also provides a path and solution.

The Pali word "dukkha" is the first factor in the Four Noble Truths that is conveniently translated as "suffering." It is one of those words that have multiple meanings and translating it into a single word would not suffice. Its literal meaning is incomplete, ever-changing, not real, hollow, and meaningless. All things with these characteristics in life tend to give us dissatisfaction and sorrow and, therefore, cause suffering within us. Suffering is any afflictions that cause a discomfort or disturbance of the mind. It is anything that we do not accept or are dissatisfied with. The three types of suffering are categorized as the suffering of suffering, the external suffering, and the acts of suffering. The suffering of suffering relates to the suffering of the physical body that passes through the four stages of life. The external suffering refers to people and our surrounding environment that contribute to our dukkha. The acts of suffering refer to the domino effect of our actions that cause one suffering leading to another. The sight of suffering in people was the reason that prompted Prince Siddhartha to seek for the truth of life.

In us, suffering affects both the physical body and the mind. There are four types of physical sufferings:

1) Birth
2) Old age
3) Sickness
4) Death

There are four types of mental sufferings:

1) Distance from our loved ones
2) Proximity to those whom we dislike
3) Not being able to have what we want
4) Fixation and attachment to the fluctuations of our Five Aggregates

Our physical body is subject to the laws of impermanence, as it progresses to changes and deterioration of forms. Our aging, sickness, and the end of life all contribute to our sorrow and mental suffering. Aging is seen in the change of physical beauty, decline in physical function, decrease in respiratory capacity, lessening of appetite, and shortening of life span. Mental sufferings are due to our dissatisfaction and attachment to our Five Aggregates consisting of the visible form, feeling, perception, mental formation (actions), and consciousness. We view physical forms and our feelings, perceptions, actions and discriminatory thoughts as real and, therefore, become mentally exhausted with their incessant inputs. We all know this, but the Buddha has to point this out so we can remember that this is the truth of life.

The second Noble Truth states that our sufferings are attributed to our cravings. The main types of cravings are wealth, beauty, fame, pleasure in delicacy, and oversleeping. It is normal for us to have the feeling of want because we live in a world driven by wishes and desires. We cannot extinguish this feeling of want, as this drive is necessary to sustain our livelihood. When our body is imbalanced, lacking water or nutrition, our autonomic nervous system creates a drive for thirst and hunger for us to drink and eat. Our desire for things in life motivates us to work to achieve a good career, maintain our physique, and accomplish a meaningful goal in life. This desire is not necessarily bad, especially when this desire leads toward a benevolent activity. We have to achieve wealth in order to perform philanthropy. We can use our beauty and fame to draw people towards fundraising activities. We need to eat and sleep well in order to nourish our mind and body to continue our mission. However, craving causes problems and turns into greed when the desire becomes excessive such that we live beyond our means and cannot live in moderation. It also creates suffering when we are not able to accept a loss after experiencing great joy from having our desires fulfilled. This is due to our attachment. The sources of suffering may originate from ourselves, natural disasters (such as earthquakes and hurricanes), or society creating prejudice and conflicts. In addition, there are ten roots in our consciousness that contribute to our suffering:

1) Greed
2) Anger
3) Delusion
4) Pride
5) Skepticism
6) Wrong view
7) One-sided view
8) Wrong view of self
9) Attachment to our view
10) Attachment to misperceptions of how the precepts should be practiced

Our intense emotions and flawed views contribute to our suffering. The key is to recognize our innate Buddha-nature to live the best kind of life, enjoy and have gratitude for our accomplishments, and be able to let go when there is a change or loss in our possessions or status.

The third factor of the Four Noble Truths states that there is a treatment for suffering. Suffering is an illness where treatment is required for our well-being to ease our mind, comfort our body, and bring satisfaction and acceptance of our conditions. The fourth factor of the Four Noble Truths outlines the Thirty-Seven Paths of practice for treatment, which is condensed into the Noble Eightfold Path. Just as when we receive the diagnosis of hypertension as well as its treatments, we acknowledge the suffering in life and its causes, accept them, undergo treatments, and overcome them.

The Dharma Wheel is more commonly seen with eight spokes, representing the Noble Eightfold Path. The Noble Eightfold Path is the fourth factor of the Four Noble Truths and is a core component of Buddhist philosophy, as it unfolds the solution to our suffering. The Noble Eightfold Path provides a guide, a solution, and an anchor for us to have a happy and peaceful life. The eight steps of the Path are organized according to the three pillars of the Buddha's teachings:

* *Wisdom*
1. Right View
2. Right Thought
* *Morality*
3. Right Speech
4. Right Action
5. Right Livelihood
* *Meditation*
6. Right Effort
7. Right Mindfulness
8. Right Concentration

The 8 spoked Dharma Wheel

Here, "Right" means true and correct because the actions are performed with mindfulness and deep reflection.

Right view is seeing things with clarity.
Right thought is thinking with righteousness.
Right speech is speaking with truth and goodness.
Right action is conducting ourselves with virtue.
Right livelihood is to work with integrity in our vocation and role in life.
Right effort is an incessant diligence and wholehearted endeavor to achieve a set goal.
Right mindfulness is the continued awareness of our thoughts, speech, and actions.
Right concentration is the ability to attain a meditative focus.

Right view is an important first factor in the Noble Eightfold Path because we develop right understanding when we can see clearly. With right view and understanding, we can develop the right thought to carry out the right speech, right action, and right work ethic. The last three factors of the path, consisting of right effort, right mindfulness, and right concentration, are mental qualities we need to cultivate toward our thoughts, speech, and actions. When we have the right diligence, awareness, and focus in each of our thoughts, speech, and actions, we can then live and carry out acts of kindness to bring harmony and benefit to our community. The result is a benevolent and happy life for us and everyone. Here, the emphasis is upon following the eight right paths instead of the eight wrong paths. When we start with the wrong view, it will lead to wrong thoughts, speech, and actions. When we have laziness (wrong effort), delusion (wrong mindfulness), and inattention (wrong concentration) in our thoughts, speech, and actions, we may hurt others' feelings and cause disharmony and unhappiness in our life and relationships with our friends and families in the community.

The Noble Eightfold Path is the Buddha's formula toward happiness, peace, and enlightenment. When we have a comfortable three-bedroom house and a functioning car, we should express gratitude and appreciation for having comfortable shelter and reliable transportation. This is right view, right thought, right speech, and right mindfulness. Working overtime or working two jobs would limit our time spent with our spouse and children; this can lead to the breakdown of our family, resulting in problems in our unsupervised children and relationship with our spouse. We should maintain diligence towards working in moderation and use our earnings for other necessary expenditures, such as saving for our child's college education, rather than compete with our peers to work overtime for the purpose of buying a bigger house or a nicer car. This is right effort, right concentration, right action, and right livelihood. Recognizing the causes of our suffering and knowing the right path to follow will help us live a more contented and fulfilling life.

Of the four factors in the Four Noble Truths, a practitioner may find that the fourth factor is the most important, as it is the key to solving our problems in life. It is not complete here just to mention the Noble Eightfold Path for the treatment of suffering, because the avid practitioner would want to know the complete Thirty-Seven Paths to practice toward the right path of liberation, similar to how a patient who has been diagnosed with diabetes will exhaustively research the treatments, ranging from prevention with diet and exercise to different types of medications. The Thirty-Seven Paths to

Enlightenment are categorized into the seven topics of teaching to facilitate learning:

1) The Four Mindfulness Foundations (4): our body, feelings, mind, and all phenomena. This is a method of practice in meditation. We want to be aware of our body, recognize our feelings and state of mind, and be aware of our surrounding manifestations.
   * We should recognize that our body, just as other forms in the universe, is subject to change and, therefore, we need to take care of it with healthy food and nutrition.
   * We should recognize our multitude of feelings that fall into the categories of pleasure, displeasure, and neutrality. Recognizing our feelings will help us to modulate our reactive tendencies and regulate our actions to respond appropriately.
   * We need to be aware of the state of our mind (e.g., agitated or calm, right or wrong thinking) so we can direct it toward actions of peace and virtue.
   * We need to be aware of the true nature of the persons, objects, and occurrences present in our life so we do not get attached to them, or easily fault or criticize them. When we are mindful in all aspects of life, we may then understand and act righteously.
2) The Four True Endeavors (4) encourage us to promote benevolence by the following acts:
   1. If a benevolent activity has not arisen, cultivate it so it will materialize.
   2. If a benevolent activity has already arisen, cultivate it so it will be enhanced.

3. If a malevolent activity has not arisen, prevent it from appearing.
4. If a malevolent activity has already arisen, extinguish it.

3) The Four Practices to achieve Transcendental Power (4): zeal, diligence, mindfulness, and contemplation. These four practices, when developed righteously, can result in the power and strength to achieve any goals to our greatest satisfaction.

* When we aspire or have the desire for a certain goal, this is our internal drive that will motivate us to fulfill our ambition. Desire is good so as long as it is headed toward well-being and not ill-being.
* Because we have this eagerness to achieve, we put in our best, continuous effort and diligence in our work to accomplish our aspirations.
* Mindfulness with right thoughts is needed to help us concentrate and focus upon our objectives, in order to make the right decisions.
* Lastly, contemplation helps us to look deeply and see clearly our goals, what is needed to achieve them, and use the wisdom we have gained to stay on the path toward completion.

4) The Five Roots or Foundations of Practice (5): the root of faith, the root of diligence, the root of mindfulness, the root of concentration, and the root of wisdom.

* Faith creates trust and understanding for us to commit to further our studies. Diligence is needed to continue our practice. Mindfulness helps us remember the Dharma teachings and create awareness of our thoughts, speech, and actions, so we know the appropriate time, place, and person to

act upon. Concentration is the focus that will help us see clearly and subsequently develop insight and wisdom from contemplation.

5) The Five Powers (5): the power of faith, the power of diligence, the power of mindfulness, the power of concentration, and the power of wisdom.

   * These Five Powers are the result of the practice of the Five Roots.

6) The Seven Elements of Enlightenment (7): mindfulness, right determination, right effort, serenity, joy, concentration, and equanimity.

   * Mindfulness helps us choose the right path in life. Once we make the right determination toward a committed goal, we put in the right effort and maintain a gentle composure to achieve the results that will bring us joy. We continue to work with a concentrated mind and can let go when conditions are no longer optimal.

7) The Noble Eightfold Path sums it all up (8). If we have the right view and understanding, we can develop and practice the other thirty-six paths to achieve happiness and enlightenment.

The elements of each of the seven categories constitute a total of Thirty-Seven Paths to Enlightenment to follow and practice for the treatment of suffering.

The Thirty-Seven Paths are the expanded version of the Noble Eightfold Path.

The Dharma Wheel, consisting of either eight or twelve spokes, is all-encompassing of the principal teachings of the Buddha—The Four Noble Truths and the Noble Eightfold Path. The teachings define the diagnosis and treatment of the suffering that we seek to understand in life. They contain the ingredients and qualities of compassion, wisdom, effort, equanimity, and joy, which are needed to practice and cultivate in order to live a meaningful and happy life. We want to ensure that this wheel keeps spinning in motion to propagate this realization.

Chapter 4

The Middle Way

The dot in the middle of the Buddha's forehead represents the Middle Way and impartiality. The dot is actually a long white strand of hair, one of the Buddha's thirty-two great features that emanates a halo of radiant light in all directions. It depicts the Buddha's wisdom spanning multidirectionally upward toward heaven, downward to the underworld, and outward onto earth. This wisdom is from the practice of deep contemplation and right thoughts, leading to enlightenment. The Middle Way, or Middle Path, is one of the initial realizations and teachings of the Buddha after his Enlightenment. Prince Siddhartha spent six years of an austere practice of physical self-deprivation that caused him to be severely emaciated to the point that his bones were prominent and visible under his skin, and he nearly collapsed. He was revived by a bowl of rice milk offered by Sujata and subsequently realized the importance of deterring from the extremes of the practice. He realized that even though our body can cause us suffering, we need to nourish a healthy mind and body in order to study and practice to achieve enlightenment, wisdom, and liberation. The Buddha observed a group of three musicians who were adjusting their violin strings and saw how the process affected the sound produced. The first musician tightened his violin strings too much, breaking them and leaving his violin unable to produce sound. The second musician loosened his strings too much and made his instrument sound out of tune when played. Finally, the third musician, learning from the mistakes of his two compatriots, adjusted his strings carefully and just right, making his violin produce beautiful music. It is in moderation that balance is found. From this insight, the Buddha teaches the Middle Path to apply moderation in everything we do in life and avoid either extreme of indulgence or asceticism. He applies this to our life's paths and in our studies. When we take care of our children, we should not stay up all night or miss a meal to care for them. If we neglect our health and become sick, we end up not being able to accomplish our ultimate goal, which is to wholeheartedly care for our loved ones. In regards to our studies, we may get burnout if we are too stringent and study nonstop. If we are too lenient, pursuing the pleasures of the material life, we will have no time to focus upon our studies. We should put all our efforts to work based on the capacity and potential of our health, so that we can bring benefit to others while not adversely affecting ourselves physically or mentally. The Middle Path also has a deeper

The Middle Way is the practice of the Noble Eightfold Path.

The three violins

meaning, teaching us to be flexible and adapt in all types of situations. We should not be fixed, attached, or narrow-minded. For example, if our friend prepared homemade food from his or her heart and brings it to us after we have eaten a full meal, we cannot be upfront, refuse the offering, and comment that we are practicing the Middle Way. We should not say, "I am full and, therefore, cannot eat your food." Instead, we need to be flexible and try a little bit of food to make him or her happy. This is the practice of the Middle Way. Avoiding the extremes, living in moderation, and having flexibility in our interactions will provide more satisfaction and fulfillment to our life.

Chapter 5

Cause and Condition

Cause and Condition is a term explaining that a precursor state with the right condition has to be sufficiently present for a subsequent state or event to exist. In Vietnamese, this term is commonly known as "nhân duyên." In other words, the manifestation of an object or event is dependent on the nature of its antecedent object or event, under the right conditions. This is how Buddhism explains why things happen the way they do and the reasons that events occur.

There are twelve interlinked factors in the doctrine of Cause and Condition. They flow through like a domino sequence, as the presence of one factor creates the presence of the next factor, and the extinction of one factor creates an extinction of the next factor. This concept is difficult to grasp, as we really need to contemplate each factor to see how each results in the next to create a recurring domino effect. The twelve factors and the corresponding treatments are:

Factors	*Treatments*
1. Delusion	1. Insight
2. Volitional action	2. Great vow
3. Consciousness	3. Wisdom
4. Forms and formless	4. The body and mind
5. The six sensory organs	5. A blessed functioning body
6. Contact	6. Purity in contact
7. Feelings	7. Purity of feelings
8. Desire	8. Compassion and joy
9. Attachment	9. Non-attachment
10. Existence	10. Nonexistence
11. Birth	11. Non-birth
12. Demise	12. Nirvana

In the life cycle, we are confined to the vicious cycle of the twelve interlinked factors that start out with delusion.

* Delusion is when there is a lack of clarity, insight, and understanding. Delusion leads to volitional actions that are not whole or benevolent.
* The volitional actions then lead to awareness in our consciousness, which gives a distinction of our likes, dislikes, or neutral sensation.
* Our consciousness sees and acknowledges the forms and non-forms (all physical and mental phenomena).
* The forms and non-forms are the objects of our six sensory organs (eyes, ears, nose, mouth, body, and consciousness).
* Our six sensory organs contact external objects and develop feelings of desire, leading to attachment, and coming to existence.
* Coming to existence leads to birth then death, and a repeat of the life cycle.

To break the cycle, we have to develop insight in order to replace the condition of delusion. This insight leads to a great vow, a commitment to a virtuous action. The great vow leads to wisdom in the actions of our body and mind that will result in a blessed, functioning body with purity in contact and feelings, compassion and joy, and non-attachment. Non-attachment leads to nonexistence, non-birth, and subsequent nirvana. In summary, the treatment to break the cycle of suffering is to start out with insight instead of delusion, so we can end up in a state of purity and serenity.

In the doctrine of Cause and Condition, the cause and the right condition form a favorable situation for consequential states to arise. For an event to arise, several conditions need to be present:

1) The precursor state, the cause
2) The right opportunity and conditions
3) The end result

	the right opportunity and conditions	
precursor state (Seed)	⟶ (sunlight, water, soil nutrients)	consequential state (fruit)
(desire to study the Dharma)	be involved in planning a retreat (transportation, good eyesight, hearing)	a retreat hosted at the temple

There are several conditions that are required to yield a good, juicy fruit. We first need a wholesome seed for the farmer to sow. For the seed to sprout, optimal conditions from sunlight, water, and fertile soil need to be available. So, given the right opportunity and conditions, a seed can yield a fruit. Other times, we have to take action to create the opportunity to accomplish a desired activity. An example is when we first develop the intention to start studying and practicing the Dharma. We need to have the blessings of good health and other external factors to engage in the activity. We need to have transportation to get to the temple, good eyesight to read, and intact hearing to listen to the teachings. However, if the temple does not host a retreat for the Sangha to convene and practice, we cannot attend and further our practice. We need to foster the opportunity and be involved with the Sangha to plan for the retreat. The initial work we invest in will sow the seed of our determination to study and practice the Dharma teachings. We need to initiate, create, and support the favorable conditions and hope to have benevolent rather than malevolent conditions. Once an event organizational group is summoned, we have to capture and maintain the energy of the group to finish the project. With much effort and work, the result is a well-planned retreat where practitioners can convene at the temple to further their study and practice of the Dharma. We should recognize and cherish the good conditions to maintain and enhance them, so we can achieve the ultimate conditions with a better planned retreat in subsequent years. At times, there may be conditions causing mishaps in the activities and events of the retreats. We just then have to accept and follow the conditions in accordance with their course. When we work hard toward a goal but cannot accomplish it, we have to realize that it is not because the conditions are not there, but the combined conditions are insufficient to achieve the end result. In life, there is a cause, but the result or effect is attributed to the heavenly powers. In Buddhist philosophy, there is a cause, but the result or effect is attributed to the right conditions. All the right conditions have to be sufficient for an event to manifest. The cause, along with the right conditions, results in an effect. This is the doctrine of Cause and Condition, which is also termed Conditioned Genesis or Dependent Origination.

Chapter 6

Cause and Effect

Cause and Effect is another important principle that the Buddha realized after his Enlightenment. Cause and Effect applies to us irrespective of our religious beliefs. Whether we believe in this principle or not, it occurs in our daily life as this is the natural law of the universe. When there is a cause, there is an effect. Nothing happens by accident or coincidence. There is a reason and cause for every event and occurrence.

One of the principal teachings that exemplifies Cause and Effect is karma. The word "karma" should not carry any negative connotation, as karma can be negative or positive. The Buddha teaches that karma is developed as a habit from our repetitive thoughts, speech, and actions. Everything originates from the mind. From our thoughts, they are translated into the words we say and the things we do. We can help and service others through our positive thoughts, kind words, and how we live and model our life. If we initiate the thought of wanting to help our friend pass a test, we express this to our friend and spend time tutoring him or her. If we have an unkind thought of not sharing an extra jacket with someone who is cold, we tell him or her we do not have an extra jacket and will not share. When we develop right, mindful thoughts, they will yield positive, wholesome speech and actions. When we develop wrong, unmindful thoughts, they will yield negative, unwholesome speech and actions. When this happens, that happens. When this does not occur, that does not occur. We can develop karma as a group working together to put on a retreat. We can develop karma filled with blessings, merits, or malevolence. This doctrine makes us accountable for the repercussion of our actions and accept the blessings of our good deeds. This is a universal law of Cause and Effect which cannot be defied.

The doctrine of Cause and Effect is omnipresent.
It applies to our life whether we believe in it or not.

There are three karmic concepts in the practice:

1) The karmic action
2) The karmic Cause
3) The karmic Effect

Our karmic actions propel the energy of karmic Cause and Effect. Our preceding actions determine the events in our current life. If we do good deeds, this will result in immense blessings; if we do bad deeds, this will result in retributions. Our material possessions may be gained or lost, but we cannot escape from the ownership of our karma. Our karma is the one and only thing that we permanently own that will follow us through the realms of our life cycle.

Our life cycle flows through the different Six Paths or realms of existence upon rebirth, depending on our karma. The Six Paths are:

1) The heaven realm
2) The asura realm
3) The human realm
4) The underworld
5) The hungry ghost world
6) The animal world

Rebirth into the heaven realm is what everyone wants, but the happiness and joy here are subject to change. The asura realm is for those who have blessings, but they do not know how to appreciate them because they are in constant strife. The human realm is where we possess a mind and sensory organs with which to study and practice the Dharma teachings to escape from the cycles of birth and death to arrive at the Four Holy Paths. The underworld is filled with darkness and suffering, assigned to those who have bad karma. The hungry ghost world is where there is a lack of food and supplies for sustenance. And the animal world is the lowest realm where there is no opportunity to study the Dharma teachings because there is constant rivalry and competition for survival. It is said that these Six Paths represent and parallel with the fluctuating state and condition of our mind in our daily life: from joy in the heavenly world to anger in the asura world, dissatisfaction in the human world, chaos in the underworld and hungry ghost world, and rivalry in the animal world. The last three realms, comprising of the underworld, the hungry ghost world, and the animal world, also correlate with the tragedies in the world. We experience the state of the underworld during a fire, the hungry ghost world during a flood, and the animal world in an assassination. The Six Paths are the realms of existence upon rebirth, which also represent the state of our mind and consciousness.

There are an additional Four Holy Paths beyond the Six Paths that, together, make up a total of Ten Realms of existence. The Four Holy Paths are the realms where we achieve enlightenment:

1) The realm of the Hearer
2) The realm of awakening from Cause and Condition
3) The realm of the Bodhisattva
4) The realm of the Buddha

The realm of the Hearer is where we achieve enlightenment from listening to the doctrine of the Four Noble Truths and have surpassed the Six Paths. The enlightenment from the realm of Cause and Condition occurs when life's events awaken us to the noble truths, and we understand the sources and etiologies of the twelve interlinked factors. The realm of the Bodhisattva is for those who have achieved enlightenment and performed the vows of a Bodhisattva to aid others in their difficulties and guide them towards liberation and enlightenment. The realm of the Buddha is the ultimate level where we want to arrive with perfect enlightenment, wisdom, and compassion. Establishing good karma during our present life will result in a fortunate rebirth into the highest realm of the Six Paths or the Four Holy Paths.

If we have ill-natured karma, we can be born into unfortunate conditions that make it difficult to encounter the Buddha and the Dharma teachings. There are eight conditions that the Buddha describes:

1) To be born in the dark place of the underworld realm
2) To be born in the hungry ghost realm
3) To be born in the animal realm
4) To be born in the heaven realm
5) To be born in a bountiful and pleasant residence
6) To be born with a deficiency of the sense faculties: blind, mute, deaf, and dumb
7) To be born with too much of the worldly intelligence
8) To be born before or after the Buddha

The underworld has suffering. The hungry ghost and animal worlds have competitive living conditions and lack the mental capacity to study the Dharma. The fourth and fifth conditions, to remain in the heaven realm and bountiful, pleasant residence, provide less motivation to study because of too much pleasure and happiness along with an extended lifespan. The lack of the senses impedes our ability to study the Dharma. We cannot study when we are unable to see or hear. The seventh difficult condition, possessing too much worldly knowledge and intelligence, interferes with our faith and acceptance of the spiritual teachings. Lastly, the eighth adverse condition is to be born before or after the Buddha, where there is no opportunity to know and learn of the Buddha and his teachings. The realm that we are reborn into depends on the karma that we develop during our present life time. This is an example of karmic Cause and Effect. We should not feel despair for existing in a less fortunate condition or having been born into a lower realm. Instead, we should transform our negative karma into a vow to do goodness, so that we can develop positive karma and be reborn into the highest level of the Six Paths or Four Holy Paths.

Karma is an important teaching in Buddhism because it is the drive for our perpetual existence. Repetitive thoughts, speech, and actions become a habitual energy that give rise to karma. These habitual energies span over three time periods: past, present, and future. Our past actions can result in retributions or rewards either immediately, months or years later in this present life, or in our future life. The results of certain actions take longer to manifest, similar to how certain trees take longer to yield fruits. Karma explains the reasons for our blessings and misfortunes in our present life. It explains how certain people possess the fortunate conditions that are difficult to attain in life. It is difficult to be reborn into the realm of human life and be able to live peacefully through the entire duration of our normal lifespan. Furthermore, it is difficult to have the capability to listen and understand the miracle of the Dharma and be able to encounter a holy person, such as one who teaches the Dharma. Lastly, it is difficult to be able to live in a good environment and have good friends and teachers. It is a blessing to be born in the human realm and possess the intellectual thought processes and complete proper function of our six sensory organs in order to study and practice the Dharma. Therefore, we should cherish the life we have and work each day to arrive towards the Four Holy Paths by using our body and six sensory organs righteously. We should envision thoughts of helping others instead of harming them. We should speak words that elicit love rather than hatred. We should act with kindness instead of causing grief to others. If we have the blessing to live the entirety of our life span, we should strive to live a purposeful life with meaning, rather than squander our valuable time on earth. We should live so that we remain in others' hearts, become dearly missed by others, and prevail in peace and triumph upon our passing. This way, we create good living conditions and lasting friendships in our life. Although we all have the innate Buddha-nature within, everyone has different levels and capabilities of understanding the Dharma. The ability to encounter the Dharma and a holy teacher is a blessing we should value highly. When we are blessed to be born in fortunate conditions, we should continue to create wholesome karma for a more favorable rebirth.

The state of our karma can be transformed toward goodness. We should be determined to create virtuous karma and not be fixated on negative karma. This is seen in an analogy of the four types of people that the Buddha points out. The first is a person who has suffering but is able to experience joy. This is a person who knows how to transform his or her karma by performing virtuous acts. He or she knows the law of Cause and Effect and understands that the current suffering is due to previous malevolent acts or the lack of benevolent acts. As such, he or she may experience bodily suffering but is not weighed down by mental suffering. The second type of person is one who has happiness but then experiences suffering. This person is not able to recognize that his or her current blessings are due to previous benevolent acts. He or she enjoys all the current blessings and does not perform any benevolent acts to maintain or create more blessings. The third type of person is one who experiences suffering and continues to suffer. This type of person does not understand why he or she suffers and does not know the law of Cause and Effect. He or she does not perform any benevolent acts but continues to bring suffering to others. The fourth type of person is one who experiences happiness and continues to enjoy happiness. This type of person shares his or her blessings with others and continues to reap more blessings. This teaching on the four types of people exemplifies the law of Cause and Effect by transforming karma. Although we cannot escape from the consequences of our actions, we should not yield to them; instead, we should alter our old, negative karma by vowing to do better so we can create new, positive karma.

Cause and Effect are seen in the three troubling processes that cause a hindrance to our practice:

1) The impediment of hardship and affliction
2) The impediment of karmic action and energy
3) The resultant impediment

These three impediments create obstacles in a vicious cycle if we do not recognize and fix them. If we did not give generously in our past life, we would be consequently less fortunate in this life. This condition can cause difficulties and sorrow in our present life, resulting in feelings of jealousy and sadness, and thereby creating a cycle of negative karmic energy where we fail to give with a kind heart. Subsequently, this results in fewer blessings and greater adversities in the future. However, if we recognize the reasons we are born in a less fortunate condition, we can give joyfully in this life to transform a negative to a positive karmic energy, which will yield blessings in the future to break this cyclic process. The karmic energy can be either negative or positive, giving rise to sorrow or happiness and their corresponding consequences.

Most importantly is to recognize the conditions and afflictions that cause us to have feelings of jealousy, sadness or anger, so we can change our actions and reactions towards a better karma and outcome. This way, we use our internal energy to change the habitual energy.

The Buddha uses the Cause and Effect principle to guide us toward a happy life by preventing the actions that would be problematic and result in sorrow and suffering. He teaches us to avoid the wrongdoings and malevolent acts outlined in the Five Precepts, which is a teaching on morality. The Five Precepts dictate as follows:

1) No killing
2) No stealing
3) No sexual misconduct
4) No lying
5) No consumption of unhealthy food or harmful exposures to the body and mind (e.g., alcohol, drugs, and violent movies)

If we knowingly smoke cigarettes, despite the warning label that cigarettes may cause cancer, we should not be aghast if we develop cancer. If we have extramarital affairs, we have to accept the consequences of ruining the happiness of our family and others. When problems arise out of our unskilled and unmindful actions, there is nothing that the Buddha or anyone can do to help us. The Buddha points out the wrongdoings (the cause), so we can prevent committing them. But he cannot and does not have any power to change the effect of our actions. We have to accept and live with the results of our actions, whether good or bad. This is the principle of Cause and Effect.

Chapter 7

Bodhisattvas and Buddhas

There are other Buddhas besides the Shakyamuni Buddha. These Buddhas and Bodhisattvas are only known through the Mahayana school (Greater Vehicle) of Buddhism, which is prevalent in the northern Asian countries such as China, Tibet, Japan, and Vietnam. The Greater Vehicle path concentrates on helping others reach liberation and enlightenment as well as practicing for ourselves. Our knowledge of the Bodhisattvas and other Buddhas is revealed through Shakyamuni Buddha's physical presence in this world in the sixth century B.C.E. The Theravada branch (Lesser Vehicle) of Buddhism, prevalent in southern Asian countries such as Thailand, Cambodia, Laos, Sri Lanka, and Burma, follows the original teachings of the Shakyamuni Buddha and does not include the Bodhisattvas or other Buddhas. The Lesser Vehicle path mainly focuses on practicing toward enlightenment and liberation for oneself. Shakyamuni Buddha is the original and historical Buddha for both Vehicles. All schools of Buddhism have in common the belief of the four Dharma Seals (impermanence, tribulations, non-reality and non-self, and Nirvana) as the core teachings of the Buddha. In a time where there was social inequality in the caste system and unrest and rivalry in society, the Buddha provided teachings to live a virtuous life through the understanding and meaning of the true essence of life. Buddhism was transformed in the Mahayana school in response to the needs of the people to have some hope of an eternal life and relief of suffering in their present life. It brought some aspects of divinity with supernatural powers to the Bodhisattvas and other Buddhas for people to worship and pray to. It also allowed some flexibility in the practice to assimilate the teachings in differing cultures. For example, in the Theravada tradition, the monastics are discouraged from singing as this activity can invoke desiring emotions which can interfere with their practice. However, in the Mahayana teaching, singing lyrics that contain the Dharma teachings provides a form of entertainment, joy, and bonding in the Sangha communal activity. This reinforces the teachings and remembrance of the Buddha and what he represents. Despite the different sectors, they both have a common thread to study, internalize, and practice the Dharma teachings.

A Bodhisattva is a great being who has attained enlightenment, but because of great compassion, delayed the gratification to Buddhahood and remained in this world to share this enlightenment to liberate humankind. Bodhisattvas provide comfort for people to turn to amidst their troubled times in life and support them in the practice to prevent regression. Bodhisattvas follow a great path to direct the mind to the highest level. They are committed to uphold the precepts and avoid malevolent acts, perform virtuous acts, and liberate others. A Bodhisattva has the characteristic of truth, virtue, and beauty and can be represented in any object, figure, or person that reminds us to live and follow the righteous path. The Bodhisattva nature can be seen in the Buddhist robe, reminding us of the practice of patience. It can be seen in the eighteen bead bracelet, reminding us to be mindful of our reactive judgment to the six sensory inputs. Or it can be seen in a stranger who stops to help us change a flat tire for our car on the side of the road, despite being late for an important meeting. Compared to the Buddha statue, the Bodhisattva statue has more of a human character with hair and other adornments to display more intimacy and closeness to us.

In the Mahayana tradition, the original and historical Buddha also revealed to us the presence of other Buddhas who have different vows. These Buddhas are known to us through the introduction from the Shakyamuni Buddha. A Buddha is characterized by complete noble wisdom and action. There is the Medicine Buddha, Vaidurya Buddha, who is frequently revered in times of our sickness. He projects the deep blue color of the Lapis Lazuli stone, which has an innate healing power. He is depicted holding a medicinal herb or a seven-level tower symbolic of the Seven Elements of Enlightenment needed to treat our mental ailments. He presides over the realm of the Eastern Pure Land where the sun rises, signaling life and the beginning of a new day. There are other Buddhas corresponding to three different time spans. The Amitabha Buddha is the past Buddha. Shakyamuni Buddha is the present-day historical Buddha. Maitreya, "the Happy Buddha," is the future Buddha. The Amitabha Buddha, who portrays purity, is the guardian of the Western Pure Land, where the sun sets at the end of the day for us to return back to ourselves with purity and serenity. The Western Pure Land

Vaidurya, the Medicine Buddha

represents a state of sublime joy and is where everyone strives to reach during and at the end of our life. There is Maitreya, well-known as "the Happy Buddha," who is depicted laughing with a jolly face and a big belly surrounded by five or six playful children. The five children represent our five sense organs (eyes, ears, nose, mouth, and body), their senses (sight, sound, smell, taste and touch), and sensory inputs that constantly prod and stir us. Sensory consciousness is the sixth sense organ that has no form and, therefore, the sixth child is sometimes not included in the statue. The Happy Buddha is commonly seen at the façade of the meditation building to greet us. His big belly contains all that life presents, but he is still able to show exuberance due to his great vow of joy and non-attachment. He is cheerful despite being bothered by the five children and exposed to the extreme weather of the outdoors. The elation that he portrays is similar to what we experience in our initial step into our study and practice. This happiness is different than the internal joy we subsequently develop from the satisfaction and realization from our study and practice. Maitreya is actually a Bodhisattva, rather than a Buddha. He is referred to as the "Future Buddha" in anticipation of his appearance on earth to reintroduce the Dharma to us if and when it gets lost. Among the different types of Buddhas, the Shakyamuni Buddha is the only one who has ever emerged into our world, through flesh and body, to teach us the Dharma and divulge the presence of other Buddhas and Bodhisattvas. There are many other Buddhas, but the Medicine Buddha, Amitabha Buddha, and the Happy Buddha are the most commonly known in the Mahayana school.

In summary, Buddhas and Bodhisattvas possess great understanding and insight. Both serve as forms in symbolism

82 *The Symbolisms in Buddhism*

Maitreya, the Happy Buddha

to remind us to develop and cultivate the differing virtues they represent. A more detailed discussion of each Bodhisattva and the Amitabha Buddha is outlined in the next chapter.

Chapter 8

The Altar

Worshiping at the altar serves to remind us of the path to attain happiness and deliverance from afflictions. The Buddha and Bodhisattva statues portray their vows of conduct and virtue for us to learn, follow, and practice. The statues merely remind us to reflect inward and see the Buddha-nature in us. At the altar, the Buddha statue is sometimes placed singly or positioned in between two Bodhisattvas. The most common arrangement is with the Avalokiteshvara Bodhisattva statue on the left side and the Kshitigarbha Bodhisattva statue on the right side of the Buddha. Another placement has the Manjushri Bodhisattva statue on the left side and the Samantabhadra Bodhisattva statue on the right side of the Buddha. A second set of statues forming the trinity at the altar is the Amitabha Buddha flanked by the Bodhisattvas Avalokiteshvara to his left and Mahasthamaprapta to his right. The most striking feature in the Buddha statue is his varying hand gestures which portray an energetic message. The hand gesture is a seal

86 *The Symbolisms in Buddhism*

The Kshitigarbha Bodhisattva *The Buddha* *The Avalokiteshvara Bodhisattva*

The Samantabhadra Bodhisattva *The Buddha* *The Manjushri Bodhisattva*

The Altar 87

The Great
Mahasthamaprapta
Bodhisattva

The Amitabha
Buddha

The Great
Avalokiteshvara
Bodhisattva

(mudra), which is an expression of the mind. Besides the statues, there are decorative displays of fruit trays, flowers, pairs of lights, and a canister holding the three incenses that convey the Dharma teachings. Let's learn what they all represent!

A statue of the Buddha is the centerpiece of the altar. The Buddha statue is usually depicted sitting in a crossed-legged lotus position with his eyes slightly looking downward to portray deep contemplation. Unlike the round Happy Buddha with a laughing gesture, the Buddha statue has a gentle smile that represents the intrinsic joy from deep concentration and peace. The Buddha has thirty-two great physical features that portray his holiness. A prominent feature of the Buddha is a protuberance at the crown of his head that has emerged from meditative concentration. There are five thin circular halos of radiant light behind his head that represent the wisdom radiating from his mind. The halos from the mind also spread to emanate the halos of light from his body to represent each step, word, and action carried out in mindfulness. And if we look closely, his hair is swirled to the right which signifies his teaching of goodness and righteousness. One of his distinguished features is a significant symbol, the swastika, on the Buddha's chest that signifies a focus of merit and tranquility that is beautiful and magnificent. The swastika forms a square shape that consists of two Z-shaped lines connected midway. In the Eastern tradition, people associate this symbol with prosperity and good luck. It is unfortunate that this symbol now carries a negative connotation for Westerners and the entire world since the Nazis took this spiritual symbol in vain and rotated it ninety degrees into a diamond figure to serve as their national emblem. While it is unpleasant to mention the Nazi emblem in the context of

The Buddha

90   *The Symbolisms in Buddhism*

The Buddha's swastika

The Nazi's emblem

Buddhism, it is a necessity to provide clarification and understanding of this significant and holy symbol situated at the heart of the Buddha, which embodies the vast serenity that is as big as the ocean and clouds. The Buddha statue also has varying positions of his arms and hands to project a spiritual seal. His left hand is sometimes seen holding an alms bowl. A position with the right palm facing up resting on top of the left palm positioned on his lap signifies a meditative state. Another position of this meditative state is the right and left fingers approximating one another with the hands resting on his lap. The touching the earth mudra has the right palm resting on the knee with fingers pointing downward, reminding us to live in the present moment. Another position, with the right open palm raised at the level of the right chest, denotes emotional support and comfort while the right thumb tip touching the index tip forming a complete circle marks the transmission of his teachings. The presence of the Buddha statue reminds us that the nature of the Buddha is in us, and that we need to reflect inward and evoke our Buddha-nature in order to bring outward the kindness and compassion in our thoughts, speech, and actions. We cannot expect to find the Buddha anywhere externally without recognizing that there is a Buddha in each and every one of us. The statue's presence is similar to that of a policeman who reminds us to slow down and adhere to the speed limit or an ambulance that reminds us how fragile life can be. So the Buddha not only serves as a figure of reverence, but he is a teacher who reminds us of the practice that we need in pursuit of transformation and improvement in all aspects of our life. The Buddha has the characteristics of enlightenment, compassion, and invincible strength that we need to emulate.

92 *The Symbolisms in Buddhism*

Meditation

Touching the earth

Emotional support

Teaching transmission

The four mudras (hand seals)

The Great Avalokiteshvara Bodhisattva symbolizes great immeasurable compassion, patience, and deep listening. All Bodhisattvas are referred to in the masculine form except for the Great Avalokiteshvara, because her great vow of compassion, patience, and deep listening is similar to that of a mother's love. Nevertheless, the masculine and feminine forms are only used as a reference of discussion, as the true nature of all forms is not real. Bodhisattvas mainly represent the mind of enlightenment and are not linked to forms of any specific gender. The Avalokiteshvara Bodhisattva is the most well-known and commonly seen Bodhisattva in the temples and books on Buddhism because many practitioners pray to her to alleviate their sufferings. She is depicted in several forms. She can be seen as a statue with a thousand eyes and a thousand hands. The thousand eyes represent immeasurable compassion and the thousand hands signify immeasurable love. Her eyes see our suffering and her hands provide support. She is able to look deeply into the world to understand and listen to the call of living people who are suffering. For this reason, she is the Bodhisattva most remembered and called upon. Another form shows the three faces of the Great Avalokiteshvara, representing the trio essential characteristics of compassion, wisdom, and great strength that every practitioner should cultivate. Here, each statue holds an object to portray these qualities. The first statue holds a sweet nectar jug representing compassion. The second statue holds the Sutra book of the Prajna Paramita, which represents wisdom. The third statue holds the Dharma Wheel spinning in continuous motion, representing great strength in the propagation of the Dharma. She is most commonly seen as a single statue, standing or sitting. In her left hand she carries a holy water jug containing sweet nectar. The nectar

94 *The Symbolisms in Buddhism*

The Thousand-hand Avalokiteshvara

The Altar 95

The three faces of Avalokiteshvara

The Great Avalokiteshvara Bodhisattva

The Altar 97

The Avalokiteshvara Bodhisattva

represents pure calmness, loving-kindness, and gentle speech as an antidote to allay anxiety, anger, and sorrow. Her right hand holds a willow branch signifying flexibility, adaptability, and perseverance. To apply this to our life, we need to use kind speech and know when and how to talk so others feel more comfortable and receptive to our advice and recommendations. For example, when someone is upset over a disappointing event, it would not help if we approach to tell him or her immediately to accept and get over it, as it has happened already. Although this may be the reality, we need to choose the right time to broach the topic and wait until he or she is settled down before empathizing and giving advice. Similarly, when a child acts inappropriately, he or she will respond more positively if we discipline him or her in a gentle tone of voice in a private environment, rather than a harsh one in a public setting. As such, the Great Avalokiteshvara statue serves as a reminder for us to practice compassion, patience, and deep listening to help our everyday interaction with others become pleasant and amicable.

The Great Kshitigarbha is the Bodhisattva of Great Vow who represents the state of our mind. When our mind is in a state of anger, hatred, and delusion, he helps us escape from the realms of suffering in the underworld to see the light of compassion and wisdom. The underworld is a place of profuse darkness and incessant suffering, and a time when we are petrified, unhappy, and confused. Kshitigarbha resembles a monastic with his shaven head and a simple robe. He is usually depicted carrying a circular jewel in his left hand to light up the darkness and illusion of the world we live in, and a staff in his right hand to guide us out of our transgressions. The staff provides a stable support to anchor and prevent the regression of our practice. The four curved designs at the tip

The Kshitigarbha Bodhisattva

of the staff represent the Four Noble Truths, reminding us of the teaching towards liberation. And on each of the four curved designs, there are three circular patterns (totaling twelve) representing the twelve interlinked factors of Cause and Condition. The twelve factors of Cause and Condition explain the genesis of the state of our mind and karma. Thus, the Great Kshitigarbha carries the two core teachings to practice towards liberation and mindfulness. He represents the mind that we need to develop to be solid and radiant so we can withstand and leave the state of the underworld. Symbolically, the underworld is a state when we have anger, hatred, and delusion. The Great Kshitigarbha works on the salvation of the deceased in the underworld while the Great Avalokiteshvara helps sentient beings. The Great Kshitigarbha reminds us that our mind can linger in an abyss due to attachment and not being able to let go, thereby motivating us to return to our innate, awakened mind to practice and develop wisdom in order to escape.

The Great Manjushri is the Bodhisattva of Great Understanding and Wisdom. He is well-known for his ability to detect unanswered and perplexing questions from assembly members attending the Buddha's sermons. He serves as a representative to ask the Buddha to clarify and expound on the subject matter in question. At the altar, the Manjushri Bodhisattva is positioned to the left of the Buddha, when coupled with the Great Samantabhadra. He is depicted holding a sword in his right hand and a lotus stem in his left hand while riding on a blue lion. The sword cuts through ignorance and delusion, transforming them into wisdom. The lotus flower is held close to his heart, supporting the book containing the Prajna Paramita Mantra of complete understanding. The lion underneath represents the robustness and strength of his

The Manjushri Bodhisattva

wisdom. Similar to the lion who is king of the jungle, the power of wisdom is supreme and can overcome all afflictions in life. The Great Manjushri's vow of deep thoughts and contemplation before each action reminds us to practice mindfulness in order to achieve understanding and wisdom.

The Great Samantabhadra is the Bodhisattva of Great Action. He helps to elaborate on the Buddha's discourses to turn them into an established sermon by asking the Buddha to assign a title and name to his talks, so they can be disseminated in their proper format. At the altar, the Samantabhadra Bodhisattva is placed to the right of the Buddha and is usually depicted holding a lotus and riding on a white elephant. The lotus represents achievements gained from overcoming adversities. The elephant signifies the great force it possesses to stampede through all difficulties and illusions. The white color of the elephant represents the purity of virtuous karmic actions. The white elephant has six tusks, instead of the usual two. These six tusks represent the six elements in the Vehicle of the Bodhisattva, which are practiced to achieve liberation and salvation. The six elements are generosity, upholding the precepts, patience, effort, meditative concentration, and wisdom. The Great Samantabhadra's imagery teaches us to develop resilience of the mind and purity of our actions, such that our actions are always sincere and undaunted. He shows us that our actions can be powerful enough to achieve any goals and eliminate any hindrances. Therefore, we need to act with mindfulness in our thoughts, speech, and actions to yield good merits.

Lastly, the Great Mahasthamaprapta is the Bodhisattva who represents the power of wisdom. He is positioned to the right of the Amitabha Buddha while the Great Avalokiteshvara is on the left. The compassion of the Great

The Samantabhadra Bodhisattva

104 *The Symbolisms in Buddhism*

The Great Mahasthamaprapta Bodhisattva

Avalokiteshvara and the power of wisdom of the Great Mahasthamaprapta both support the Amitabha Buddha's mission to liberate human beings by encouraging us to study and practice with the ultimate goal of achieving purity and serenity in the setting of the Western Pure Land.

Bodhisattvas represent the vows that we need to commit to and apply to practice.

Amitabha is the Buddha in the past era who represents purity and serenity. He is depicted with his left palm holding a lotus which conveys concentration, and the right open palm extending downward for us to clasp and follow him to the realm of the Pure Land. He presides over the Pure Land situated in the Western Hemisphere. It has a lotus pool covered with an array of lotus flowers of different colors and seven types of cherished jewels. Each lotus emits the radiance of its innate color, signifying that each of our innate feelings and thoughts similarly projects onto our physical appearance. When we are angry, people can see that we are angry. When we have a sincere heart, others can see our kind nature projected onto our physical appearance. The seven jewels covering the lotus pond consist of gold, silver, lapis lazuli, crystal, nacre (mother of pearl), red pearl, and carnelian. These jewels remind us of the seven cherished jewels a devoted practitioner should cultivate. They are faith, morality, repentance with self, repentance with others, deep listening, release of attachments, and wisdom. Unlike the seven worldly

The Amitabha Buddha

jewels, these seven assets of a practitioner are enduring and perpetually flourish as we foster them. Figuratively, the Western Pure Land is the time and place in us where our mind is pure and calm, happy, and not subjected to any further distress. The Amitabha Buddha has three characteristics:

1) Immeasurable radiant light
2) Immeasurable meritorious deeds
3) Immeasurable longevity

We usually greet one another with Amitabha Buddha's name in Vietnamese as "A Di Đà Phật," as a way to wish each other to develop these three attributes. Immeasurable light is the insight needed to make prudent decisions which will lead us to perform good deeds and make right decisions. Immeasurable longevity does not mainly mean long life here, but that we will always be present, loved, and remembered in the remaining lives of people when we act with compassion, insight, and mindfulness. It is easy to have our name on others' phone list, but it is harder to have our name remain in someone's heart. When we take refuge in the Amitabha Buddha, his image, character, and vow lead us to a state of purity and tranquility in our present state and future destination.

At the altar, there are six offerings to the Buddha:

1) Straight incenses
2) Trays of fruits
3) Vases of flowers
4) A pair of lights
5) A pair of cups of water
6) White rice

The offerings are displayed evenly on the right and left side of the altar. This pairing represents the balance of religion and life, and the Buddha and the Buddha-nature that is in all of us. The straight incense represents the mind following a straight moral path and a life with discipline. The cup of water represents purity of the mind, concentration, and our potential as we have the Buddha-nature in us. The pair of lights represents wisdom and enlightenment, the ultimate goals of our practice. The lights have the fire of wisdom that can transform the fire of hatred. This wisdom helps us to mindfully know the right place, time, and person to talk to in the middle of a conflict. The flowers and fruits symbolize Cause and Effect, such as flowers blooming to yield fruits. The vases of flowers represent impermanence, as their beauty eventually wilts. Therefore, we take care and water them, so we can enjoy them while they are still beautiful in the present moment. Our body is of the same nature as the flower, and we should nourish it in the same manner to live as beautiful as the flower. Similarly, we should enjoy each other's company and be mindfully present for one another when the opportunity permits. Because when our encounter ends, we have no idea whether we can or will ever meet again. The trays of fruits are positioned with a strong, wide base with each row narrowing upward to the highest point. This arrangement represents a strong foundation toward higher achievement and merit. We select fruits that are sweet and tasty to arrange them in an upward rising position, representing our continuous effort to cultivate our benevolent actions. This can be accomplished through acts of kindness that build up our merits to give us a fruitful life. Lastly, the white rice represents the sweetness of the path towards awakening. These six offerings at the altar comprise a display of our reverence and deep sincere thoughts

The altar

toward the Buddha and also awaken us to the teachings of the Dharma.

The two common rituals performed at the altar are lighting the incense and bowing to the Buddha. Formal rituals are performed to display our respect to the Buddhas and Bodhisattvas. Lighting the incense is an expression of our vow to commit and follow to live our life with discipline and order. Many practitioners feel the need to light up their own three incenses at the altar despite the many that have been lit, creating heavy smoke in the meditation hall. If it is already too smoky, or if the incense is not available or cannot be lit at the altar due to building regulations or medical reasons, the inability to offer a lit incense should not be a concern. What is important is that we light our mind to represent the lighting of the incense and elicit its five natures. The five natures of the incense are:

1) Morality
2) Concentration
3) Wisdom
4) Liberation
5) Liberation from our fixated view and understanding

Each of the Five Precepts that we are able to keep is an act of lighting the incense offering to the Buddha. The time we spend in meditative concentration is an act of lighting the incense offering to the Buddha. The wisdom we use to make the right decision with every action is an act of lighting the incense offering to the Buddha. Attaining liberation devoid of emotional and physical strap is an act to light up the incense offering to the Buddha. Attaining liberation from our fixated, narrow point of view and understanding is an act of lighting the incense offering to the Buddha. Furthermore, when we treat others with kindness is when we light up our incense fragrance. These five acts of lighting the incense produce the light, beautiful fragrance that will rise and permeate in all directions.

The second ritual performed at the altar is bowing three times to the Buddhas and Bodhisattvas. Bowing is an act of putting down our pride to be humble. It is performed with the union of our mind and body in utmost reverence to the Buddha. The three bows have several significances to remind us to:

1) Pay homage to the Buddha, Dharma, and Sangha (the Three Jewels)
2) Pursue toward mindfulness, concentration, and wisdom
3) Overcome greed, hatred, and delusion

Taking refuge in the Buddha, Dharma, and Sangha is the first step that each practitioner learns, as the Three Jewels are the foundation of belief and reverence in Buddhism. Developing mindfulness, concentration, and wisdom are the main goals of our practice. If we see a Rolex watch on the ground, mindfulness helps us to be aware that the owner of the watch is bothered by his or her loss. Concentration helps us to remember the second of the Five Precepts, teaching us not to take what is not ours. Right concentration leads to wisdom, leading us to make the right decision to turn the watch into Lost and Found instead of keeping it. Greed, hatred, and delusion are referred to as "the three poisons." They are the sources of our sufferings that we need to subdue. There are a series of steps in the bowing ritual at the altar. First, we stand upright and join our hands in prayer against the chest. Standing upright represents our steadfast concentration. Our palms clasped together focus our mind. The ten fingers jointly placed together direct the mind to the ten directions of the entire universe (North, South, East, West, Northeast, Northwest, Southeast, Southwest, up and down). Theoretically speaking, the ten directions in Buddhism are virtuous places like the Pure Lands throughout the universe where we can direct our mind as we practice. The praying hands at the chest invoke our mind to serenity and harmony with the precepts. The hands are then brought to the forehead, directing toward the highest level. The praying hands are then lowered from the forehead, to the mouth, and then the chest to remind us to stop and reflect our thoughts, speech, and actions so all three are in unison and pure. We then lower the body to bring our two elbows and knees to the ground. As our head bows down to touch the floor, the clasped hands spread open and the palms face down to the floor, symbolizing the release of attachments and subduing our pride. This is followed by flipping the hands over to cup the forehead into our palms, which represents the opening of ourselves with a warm heart to receive others. There are rituals where two, three, four, or five bows are performed and each has its significant meanings. The two bows recognize the relative and absolute truths. A memorial service for the deceased is an example of the relative truth, while the recitation of the Sutras during the ceremony to elucidate the nature and understanding of life is the absolute truth. The funeral ceremony and gathering create an opportune time for families and guests to hear the teachings in the Sutras. The three bows represent gratitude for our parents, teachers, and government. The four bows show respect to our four parents (parents and parents-in-law) and

The Altar 113

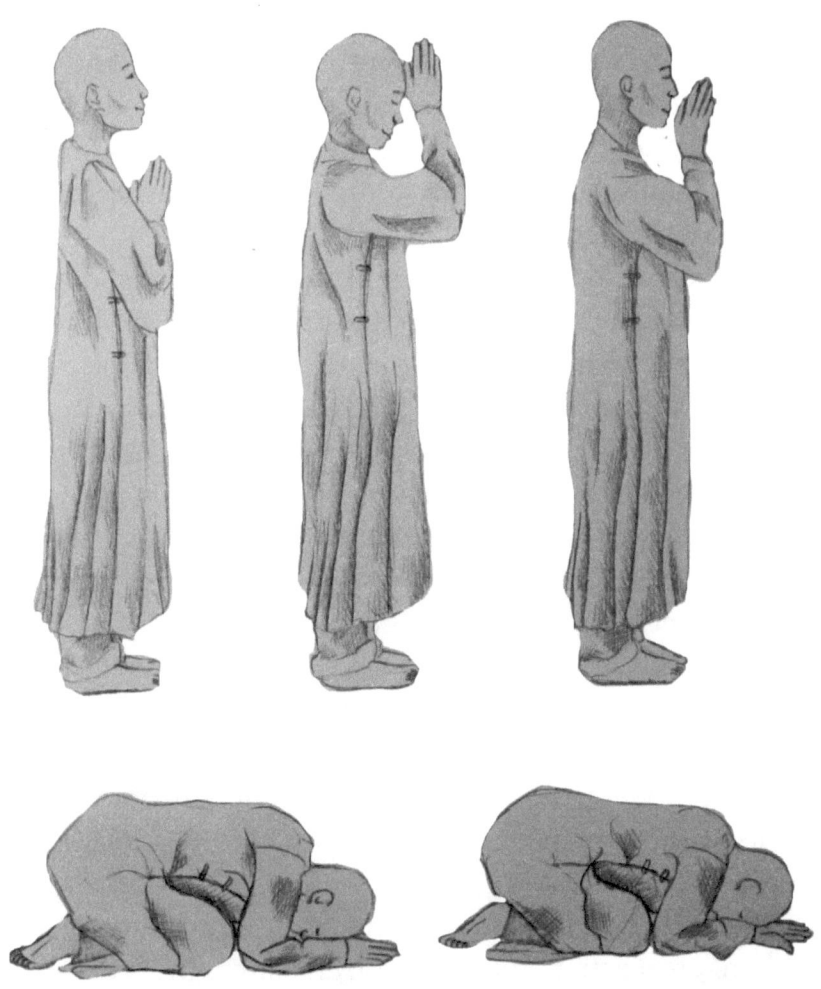

The sequences in the prostration ritual

the four cardinal directions. And the five bows direct our attention to the north, south, east, west, and central direction. Bowing also represents a greeting and gesture of appreciation and respect. Because it symbolizes many things, oftentimes we do not need to say anything but just to give a bow. When we greet each other with a bow, we are recognizing the nature of the Buddha in each of us. The rituals of bowing and lighting the incense are ways for us to show respect, exhibit our humility, and kindle our vow to further our practice and be mindful of the teachings.

Rituals and ceremonies are routinely performed at the altar. One of the reasons we show respect and pray to the Buddhas and Bodhisattvas is to study each of their vows and put them into practice. The Shakyamuni Buddha has an attribute of great effort and endeavor, the Great Manjushri his wisdom, the Great Samantabhadra his great action, the Great Avalokiteshvara her compassion, the Great Kshitigarbha his great vow, the Great Mahasthamaprapta his potency and strength, and the Amitabha Buddha his purity. The word "great" means numerous or enormous. However, the word "Great" that is referenced to the Bodhisattvas means that their heart and vows are extraordinary. "Great" also means that each of the Great Bodhisattvas represents all other Great Bodhisattvas combined. Each of their vows encompasses all the other vows. When we practice the vow of compassion, this also leads to the development and inclusion of the vows of wisdom, great action, commitment, and strength. The display of the altar has much symbolic significance with the statues and many decorations, and it is a place where we need to go and pay respect each time we visit the temple.

Chapter 9

The Ambience at the Temple

The presence of peace and tranquility can be felt as we first step into the entrance of the temple. The temple has the three doors of light to provide us blessings, insight, and wisdom. It is a place where we come near benevolence and distance ourselves from malevolence. It is where our body is nourished with food and our mind is nurtured and fulfilled by the Dharma. In between the Dharma lectures and prayers, we can always count on eating a good vegetarian meal at lunch or dinner time during our visit. What's most impressive, however, is the array of forms and figures throughout the temple's worship hall and landscape that reminds us of our mindfulness practice.

There are many different sounds and decorative objects seen throughout the temple that subtly display the Dharma teachings. The drum and bell are the two instruments sounded to elicit our wisdom and compassion, respectively. In the morning, the pounding drum awakens us to live each new day to the fullest. In the evening, the sound of the drum denotes that one more day has passed, and we need to reflect on what we have not accomplished during the day so we can improve tomorrow. The strike of the bell wakes us in the early morning from our deep, sound sleep and has the potential to awaken each and every one of us out of our delusion. Its robust sound can pacify our hearts and reverberate great distance as far as the underworld. When the bell is struck, its resonating sound steers us to the practice of mindfulness as we all silence from our activities. There are three kinds of bell: 1) the bell that concentrates and maintains our mind and attention while chanting the Sutras, 2) the bell that is sounded for announcements, and 3) the bell tower that is grand and magnificent. Another characteristic sound heard at the temple is the rhythmic striking of the drum meditation instrument accompanying the chanting of the Sutras in the meditation hall. This constant and continuous sound of the wooden instrument reminds us to practice progressively with diligence and steadfastness. The rising timbre of each strike directs us to chant in unison and maintain vigor and attention to the recitation of the Sutras. On the drum meditation instrument, there is an engraved fish emblem that represents a practitioner in a constantly awakened state, as a fish always has opened eyes, even during sleep. The fish also meanders through the currents and crevices in the water, whether deep or shallow, dirty or clean. This parallels how a practitioner should skillfully navigate through the up-and-down changes in life. There is the typical architecture of the meditation hall and its curved roof and an array of colorful Buddhist flags along the temple's walkway. The curved roof exemplifies the flexibility that is needed in our interaction of daily life with others. The Buddhist flags flank the sidewalks, leading us toward the meditation hall. The

The drum meditation instrument

*The ambience at the temple:
the curved roof, lion statues,
wavering flags, and lotus pond*

flag's design was introduced in 1885 and was formally accepted internationally in the early 1950s. It has five colors consisting of blue, yellow, red, white, and orange. The colors are arranged in large vertical rectangular blocks, followed by a short end segment with the five colors arranged horizontally to embody our collective practice. The Buddhist flag is a symbol that represents many different aspects of the Buddha's teachings through its five colors:

1) The Five Precepts
2) The five colors of the circular halo lights at the crown of the Buddha's statue, which is symbolic of enlightenment, awareness, and wisdom
3) The Five Roots of Practice: faith, diligence, mindfulness, concentration, and wisdom
4) The five organs of our body: blue for hair, yellow for skin, red for blood, white for bone, and orange for bone marrow
   * Therefore, the five colors represent our living body.
5) The five main continents of Asia, Europe, Africa, the Americas, and Australia
   * When the people of all five continents utilize the Five Roots of Practice and follow the Five Precepts, the world will be a better place with peace and harmony.

There are animal and flower imageries at the temple, such as the lion, elephant, and lotus decorations that silently but powerfully portray the Dharma teachings. The lion sculpture represents the strong, roaring voice of the Buddha to awaken us from deep sleep and delusion. The elephant statue exhibits the natural, strong force of the Buddha and his teachings. There are lotus flowers floating above a muddy pond, which

*Symbolic objects at the temple:
the drum, bell, elephant, and flag*

symbolize achievement and success over our difficulties. The mud is our difficulties. The lotus flower represents the beautiful end result arising from our diligent effort. One of the important symbols we witness at the temple is the exchanging of the rings for the newlyweds during their wedding vow. The word "ring" in Vietnamese is "nhẫn." The word "nhẫn" also means patience and tolerance. Rings are round and are usually made of solid metals of silver or gold. So the wedding ring worn on our finger serves to constantly remind us to build a marriage that is solid, complete with love, compassion, and patience. From the activities at the temple to the sounds of the instruments and the animal and flower imageries, the ambience at the temple has many symbolisms that remind us of the Dharma teachings. It is a miracle to be able to encounter the Dharma teachings and walk peacefully on earth. And it is the environment of the temple that fosters this.

Chapter 10

No Mud, No Lotus

The lotus is such an important and significant symbol in Buddhism that it deserves a chapter of its own. It symbolizes the Buddhist practice in its character, form, and effect. Each part of the lotus can be used to prepare different dishes and its characteristics provide lessons for our practice. Its form is beautiful and is copied in our hand gesture and sitting posture. Its effects to yield a fruitful flower above its muddy environment signify that our innate Buddha-nature can surface to attain enlightenment in this challenging and adventuresome life.

One of the distinct characters of the lotus is its ability to remain pure and uncontaminated despite growing in mud. Just like mud is needed for the lotus flower to surface, we need to experience hardship to become wiser and overcome impediments to realize answers. When we are living in delusion, we only see mud as mud and money as money. When we are awakened, we see a lotus flower in the mud and the potential to use our money to benefit others. In polluted water, the lotus is able to purify its environment by settling the dirt to the ground, making the water transparent and clear. Similarly, practitioners aim to purify their thoughts, speech, and actions amidst life's tribulations, calm any commotions at gatherings, and shine light to positively influence others. We should bring fragrance to wherever we go and whatever we do so others would welcome us again in the future. Besides these two qualities, the lotus is highly revered and unique in six other aspects:

1) Unlike roses and carnations, the fresh lotus flower is not used to adorn formal outfits. However, the engraving of a lotus flower with eight petals are commonly seen on the top left side of the uniform shirt worn by the family of Buddhist practitioners at the temple. The top five petals represent diligence, compassion, forgiveness and non-attachment, joy, purity and wisdom. The bottom three petals represent the Three Jewels. All eight characteristic points of the practice remind us of the qualities we need to achieve.
2) The lotus flower is ethereal and distinguishes itself by growing on its own stem, separate from the leaf.
3) Unlike other fruit trees where the flowers wilt before their fruits emerge, the lotus flowers and fruits (seeds) coexist, symbolizing the coupling presence of Cause and Effect. Our life consists of Cause and Effect. For every action, word, and thought, there is a corresponding effect and consequence. When we perform positive wholesome deeds, we receive positive wholesome outcomes, and conversely.
4) Each part of the lotus serves a function; it can be prepared into a dish or provide a life lesson. The lotus

The eight lotus petals

root, cooked in stew, provides a restful sleep and cools the flame of afflictions. The root is anchored deeply in muddy water, mirroring our tendencies to be submerged in life's afflictions. The leaf can be used as an outer covering for sticky rice cakes or rolled up with flour to be fried and eaten with sweet-and-sour sauce. The lotus leaf is known to have remarkable water-repelling properties. The leaf never gets wet as the water just rolls right off. We should learn from the lotus leaf to allow the unimportant mishaps to roll off our sleeves. Once we transform and learn from our mistakes, we should not keep the problems brewing within us. Instead, let them sprinkle on us like the droplets of water on the lotus leaf that subsequently roll off. As such, the lotus leaf symbolizes the process of detachment from our attachments. Another important part of the lotus is the seed, which sits in the seed pod. The seed can be baked to make moon cake paste and served as a dessert. The heart of the seed is bitter but can be cooked into a drink to aid in sleeping and calming our aggravation. Similarly, life's problems can give us good lessons. Coming out of any failed relationship or venture, we can reflect on how we can do better in subsequent ones rather than brood over our past failures. Maybe we can improve to become more thoughtful and understanding of other people. Nevertheless, we learn that a successful relationship or venture requires collaborative participation between everyone involved, and we should not place all the blame on ourselves.

5) Under optimal conditions, the lotus will emerge above the water at the right time and place; this represents the characteristic of patience and tolerance.
6) Lastly, the lotus stem is hollow with multiple holes that give a decorated look when sliced horizontally and served on a dish. The hollowness reminds us to let go of our problems and difficulties that overfill and weigh down our mind and heart.

Because each part of the lotus has special characteristics, we can apply its attributes to all aspects of our life.

*The lotus remains beautiful and pure
despite growing in the mud.
So too can our thoughts, speech, and actions
be virtuous despite the surrounding impurities.*

The lotus is a prominent symbol in Buddhism as its form is used in greetings and salutations, hand gestures in prayers, and meditated sitting postures. As we bow to greet each other, we form a lotus bud by joining the palms of our hands and fingers closely together at midchest. The lotus bud gesture symbolizes an offering of a lotus flower to our friend and recognizes the Buddha-nature in him or her. Its position against the front of our chest represents the flower coming from our heart. We form the same lotus bud with our hands in prayer to show respect as we offer our lotus flower to the Buddhas and Bodhisattvas. Another way the lotus is applied in our practice is forming the lotus posture in sitting meditation. The position consists of sitting with the back upright and both shoulders relaxed to facilitate the passage of our breath to flow in and out. The legs are crossed together and the arms straightened out with hands resting on our lap or knees. This seated pose represents our potential to achieve mindfulness and inner peace, despite surrounding distractions. Because the lotus flower is beautiful, we imitate its form frequently in our daily practice.

The lotus is fruitful in its effect. The lotus flower blooms beautifully despite being immersed in the muddy water. We, too, can be like a lotus and emerge from the impurities in life. The lotus is the symbol of our successful practice. The dirt is the trials and tribulations of life's challenges. The lotus flower is an important symbol that teaches us that something good can arise from any affliction or hardship.

The lotus is of such significance that the Buddhas and Bodhisattvas are usually depicted sitting or standing on a lotus pedestal, symbolizing their supreme attainment of wisdom and enlightenment. The lotus and its characteristics provide essential lessons. If there is no mud, there is no lotus. Similarly, if there is no hardship, we would not be able to achieve wisdom and enlightenment. From the lotus, we learn to transcend our difficulties and problems in life so we can continue with determination, persistence, and practice.

Chapter 11

Robes and Prayer Beads

The Buddhist robe worn at the temple is light in color and texture and represents simplicity in the practice. The Kasaya robe worn by the monastics provides an enduring and harmonious reminder to reinforce the teachings. It represents patience, liberation, purity, and a fertile field to cultivate benevolent seeds. The Kasaya is a rectangular piece of fabric divided into either five, seven, or nine columns of rectangular patterns that are outlined by narrow strips that resemble the rice paddy field in Magadha, India. The number chosen to wear can range up to twenty-five columns, depending on the significance of the activity and the rank and level of the monastic. The Buddha requested his personal attendant, Ananda, to design a robe that would mirror the image of the rice paddy field. The robe's design in connection with the rice paddy symbolizes the interbeing inherent within our connection and relationship to earth and our community. As with any form, an object cannot sustain or appear by itself.

The Kasaya robe and rice paddy of Magadha

The rice crop needs sunshine, soil, water, and a farmer to cultivate the crop. We, in turn, are nourished by the rice. For practitioners, the Buddhist robe consists of five pieces sewn together with a straight seam at the front midline. The five pieces represent the Five Precepts, and the straight seam symbolizes the only One Vehicle to direct us in the right path, the Dharma teaching. The collar is two-layered, which represents the two truths: the relative and absolute truths. There is a small piece of fabric centered in the upper back of the robe that is square in shape. The square shape is symbolic of a practitioner living within the confines of the precepts, just like an object is contained in a square. The robe commonly has the colors of gray, brown, and yellow. The gray color represents the light smoke of incense rising in the air. The weightlessness of the smoke enables us to escape this mundane life toward enlightenment. The brown color resembles the ground and earth, reminding us to be humble. The yellow color is associated with the dirt in the ground that is often blown and embedded in our clothing by the wind. Both brown and yellow are colors of the earth. The earth symbolizes patience and endurance as it receives everything we do, from stomping on the ground with our feet to spilling contaminants into the soil. The robe serves as one of the Bodhisattva reminders for us to practice mindfulness. For example, when we are late getting to the next connecting flight, we are quick to grab our bags and charge to the front of the line. This is our immediate reactive tendency. But when we see the facial expressions of others in response to our actions, we stop to reflect that we need to slow down and be courteous toward others and act accordingly to represent the robe that we are wearing. Wearing the robe reminds us to accept all situations with acts of perseverance and kindness instead of reactions of anger and disengagement.

Prayer beads are one of the articles that practitioners use to keep count to be mindful while reciting the Sutras and mantras. They come in 18 or 108 beads. The 18 bead bracelet represents our six sensory organs, their object of the senses, and sensory consciousness. The six sensory organs correspond to their object of the senses and are as follows:

1) Eyes – form
2) Ears – sound
3) Nose – smell
4) Mouth – taste
5) Body – contact or touch
6) Mind – mind consciousness

Each sensation is then registered into our consciousness, which gives way to sensory consciousness, such as a fragrant or odorous smell, or a sweet or bitter taste. We become aware of each sensory consciousness, allowing us to develop our opinion towards it. Upon seeing a painting, our sensory consciousness provides feedback on the properties of the painting, whether it is square or round, large or small, gray or colorful. From this, we develop judgment as to whether we like it, dislike it, or have a neutral feeling. Another example is when our ear hears a pleasant tune; we perceive and recognize the sound consciousness, whether it is loud or soft, melodic or dull, soothing or provoking. We then distinguish and develop a reaction and an opinion as to whether we like or dislike the sound. This occurs similarly in the sensations of smell, taste, and touch. It is great that our sensory consciousness provides the differing sensations for us to experience, but it is when we become attached to what we see, hear, smell, taste, and touch that we may become disturbed. When we perceive the sensory consciousness, we tend to judge. We rarely take things as they are. We compare the fried noodle dish that we had the last time we were at the restaurant was much tastier and crunchier than this time. To prevent discontentment and dissatisfaction, we should practice gratitude for having food and being healthy enough to taste, eat, and enjoy it. We can have happiness if we are aware of our emotions that are aroused by these sensory inputs and adjust our subsequent thoughts, speech, and actions with gratitude and contentment. The six sensory organs, their six corresponding object of the senses, and the transpiring six sensory consciousness together add up to the number 18 that is present in the number of beads on the 18 bead bracelet. There is a longer prayer bead that consists of 108 beads. It is used to keep count in Sutra chanting and recitation and to develop a one concentrated mind. The number 108 derives from the number 18 applied to the six roots of afflictions (greed, hatred, delusion, pride, skepticism, and malevolent views). In summary, the numbers 18 and 108 in prayer beads have significance that refers to our discriminatory reactions to the objects of our senses.

The Buddhist robe and prayer beads are two of the most important articles in the practice. They help to remind us to maintain humility, patience, and awareness of the constant triggers from the multitude of external sensations that can cloud our mind. They both are the Bodhisattvas that remind us to think, speak, and act mindfully to reflect the teachings of the Dharma.

Chapter 12

The Five Aggregates

The Sanskrit word "skandha" means to combine and contain as a whole. It refers to the form and sensations that make up our human existence, so called "the Aggregates." There are Five Aggregates that form a continuous stream and are in constant flux feeding into our mind:

1) Form, including the five sensory organs and senses
2) Feeling
3) Perception
4) Mental formation
5) Consciousness

The first Aggregate is form, the visible object. It consists of all physical forms, including our body, the sensory organs, and their senses. The second to fifth Aggregates correlate with our mind; they are known for their given name but are not visible to the eyes. As discussed in the last chapter, the sensory organs and their object of the senses first have to form sensory consciousness for our mind to act upon. For example, when the ear hears the sound of music, our consciousness elicits the sound consciousness so we recognize the tune. From the awareness of the music, our feelings and perceptions produce a positive, negative, or neutral experience and trigger our actions. The second Aggregate, feeling, allows us to feel whether we like the sound, dislike the sound, or have a neutral feeling towards the sound. The third Aggregate, perception, is our thoughts and awareness of objects and phenomena. It tells us how we perceive the sound, whether it is too loud, too soft, or just right. The fourth Aggregate, mental formation, is our volitional activities, habitual actions, and impulses. It allows us to either react to the sound, dance to the pleasant tune, or block our ears from the unpleasant noise. These four Aggregates act on the sensory consciousness developed from the sensory inputs, and our consciousness then distinguishes the experience as a memorable sensation. And these experiences are what make up our human nature.

The Buddha delves into the topic of forms at length because they serve as a convenient method and symbolism for our studies and are a source of our attachments. There are five features of an object that can cause afflictions in us if we are not awakened to see their true nature:

1) Its form or figure
2) Its designated name
3) Its distinguishing characteristics
4) Its true nature
5) Its purpose

A flower is an example of a figure. To communicate with each other, we give a descriptive name to this object, defining it as a rose. We further distinguish it by its red color to impart an emotional component, as it is an expression of love. When we develop an emotion toward an object, we get pulled into life's pleasures and displeasures. If we have the wisdom to see that a red rose is just a flower made up of individual constituents as its true nature and do not associate any emotional attachments or possessiveness to it, we will not be caught up in the cycle of cravings and sufferings in life once the rose decomposes. When we designate a flower as a red rose and place our mind and practice to absorb its representation of the Dharma teaching on impermanence, the red rose becomes a practical object for us to enjoy and learn. Our mind will be able to see the true nature of things and remain stable and unshakable. Another example is a house. The true nature of a house consists of columns of wood, shingles on the roof, and concrete for the foundation. All these elements together form a figure of a place of dwelling, which we assign a name and call it as a house. We further distinguish it as a log cabin or mansion where it serves its purpose as our home, and so it then becomes an object of possession and attachment. If we lose our home through fire or the wear and tear of time, we will be greatly disappointed and sorrowful. But when we have the wisdom to see the true nature of the house, which actually is made up of different elements and components, we do not develop an attachment to the named object because we understand the Dharma teaching on Conditioned Genesis whereby objects manifest or cease to exist under the combination of right conditions. Therefore, we will be able to maintain a stable affect and composure during its degenerative natural changes throughout time. The goal is to transform our distinctions of pleasure and displeasure in response to the forms and phenomena into the wisdom to see their true nature and symbolism of the Dharma teaching.

Forms are one of the three realms of the universe. The three realms consist of cravings, forms, and non-forms. The realm of cravings consists of the Six Paths or realms of existence where there is desire for things. The realm of forms, a level above cravings, contains all the wonderful objects for us to see and enjoy. The realm of non-forms is the highest level where we recognize the impermanence of forms and attain the realm of pure spirit. All forms and phenomena have four characteristic marks of life. They are impermanence, tribulation, non-reality, and non-self. Forms are subject to decay and changes and are not permanent. The presence of forms is the result of a combination of all conditions that are present. Therefore, each form does not have a true identity and is not real. When conditions are not maintained, the form disintegrates. For example, a house cannot be a house by itself without the components of wood, shingles, nails, etc. After twenty years, if the house is not maintained with a new roof or a repair for a slanted foundation, the house may collapse. All forms present are not real, as they are formed by a combination of other elements and constituents under favorable conditions. When we are attached to worldly possessions, we become troubled when we do not recognize and accept their true nature.

Every day we are bombarded with an infinite amount of sensory information that can stimulate and overwhelm us. They give rise to the seven emotions that stir us from within. The emotions of joy, anger, happiness, sadness, love, hate, and cravings cause our Five Aggregates to fluctuate. They form a cloud and covering over our innate purified mind, creating foggy and unclear thinking. The tainted mind leads us to stray away from proper thoughts, speech, and actions. This covering is similar to the layers of dust that can accumulate on a mirror over time. It then takes multiple efforts to wipe the dust off to see ourselves clearly in the mirror. Similarly, our mind is clouded by the multitude of sensory stimuli and biased personal experiences that we develop in response to these sensory inputs; they can cause our mind to react with feelings of desire, anger, and delusion. The Buddha uses the metaphor that our body is a basket that contains the four snakes of earth, water, wind, and fire. We are constantly juggling to balance our four non-self elements so each snake does not overpower the others and cause us mental and physical sickness. When we are angry, the fiery snake takes charge. We then need the aqueous snake to pacify the basket. When we are in a hurry to rush through a task, the earthly snake is needed to calm the snake of the wind. Our natural existence is comprised of the sensations and emotional judgments. Our temperament is dependent on how we react to these sensory inputs. We are not at fault for enjoying a beautiful picture, hearing the nice melody of a song, or feeling an attraction towards someone. What is important is for us to apply mindfulness to be aware of our feelings and perceptions, and be able to regulate our thoughts, speech, and actions in response to these feelings and perceptions. For example, we recognize the $5,000 framed painting is beautiful, however, it is too expensive, and we should not buy it in order to avoid debt. Likewise, when our eyes see an attractive person, we should recognize that this is our reaction to the first Aggregate, the form. Although that person may appear attractive to us, we should not pursue a romantic relationship as this will destroy the happiness of our family and spouse. On the other hand, when we hear a critical remark that our book report is not well-written, we reflexively get upset and become distant. Instead, we should mindfully reflect and understand that our friend may be trying to help us in telling the truth. We should see the painful truth as a lesson for us to practice, transform, and improve. We can thank our friend for giving us sincere feedback on the book report so we can work to edit it. This way, we do not end a good friendship and, in return, have a better book report to submit.

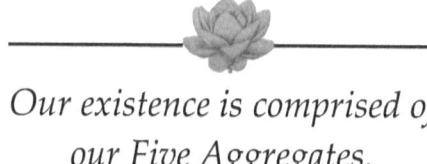

Our existence is comprised of our Five Aggregates.

We live in ignorance and delusion when we do not recognize the extreme nature of our reactive emotions that can pull us down the road of desire and improper actions. We need the radiant light of the Dharma teachings to wash away the accumulated dust for our purified mind to emerge and have the clear thoughts, awareness, and mindfulness to act accordingly. These Five Aggregates are not necessarily bad, as they are needed to achieve good things also. We need our eyes, ears, and mouth to learn the Dharma teachings. We need feedback from our feelings and perceptions to understand the Dharma teachings. We use our actions to practice the teachings. We use our consciousness to apply our mindfulness training. These are the Five Aggregates that make up our existence. The key is to not let these Five Aggregates or skandhas go unchecked and dominate us. Instead, we want our awakened mind to regulate our expressions and actions based on the feedback of these sensory inputs. This is how the Buddha teaches us to create happiness in our life. He cannot change the outcome of the results of our karmic actions. He can only provide us a guide on how to live, to prevent committing the cause that results in an unwanted effect.

Chapter 13

Planting the Positive Seeds

The mind is like soil in the ground. We have to tend to it, water it, and remove unwanted weeds and garbage from it in order to create a favorable condition to cultivate and plant a seed. We need to plow it to soften the soil so water can creep through and moisturize the ground. There are many types of negative and positive seeds in our mind consciousness. Negative seeds are unwholesome seeds which include greed, hatred, and anger. Positive seeds are wholesome seeds that include generosity, joy, and forgiveness. The Buddha-nature in our mind is inherently pure and radiant, and the positive and negative seeds are naturally dormant. It is through the interactions in our daily life that we stir up the negative seeds when we perceive things and situations that we dislike and are not to our satisfaction. We need to recognize this so that we can mindfully stimulate the positive seeds and repress the negative seeds. Because we have not attained perfect enlightenment, we should look for events and situations to reside in that will bring us peace and happiness, which will reinforce the positive seeds such as compassion and forgiveness. We want to avoid the impure environments, such as going to the casino, which can stimulate the negative seeds of a gambling habit and uncontrolled actions of spending money. In our life, we want to cultivate the positive seeds so they can surface more easily in all situations. We can water the positive seeds by remembering to repent our faults and practicing the vows of the Buddhas and Bodhisattvas. We can practice mindfulness to evoke the wholesome seeds by having an attitude of acceptance and forgiveness in all circumstances, even when we are presented with an unpleasant situation. When someone cuts us off on the freeway, instead of getting angry and watering the negative seeds, we should consider that the other person must be in a hurry to drive recklessly and cut in front of us. Or when our friend accidentally drops and shatters our favorite plate, we should adjust our reactive tendency to get upset and angry. Instead, we should apply the positive seeds of understanding and forgiveness: understanding that our friend did not intentionally break our plate and forgiving so we can release our anger and make our friend more comfortable. As we cultivate the positive seeds, we will suppress the negative seeds and prevent them from sprouting.

We have to constantly monitor the type of seeds sown in our mind consciousness so the plants and trees will grow favorably. Nothing can be set on cruise control to yield optimal results. If we recognize that we have sown the negative seeds, we can remove and pull them out before they sprout into big plants or trees. But once the negative seeds have grown into plants or trees, it is still not too late to work on them. We can trim the plants and trees while they are growing and mold them toward the right direction. Similarly, we need to cultivate the positive seeds so they can grow into big, healthy plants or trees toward a positive direction. We use mindfulness and our awakened state to alter and transform the negative and positive seeds, which can then change and result in wholesome, karmic fruits. Let's choose to mindfully plant and water the positive seeds of kindness, forgiveness, and great tolerance, so they can be more easily accessed to apply to our thoughts, speech, and actions.

Just like the farmer, the Buddha's teachings have all the ingredients to plant the positive seeds to yield a good harvest. Upon seeing the Buddha on alms round for food, the farmer asked the Buddha how he works to earn his livelihood. The Buddha compares his teachings to the process of farming. The

The practitioner's farmland

practitioners are the farmland. Our faith is the seed. The Dharma is the rain needed to cultivate our faith. Wisdom is the sun needed to provide the energy for the practice. Upholding the precepts is the work of plowing the soil. Our effort is the ox that propels the practice. Mindfulness is the harness that straps the ox to the cart and is the key and heart to our practice. Afflictions are the weeds that we want to remove. Purity is the fruition of our farming. As practitioners, we have to work as hard as the farmer to plow the land and plant the crops to yield a good harvest.

Chapter 14

Impermanence

It would not be a complete writing on Buddhism without a discussion on the doctrine of impermanence. Impermanence is an infallible and ordinary phenomenon that contributes to why we have sorrow or joy in life. This fundamental truth is the law of the cosmos, irrespective of our religious beliefs. All things in life are continuously ever-changing. The forms and non-forms are impermanent and are subject to degradation and change. Man-made objects are subject to change like a dream, an inauthentic object, a foam, a blinking light, a shadow, and dew on the grass. Our body is impermanent. Our wavering mind and thoughts are impermanent. All circumstances and situations in life are impermanent. The only thing that is permanent in life is the notion of impermanence.

Anything that has form is impermanent and can cause us distress, as it is difficult for us to accept change. We become discontent with the negative changes in life. Impermanence applies to four categories in life: our flesh and body, our mind, our situation and circumstances, and the forms and non-forms. Forms continuously disintegrate and cannot remain in their original form indefinitely. Our body is a type of form. It does not stay young and beautiful forever. Our physical body is sure to age with deterioration of all our organs. We age, progressing from infant, to teenager, to adult, and to senior citizen with gray hair and wrinkles. We cry over the deaths of our loved ones. We get depressed over our illnesses. If there were permanency in life, we would not have births or deaths, get sick, or recover from illnesses. Impermanence may be a pessimistic thought, but it is the truth. We can acknowledge this now or be surprised and dismayed when we experience a sudden tragedy or change in the future. Our mind changes by the second and minute as we develop differing opinions, likes, and dislikes. We should enjoy the blessings that come our way, as they are transient. We should not brood over unfortunate circumstances, as they will pass. All objects and experiences in life that serve as Dharma teachings also come and go. The Buddha teaches the practice of non-attachment in light of the revelation of impermanence. Non-attachment is the act of not clinging to an object or a situation, or releasing our attachments. We can enjoy being in a relationship but must learn to let go when its requisite Cause and Condition no longer exist. Although we enjoy the beauty and true nature of the flower, which is made up of sunlight, water and nutrients from the soil, we do not become disheartened when the flower wilts and decomposes back to the ground. When we see someone mourning over the sudden death of his or her loved one, we can take the opportunity to empathize and recognize the impermanence and transient nature of worldly phenomena. Forms appear real in that moment in time, in the right situation, and experienced by a particular person. But their presence is only temporary, as all necessary conditions have to be present for forms to exist. And when conditions are no longer sufficient, the presence of forms disintegrates. We accept the good things that impermanence has to offer and practice to overcome its negativity.

Impermanence can bring us joy when the changes are positive, depending on our perspective. Impermanence is needed for transformation and growth. The planted seed can sprout and yield a delectable fruit. The dry grain of rice can be cooked into steamed, aromatic rice. For children, they look forward to becoming independent, meeting their life partner, and establishing a family. As parents, we rejoice in our children's wedding celebration and welcoming our grandchildren. Changes can yield a positive event in our life, such as the achievement of a doctorate degree or buying our first house. Because of impermanence, we can enjoy the different stages of our child's life, from a newborn to an infant, to a toddler, to a youth maturing into an adolescent and young adult. On the other hand, we age toward our mortality to balance with this change. Life comes in pairs. Impermanence is normal and ordinary. We recognize impermanence so we can live the expected ordinary life.

Impermanence results in a negative or positive change.

Impermanence becomes a problem when we cannot accept changes in life. Change can result in a negative or positive outcome. Because of impermanence, we do not want to waste the precious time we have in this life. Our life is only in a single breath. If we breathe in and do not breathe out, our life ends. We want to live each day to the fullest to create a meaningful life. We want to live wholeheartedly like a fully bloomed rose. Just because a rose is impermanent does not mean we should not enjoy it. We should relish the sight of a beautiful red rose and its fragrance, but be cautious of its thorns. The Buddha did not create the principle of impermanence, nor did he form the doctrine of karma, non-reality, non-self, or interbeing. Rather, he is the fully Enlightened One who realized the laws of the universe and revealed them to us.

Chapter 15

Crossing Over to the Other Shore

The Prajna Paramita Mantra is a perfectly wonderful and completely understanding mantra in the Heart Sutra. A mantra is a phonetic phrase that is repeatedly recited during meditation to help develop concentration. Prajna means great wisdom. This wisdom is not the same as intelligence or knowledge obtained from studies. Prajna is a unique, immense, and an amazing type of wisdom that is attained from deep thoughts, contemplation, and practice. This wisdom is comparable to a sword that is so sharp and powerful such that it can eliminate all afflictions. "Para" is the other shore, and "mi" is to arrive. Paramita or parami means crossing to the other shore. Figuratively, it means achieving a set goal to perfection and completion. We cannot stop midway any time we start a project but need to arrive to the end so it is perfectly completed. The mantra is written as follows:

In Sanskit:
Gate Gate
Paragate
Parasamgate
Bodhi
Svaha

In Vietnamese, a phonetic translation from Sanskit:
Yết đế Yết đế
Ba la Yết đế
Ba la tăng Yết đế
Bồ đề
Tát bà ha

Meaning:
Try your best
Try a little more
Try harder
I have arrived and awakened
Bravo, I have achieved.

This mantra emphasizes that our continuous practice will lead us to cross to the other shore, from suffering to happiness, and delusion to awakening. It elucidates the important tenet of emptiness. Here, emptiness does not mean totally nothing, but that the true form of all things is not real. Things that are real do not change. The presence of objects in the universe, including our body, is not real because this presence is only temporary and arises when conditions are optimal. The objects do not have a true nature because they are made up of constituents and exist only under the right conditions. All things are interbeing and interdependent. Everything is

Crossing Over to the Other Shore 151

The Prajna Paramita Mantra

dependent on each other in life. Every object or activity is formed when conditions are sufficient and disintegrates when conditions are insufficient. For example, a flower is beautiful and enjoyable while it is in bloom but will eventually decompose and be recycled back to the earth. The flower is not really a flower by itself; its true nature is made of a combination of non-flower elements. The beauty of the flower is made up of sunshine, clouds, water, and soil. The flower then becomes part of the ground at the end of its life. There is a balanced shift from the dissolution of an object to the presence of another. We realize that all things come together to form an object, which then decomposes to its individual, natural elements over time. We cannot exist or accomplish any act independently by ourselves; we are part of everyone and everything in this cosmos. If we say this book was published by ourselves alone, it would not be completely accurate. Without the clouds, trees, ink, the people and machine to bind the book, the book cannot be made. We ourselves are not real, as we are made of the Five Aggregates and the four great non-self elements of the earth. The Five Aggregates that make up our existence are not real. Therefore, our form, feeling, perception, mental formation, and consciousness are not real.

The Five Aggregates that make up our existence are not real.

So do not become too fixated and preoccupied with our emotions of sadness, anger, likes, and dislikes. The four non-self elements that constitute our body are earth, water, wind, and fire. Our hair, teeth, bones and muscles are made from the resources of the earth. Our blood and urine are made of water. The air in our lungs is the wind. The warmth of our living body is the fire. All our organs are returned to and become part of the earth again once they are decomposed. To be exact, everything belongs to the great four elements of this world. Everything we use, we have to give back. We are just borrowing the resources of the universe. We drink water and urinate it out. We eat the food grown from the earth and subsequently excrete it. We breathe in fresh air with oxygen and expel carbon dioxide for the plants. Our body is borrowed from this earth. This is the absolute truth. Is it by chance that the word "human" describes our true substance? Dr. Myles Monroe explains that the word "human" is combined from two derivatives: "hummus" and "man." Hummus means dirt and soil. Man is a spirit being. As humans, we are a spirit being in a dirt body. Similar to the flower, our body returns back to earth upon our demise, but our spirit being persists with our accumulated karma. Our body and material possessions will be left behind upon our passing, but the one certain belonging that will follow us is our karma. We discern that the visible forms and our body are not permanent and, therefore, do not become attached to things in life. This understanding will help us grieve through our losses and accept the concept of death as a natural process of life, so we can celebrate life rather than mourn over it. In essence, from this realization, we have crossed to the other shore with joy and celebration. The Dharma teaching is the raft that helps us cross to the other shore. The body of water is the hardship and affliction that form the barrier opposing the process of crossing over to the other shore. The practice of mindfulness, contemplation, and reflection is the work needed to put in to row the raft to the other shore. Once we cross over to the other shore, we achieve the results of our practice and attainment of wisdom and enlightenment. The emphasis is on the arrival at this goal. It is accomplished by using the Dharma teachings as the convenient vehicle. Once achieved, we should not become attached to the Dharma or the practice, as it is merely a vehicle to cross to the other shore. Similarly, we would not continue to hold on and carry the raft once we cross over to the other shore. This wisdom allows us to see things in life differently, similar to a raft that flows upstream. The worldly person sees this life is real, such that there is a need to engage in rivalry and gain. This is the ordinary view. With this wisdom, we see the reality and truth of this life and, therefore, relinquish the need to dominate others and allow ourselves to live with harmony and serenity. This is the extraordinary view. It is the understanding of the noble truths

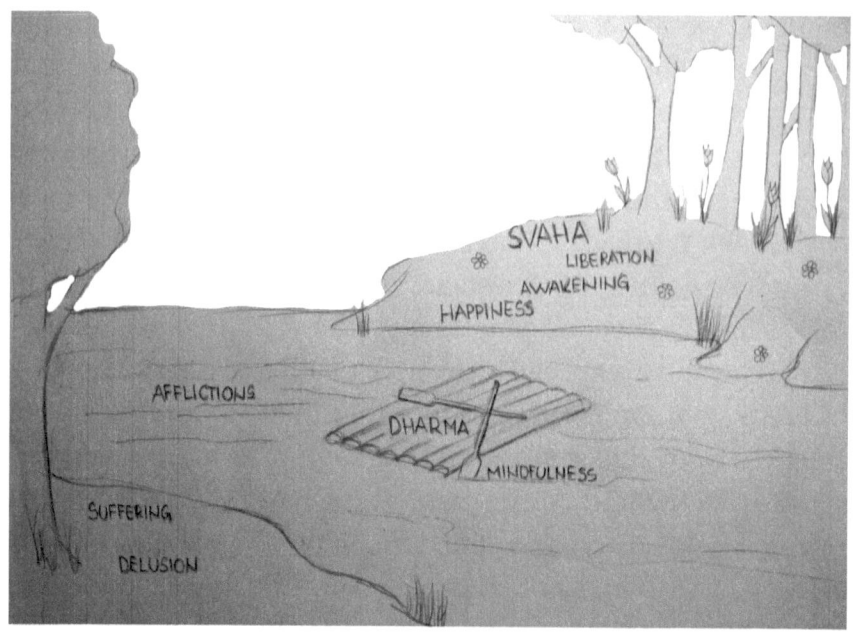

Crossing over to the other shore

of life in the concept of emptiness, non-reality, impermanence, interbeing, Cause and Condition, and non-self that we can let go and rejoice in our triumph and liberation. Recognizing the principal hallmarks of the Buddha's teachings of impermanence, tribulations, non-reality and non-self will lead us to Nirvana. These are the four Dharma Seals of Buddhism. The Prajna Paramita Mantra is a great and radiant mantra that elucidates the noble truths. It has the potential to help us eradicate all sufferings and overcome all attachments. There are no other mantras comparable to the Prajna Paramita Mantra.

Chapter 16

Pairs of Words and Opposites

Pairs of objects, words, and opposites are interbeing. The pairing of decorations at the altar on opposite sides, left and right, represents life and religion and the relative and absolute truths. The concept of interbeing explains that no one thing can exist independently from another. The presence of the two extremes is related and in each other. Nothing appears in isolation. The presence of one thing means the absence of another but remains in a continuum. Brightness is the presence of light, and darkness is the absence of light. What goes up must fall down to where it came from. For every beginning, there is an end, and for every ending there is a beginning. When we experience a loss of a job, there is another job available for us to advance in our career. When we hit rock-bottom from the breakup of a relationship, there is another person waiting to meet us who will be a more fitting partner. There are opposites such as old age in youth, death in birth, sickness in health, and sadness in happiness. They are inseparable as they are a continuum. At the moment of birth, the process of aging has also begun; the cells in each organ undergo a constant turnover. Life is just a cycle. There is no birth or death, just transformation. The flower decomposes to form compost, which in turn fertilizes another plant to give rise to another flower. In regards to sickness, high blood pressure is a silent disease in a seemingly healthy person until the blood pressure reaches an extremely high level, which then may lead to strokes or other complications. For our health, we can practice mindfulness by consuming food that will nourish our body and attending annual physical exams to detect silent illnesses early in order to prevent them. When we express "tears of joy," there is an emotional heartache in our happiness. We need to understand that when we experience the joy in life, there will necessarily be moments of sadness. Even in Nirvana there are pairs of opposites, the presence and absence of our emotional disposition. Nirvana is a state of having sublime inner peace when there is generosity, compassion, and wisdom while there is an extinction of greed, hatred, and delusion. Even in times of difficulty, we can choose to let the experience cause either suffering or strength in us. Remember that everything exists in pairs of opposites, including transformation and change. It is through practice that we can recognize the presence of the opposites, so that we can cultivate the presence of the positives and not allow their corresponding negatives to tear us down.

Here are pairs of the causes of suffering with their corresponding treatments:

1. Greed and desire – generosity and philanthropy
2. Hatred and anger – loving-kindness and compassion
3. Delusion and ignorance – wisdom and understanding

The treatment for greed and desire is to give and donate cheerfully. The treatment for hatred and anger is to practice loving-kindness and compassion. The treatment for delusion and ignorance is to develop wisdom and understanding. These pairs of words and opposites bring us back to the concept of interbeing, that all things in life are related and dependent on one another. We recognize this so we can practice with an emphasis toward attaining the more positive side of the pairs of opposites.

The Dharma has four pairs of teaching points:

1) Cause and Effect
2) Symbolic forms and their representation of the teachings
3) Minuscule and grandeur
4) Self-reliance and reliance on others

Flowers and fruits are an example of Cause and Effect. A flower has to be present in order to produce a fruit. One condition evolves into another, continuing the chain reaction that occurs in all events in life. The symbolic forms and their representation of the teachings are convenient ways to study Buddhism. A flower represents the teaching of impermanence. A pair of lights represents wisdom. There are small things and big things in life, and we need to enjoy them all as each has its own special, unique qualities. Sometimes we have to forego the small things and hold back our dissension, for the sake of harmony in a big group so we may get things accomplished. Self-reliance is required in certain circumstances. For example, we have to spend countless hours of studying in order to attain a degree on graduation day; no one else can do it for us. On the other hand, we cannot live in isolation. In order for us to exist, we rely on one another in the community. We rely on farmers to grow food, truckers to bring food to the market, the supermarket to sell the food, and the sequence of interdependencies continues.

The most perplexing statue seen at the temple is that of the Bodhidharma who is typically portrayed carrying one shoe. Bodhidharma is one of the spiritual ancestors who is highly regarded in Chinese history for bringing the teachings on meditation from India to China. Usually, shoes are not complete unless they are in pairs. The picture of one shoe that he carries suggests that the pair is already represented in one. If both sides are presented, we will more likely develop judgment and discrimination in our viewpoint. This statue is symbolic of the teaching of the pairs of opposites in one.

The one shoe Bodhidharma

Chapter 17

Wisdom versus Knowledge

The reason we study and practice Buddhism is to develop wisdom and transform ignorance. When we are in darkness, we look for a source of light in order to see. Enlightenment or awakening helps us to develop wisdom. Wisdom provides more than just the visual light compared to that of the fire, moon, and sun. Wisdom has a bright light that is clear with the energy of mindfulness. Wisdom allows us to see and acknowledge our innate Buddha-nature and improve our negative karmic status. Wisdom is the mental quality to make good judgment based on our knowledge, mindfulness practice, and experience. Wisdom is gained through study and practice. Knowledge is not the same as wisdom. Knowledge is attained from learning new facts, such as one plus one equals two or learning the Five Precepts. Of all the knowledge that is pursued in life, the knowledge from the Dharma teachings provide the ultimate true knowledge and right view to learn other types of knowledge, such as multiple languages, STEM courses (science, technology, engineering, and math) and vocations, medical science and medications, and the worldly life. The two components in obtaining knowledge are to gain knowledge of subjects that we do not yet have and relearn the knowledge that has been forgotten. For example, if we have never heard of the Five Precepts and learn it for the first time, this is acquiring new knowledge. If we forget one week later and relearn the significance and meaning of the Five Precepts, this is relearning the knowledge forgotten. But not until we apply and practice the teaching of the Five Precepts can we attain wisdom and the potential toward enlightenment. There are three steps to develop wisdom:

1) To listen and learn
2) To think and reflect clearly
3) To practice and complete the committed task

We have to practice these three steps skillfully and with goodwill in order to attain the wisdom of listening, contemplation, and practice. For example, we listen attentively when our friend is agitated and need to know when to argue and when to hold our tongue in a conflict. When we think with mindfulness, we are careful not to immediately confront him or her with our skepticism as to whether he or she is telling the truth. We wait until he or she is in a calm state of mind before we present our point of view. Therefore, we use the knowledge learned to develop wisdom to provide intellectual judgment and reasoning for us to make the right decision in order to promote harmony and happiness within the relationships in our life. We need to use wisdom to know what we should listen to and what we should not, and what to retain from what is heard. When we listen and learn with mindfulness, we think with mindfulness, which leads to actions performed with mindfulness. Similarly, the Buddha selects what he preaches depending on the circumstance, time, place, and person. His knowledge and wisdom are vast and broad like the amount of leaves in the forest, but the amount of knowledge he reveals is just like a handful of leaves. The Buddha only says what is necessary and pertinent to the situation at hand. Through practice, we can train and cultivate ourselves to develop wisdom. Listening, contemplation, and practice are the wisdom of a novice practitioner. As we mature in our practice, we achieve morality, concentration, and wisdom. This wisdom gives us understanding and insight. By following the precepts and concentrating on what is right or wrong, we develop the wisdom to carry out the right decisions. This is the reason why we practice and study Buddhism, to attain this wisdom.

Wisdom is not the same as knowledge. Wisdom is gained from listening, contemplating, and practicing.

There are three methods of how we process the knowledge that is learned to attain wisdom:

1) Unretainable
2) Inside out
3) Vast and monumental

Unretainable knowledge refers to the inability to retain the study of a teaching or grasp everything in life. Some of us go to the temple on a regular basis to pray, chant, and listen to the Dharma teachings, but we are unable to absorb the information and put them into practice. This is similar to having a bunch of candies on our lap while sitting, which then drop to the floor once we stand up and walk away. It is the wisdom just like on our lap. We do not want this type of wisdom but can utilize another concept of unretainable wisdom to recognize that sometimes we cannot grasp everything in life. For example, when we are carrying a handful of beans and happen to drop a few, we should continue toward our path rather than stop and try to pick up the few that were dropped. If we stop, we may not be able to gather all the dropped pieces, but instead we may lose more than the few that were dropped while holding onto the remaining beans. In other words, we need to learn when to let go and be content with what we have. From the unretainable wisdom, we learn to cultivate the wisdom that is retainable and put our study into practice. We also learn to let unpleasant events pass with a positive attitude and develop gratitude for the blessings that we do have in life.

Inside out wisdom is the wisdom that is spilled out, such as when a box is turned inside out. We all have experienced when no matter how much we pray and study, we still cannot contain or understand the information. It feels like the knowledge just spills out of our mind. We do not want this type of processing of knowledge and wisdom, but we can apply its symbolism of reflecting inward to bring out the shining wisdom. We can practice the "inside out" concept by reflecting inward with the light of wisdom to bring our goodness outward. This is a powerful exercise. Before criticizing someone else, we should look at ourselves first to see whether we would act similarly under the same circumstances. When sharing a secret recipe, we may want to keep certain ingredients a secret and not share the entire recipe. If we stop and reflect inward, what good will it be if we keep the recipe to ourselves? When we pass away, the recipe cannot be shared with others to enjoy. Once we realize this, then we will be happy and more willing to share the entire recipe. We can see that every event in our life provides the opportunity for us to reflect inward to yield a positive outcome outward.

Wisdom that is vast and monumental can fill and contain an infinite size in our mind. This is the wisdom process that we want to pursue. With persistent listening, learning, and practice, our mind calms down one step at a time. Each lesson can diminish our suffering gradually, like removing one grain of sand at a time from the desert. As we study, we become more immersed in the teachings and develop a deeper conviction to study more. This creates a positive feedback loop to fill and grow our wisdom box. This is the wisdom that is vast and monumental.

The Buddha encourages us to transform our discriminatory judgment from sensory consciousness to develop four types of wisdom. The four types of wisdom are:

1) The wisdom of clear reflection
2) The wisdom of impartiality
3) The wisdom of deep contemplation
4) The wisdom of perfect achievement

The wisdom of clear reflection helps us see and understand the true nature of things, similar to how a clear mirror reflects images accurately and without distortion. An example is seeing that a table is a name we assign to an object that provides support. The table's true nature is made of several pieces of wood that are nailed together. The wisdom of impartiality is not compromised by attachment to ourselves, our views, or other objects; it allows us to see the other person's point of view without discrimination. The wisdom of contemplation allows us to look deeply and see everyone's weaknesses and strengths. The wisdom of perfect achievement gives us the potential to accomplish any tasks despite adverse conditions. These four forms of wisdom can help us change our tendencies for attachment and narrow-mindedness, and they can help us achieve the fulfillment of our aspirations.

The ultimate wisdom we want to attain is the wisdom arising from deep reflection and clear perception. This is Prajna. In order to practice, our mind has to be pure. And for our mind to be clear, we have to stop and settle down. To stop and settle down is the practice of meditation. So in order to contemplate, we need to practice meditation. There are three important steps to gain in the practice toward Prajna:

1) Wisdom from learning through listening
2) Wisdom from contemplation and deep reflection
3) The enlightened wisdom from practice

The three steps can be seen in the metaphor of the Prajna Paramita Mantra, the teaching of "crossing over to the other shore." The act of listening and reading refers to the raft that is used to carry us over the water of affliction. The act of contemplation and deep reflection refers to the work needed to row the raft to get us across. And the enlightened wisdom of the Buddha refers to the practice resulting in the achievement of crossing over to the other shore. Knowledge is first attained by reading and listening to the Dharma teachings or hearing what others say. Contemplation and deep reflection require thought and reasoning to understand what is learned and see the Cause and Effect. The enlightened wisdom is the ultimate truth obtained through diligent practice and experience. For example, we can hear people describe how a lemon is as juicy as an orange and sour like vinegar. Through contemplation, we can imagine that a lemon tastes like eating an orange dipped in vinegar. But only when we actually taste and eat the lemon ourselves can we absolutely know the true nature of a lemon. This is acquiring the ultimate truth through actual experience. In another example, when we hear someone tell us that a shaved head gives a cool and light feeling; we learn this knowledge through hearsay and can share it with another person. Through reasoning, we can deduct that a lack of hair or covering on a head would feel colder than a head that has hair. We do not know the true sensation of what a shaved head feels like until we actually experience it ourselves. It is only when we shave our own head that we can experience the ultimate wisdom of what it is like to not have any hair. This is the enlightened wisdom. In order to understand and know the true nature of things, we have to practice and experience them ourselves.

Throughout life, we encounter opportunities that come our way where we can apply these three steps of practice. When we hear of someone developing a terminal illness, this is knowledge gained from listening. Hearing such news provokes us to contemplate that life is short and fragile. This leads to our awakening to have gratitude for our good health and be mindful to feed our body with good nutrition, as well as exercise regularly to maintain our health. In another example, we hear of people complaining of their unfavorable circumstances, such as losing a job, which brings us to contemplate and reflect that our situation may not be as bad as compared to that of others. Although we face conflict in the workplace, we still have a job to pay our bills. Compared to the constant changes and catastrophes in the universe, the problems we have are minuscule. Our problems are like small grains of sand in an entire desert, and we should not feel discontent for every little thing that is not to our satisfaction. This realization is the ultimate wisdom. This practice can also be applied in our daily life while interacting with others. When our mother invites us over for a meal and happens to season her soup too salty, instead of complaining, we should appreciate her effort in making a meal and preparing it for us to eat. Once we stop to reflect and see clearly, we understand and are then able to be liberated from our dissatisfaction so we can accept the situation gracefully. To achieve Prajna, we have to use the phenomena in our daily life as objects for our contemplation and deep reflection in order to practice and attain the complete and perfect wisdom. Similar to the Buddha, we want to practice so we can develop the five thin circular halos of radiant light radiating from the mind and body to elicit the wisdom from right thoughts, which then give way to right speech and actions from mindfulness practice. This treasured wisdom is attained by acknowledging the noble truths, practicing equanimity, achieving serenity, and developing the three wisdoms of listening, contemplation, and practice. We have to do the work and practice. No one can do it for us. In essence, once achieved, we will cross to the other shore of liberation after putting in the work to row the raft.

Chapter 18

The Five Vehicles

Buddhism uses forms as symbolisms to transmit teachings. A Vehicle is a method to explain the teachings and institute them into practice. It is a convenient way to carry us from one place to another, from delusion to enlightenment. Each Vehicle has different levels of practice and allows the practitioner to start at the most basic level and advance accordingly. There are Five Vehicles for us to progress in the studies:

1) The Vehicle for the Worldly Person
    a) The Three Jewels
    b) The Five Precepts:
        1) Do no harm to living beings
        2) Do not take from others
        3) Avoid sexual misconduct
        4) Refrain from unkind speech

5) Abstain from the consumption of unhealthy food and harmful exposures to the body and mind (e.g., alcohol, drugs, and violent movies)

2) The Vehicle of the Heavenly Being (Ten Benevolent Practices to train the three karma)
   a) Body (3 precepts):
      1) No killing; do preserve life
      2) No stealing; do charity
      3) No sexual misconduct; do have faithfulness
   b) Speech (4 precepts):
      1) No lying; do have truthful speech
      2) No forked tongue; do have harmonious speech
      3) No malevolent speech; do have benevolent speech
      4) No frivolous speech; do have constructive speech
   c) Mind (3 precepts):
      1) No greed; do have generosity
      2) No hatred; do have compassion
      3) No delusion; do have wisdom

3) The Vehicle of the Bodhisattva (six paramitas)
   a) Generosity
   b) Morality
   c) Patience
   d) Effort
   e) Meditative concentration
   f) Wisdom

4) The Vehicle of the Hearer
   a) The Four Noble Truths
   b) Awareness of the four physical and four mental afflictions
      1) Birth
      2) Old age

3) Sickness
4) Death
5) Separation from our loved ones
6) Proximity to those whom we dislike
7) Unable to obtain what we want
8) Attachment to our Five Aggregates

5) The Vehicle of the doctrine of Cause and Condition

There are different paths to study and practice in Buddhism, depending on the level of the practitioner. The novice usually starts with the first Vehicle of the Worldly Person to take refuge in the Three Jewels and uphold the Five Precepts. This is the foundation of any initial training. Taking refuge in the Three Jewels, consisting of the Buddha, the Dharma, and the Sangha, is one of the most important teachings for all beginners. The Buddha signifies enlightenment. The Dharma represents truth. And the Sangha embodies peace and harmony.

The Five Precepts are the fundamental practice for every practitioner. Precepts are a set of rules that help prevent us from doing harm and halt concurrent harmful acts. The five basic moralities to follow are:

1) Avoid harming living beings
2) Avoid taking from others
3) Avoid sexual misconduct
4) Avoid unkind speech and deception
5) Avoid consumption of unhealthy food and harmful exposures to the body and mind (e.g., alcohol, drugs, violent movies)

Every practitioner should commit to following these five basic moral conducts and review them each month. Because the Buddha sees that these five issues in life are the cause of our sorrow and unhappiness, he established these precepts to be the guidelines for us to live by. They are not meant to suppress us; they are to prevent us from doing harm to ourselves and others, and halt ongoing malevolent acts. We should not hesitate to commit to follow the Five Precepts for fear of being faulted if we cannot carry them out to completion. The Buddha recognizes our character flaws and, therefore, categorizes different levels of people who are able to adhere to one, two, three, four, or five vows of the precept. More importantly is our initiation of commitment and to steadily work on keeping each vow until they are all upheld. Buddhism always speaks in pairs. The steps the Buddha teaches in observing the precepts are to first prevent the wrongful deeds by stopping and not performing the actions; once we maintain this practice, we then perform the mirror counterpart with virtuous deeds in the Five Mindfulness Trainings:

1) Preserve life
2) Practice generosity
3) Build faithful relationships
4) Speak truthfully and with loving-kindness
5) Consume nourishment for the body and mind

Both the Five Precepts and the Five Mindfulness Trainings are incorporated in the next progression to the Vehicle of the Heavenly Being, where we not only avoid committing wrongful acts but aim to perform benevolent acts.

The Vehicle of the Heavenly Being has Ten Benevolent Practices to train the body, speech, and mind to yield good karma effects. The Five Precepts and the Five Mindfulness Trainings are emphasized here again, in addition to delving into regulating our speech and taming the three negative roots of the mind. It reinforces the ten modes of conduct to prevent bad karma, create good ones, and transform the unfavorable karma to favorable ones.

1) In physical action, we should abstain from killing, stealing, and committing sexual misconduct. Instead, we encourage preservation of life, charity, and faithfulness.
2) In mindful speech, we should avoid lying, speaking with a forked tongue, speaking maliciously, and gossiping with non-purposeful speech. Instead, we encourage truthful speech, praise, and benevolent and constructive speech. We all want to teach our kids not to lie. But we have to be careful not to model the opposite of what we preach. If we see a person's name who we do not want to talk to on the caller ID, telling our children to say that we are not at home would teach our children to lie. Our children will learn from what we do rather than what we preach to them.
3) In thoughts, we should avoid maintaining a mind of greed, hatred, and delusion, and instead, develop ideas of generosity, loving-kindness, and wisdom.

The Vehicle of the Heavenly Being works on the karma of our body, speech, and mind to create a virtuous life for us.

In our initial study, we are considered as "the novice Bodhisattva." The novice Bodhisattva has to develop certain qualities in order to commit to the study and practice. There are four qualities they should cultivate:

1) A stable and solid practice
2) Purity in the body and mind
3) Boundless deeds
4) A direction toward the supreme level of enlightenment

As we achieve the Vehicle of the Heavenly Being and advance to the Vehicle of the Bodhisattva, we want to become "the Bodhisattva of non-regression" who is steadfast and does not regress in the practice. Here, we aim to follow the vow of a Bodhisattva by serving others to enable happiness, liberation, and enlightenment.

The Vehicle of the Bodhisattva is the ultimate practice in the pursuit of the perfect and complete attainment toward the enlightened path. The Vehicle of the Bodhisattva encourages us to serve and help others through the six paramita practices consisting of generosity, morality, patience, effort, meditative concentration, and attainment of wisdom. Each quality encompasses one another and, when practiced with an emphasis on effort, we will develop transcendental wisdom. Paramita means to cross to the other shore. These six paramita practices will help us cross from the shore of delusion to awakening and from the shore of suffering to happiness and liberation. The Vehicle of the Bodhisattva is considered as a Great Vehicle since the practice is to achieve self-enlightenment and to share and reveal this enlightenment to others.

The first paramita, generosity, teaches us to give without discrimination. It is the antidote for greed. The Buddha preaches at length regarding generosity and expounds on different ways it can be practiced. We can express our generosity not only by giving material possessions but also by giving our patience and great effort. The act of generosity increases our blessings and merits. Blessing is attained by the giving of our material possessions. Merit is the virtuous quality we develop by how we think, speak, and act mindfully and righteously in the process of giving. We gain blessings when we donate food during a food drive. We generate good merits when we give with all our heart, without discrimination or regret. However, we lessen our merits when we give expired food or have contempt toward the people receiving the food. The Buddha makes it easier to give by pointing out that our possessions are not permanent and cannot be taken with us upon our passing. Our houses and real estate, monies, jewelries, and land are all temporary assets and are subject to change in nature and possession. Our estate will eventually return to their five true homes: washed away by water, burned by fire, stolen by thieves, confiscated by the government, and squandered away by future generations. Although we can fight over the borders of our land or outbid another person for a special painting, our possessions ultimately belong to these true homes. They are commodities in our worldly life, but we need to recognize their true nature so we do not become possessed by them, thereby watering our three poisons of greed, hatred, and delusion. Despite the impermanency, the Buddha teaches us to allocate our possessions into daily expenses and miscellaneous use, savings, investments, gifts for dear friends and family, and charity. This gives a balance to take care of ourselves and family and share with others. We do not have to be wealthy to give; we can give generously with whatever resources we have. Material possessions are categorized into external and internal possessions. The external possessions are what we own outside of our body, such as monies, food, or clothing. The internal possessions are what we have in our body, such as the blood we give for transfusion or hair for cancer patients. We can also give emotional and verbal teachings, affirmations, and support. Donating monies and material possessions require the least effort. More energy is needed to offer our service in sharing the Dharma teachings and providing actions of fearlessness. Sharing the teachings is not only about the Sutras but includes the encouragement of others to live righteously, give generously, and have mutual concessions and compromises in our relationships. We can offer emotional support and allay fear in times when our friends are anxious about their sickness, family plight, or financial distress. Our giving can be as simple as a happy smile, a caring act, or words of kindness. We can provide service by helping an elderly woman cross a busy intersection or reassuring a friend that things will improve with time. The three ways of giving are to give magnanimously, reciprocally, and respectfully. Magnanimous giving is to give wholeheartedly without prejudice or calculation of the object to give or showing favoritism to whom we give. Reciprocal giving is to give in return for others' services or gifts. Respectful giving is to make offerings to teachers, Bodhisattvas, and Buddhas who we have high regards for. It is said that we are making offerings to the Bodhisattvas and Buddhas when we provide services to others. We should display loving-kindness and give without expectations. It is important that we give with understanding, love, and mindfulness so we are giving others happiness rather than sorrow. At times, we unknowingly pass on our anger to our children when we argue in front of them. Because of this, it is important to acknowledge that we are giving in our daily life both verbally and nonverbally, whether intentionally or unintentionally.

The second paramita, observing the precepts, is so important that it is included in all three Vehicles of practice: the Vehicle of the Worldly Person, the Vehicle of Heavenly Being, and the Vehicle of the Bodhisattva. Observing the precepts serves as the first step in the Dharma studies for the novice Bodhisattva and as a foundation of practice for the Bodhisattva of non-regression. It is an important practice for disciplining our karma in thoughts, speech, and actions.

The third paramita, patience, is a necessary quality we must have to create harmony in our life. Patience is the great endurance applied in all situations. It is needed in order to practice the other five paramitas of the Vehicle of the Bodhisattva: generosity, upholding the precepts, effort, concentration, and wisdom. Practicing patience and tolerance is one of the methods of conveying generosity. It doesn't necessarily mean we have to hold back and suppress the troubling issues within us. We have to choose the appropriate place, time, and situation to mindfully express our discontentment in a way so that our peace of mind is not disrupted. We can hold off from making a scene, speaking in anger, and thinking of spite when we are upset. Instead, we wait to calm down before we share our distressing thoughts to the person who upsets us. The ability to practice and carry out patience with one another, in difficult situations, and effortlessly is a great virtue. When we are unhurried and can wait for our friend without becoming annoyed is to practice patience with a person. When we can tolerate a cramped space or a hot room without complaining is an example of practicing patience in all circumstances. The natural tendency to be patient and forgiving allows us to practice patience without much effort. We have to be careful that we develop patience that brings us peace rather than unrest. If we decide to wait for our friend, we should do it with a giving heart and joy instead of getting upset over it, as patience is needed to release us from anger.

The fourth paramita, effort, is the perseverance and endeavor put forth without giving up; it is the most important element, as it is the drive for us to carry out the other five paramitas. Effort is putting dedication and persistence in our work. The four types of endeavors needed to maintain our practice are:

1) A stable and strong endeavor
2) A pure endeavor
3) A boundless endeavor
4) A supreme endeavor

To succeed in our practice, we need to develop these four endeavors which constitute our self-nature gem. A strong and stable endeavor is required so nothing can distract and stray us from our practice. We need to have a pure determination of the mind and heart that can tend to any disruptions from external afflictions. We should develop a boundless endeavor to target the obstacles and difficulties in our path of practice. All these endeavors combined will result in an extraordinary and supreme endeavor that will lead to enlightenment. Developing the perfect endeavor can be achieved in various ways:

1) Wear a coat of armor for diligence
2) Work steadily and continuously toward benevolence
3) Always strive to do better and not remain content with the status quo

Here, the Buddha emphasizes diligence as one of the most important factors in our practice, as it is the factor included in the Vehicle of the Bodhisattva and the Noble Eightfold Path. We should develop and wear a protective metal coat of diligence to overcome obstacles and prevent any negatives from penetrating into our endeavors. Just like the steady rhythm of the drum meditation instrument, we should work with constant, unceasing effort toward concentrated benevolent work. The accumulations of benevolent work will nourish and further additional benevolent goals. Thinking of how the end result will benefit and bring happiness to others will give us the persistence and determination to follow through with the committed tasks. The Buddha teaches us to be satisfied and content with what we have, except in the practice of diligence, where he encourages having an eternal drive to study and practice. Constant effort and endeavor are the antidote to subdue our laziness.

The fifth paramita, training on meditative concentration, will calm our turmoils, leading to a focused awareness with purity and tranquility. This, in turn, will help us make prudent decisions and speech. Developing concentration will help us carry out the other paramitas with mindfulness.

The sixth paramita, wisdom, is the knowledge and insight gained through contemplation and practice, and its attainment will end all delusions. There are seven objectives to complement this practice in order to achieve enlightenment to perfection and completion:

1) To peacefully reside in the compassionate character of the Bodhisattva
2) To take refuge in the mind of enlightenment
3) To consistently exhibit compassion and generosity

4) To establish merits and virtues in our designated vocation
5) To be skilled and mindful in the nature of all phenomena
6) To direct oneself toward the supreme level of enlightenment
7) To develop purity in character to overcome afflictions and impediments

We should aim to develop the characteristics of a Bodhisattva so we can promote compassion, generosity, and purity, and direct our practice toward the supreme level of enlightenment. From the practice of the Vehicle of the Bodhisattva, we want to achieve the ultimate perfection of giving, the perfection of morality, the perfection of patience, the perfection of effort, the perfection of meditative concentration, and the perfection of wisdom.

Besides the three Vehicles of practice, there are two Lesser Vehicles of study that elucidate the noble truths of the universe and the laws of Cause and Condition. They are termed the Lesser Vehicle because the practice is to attain enlightenment mainly for oneself. The first is the Vehicle of the Hearer where enlightenment is pursued by listening to the Dharma studies. These studies are pointed out for us to recognize the true natures of life and accept them gracefully when we experience them. The study of the Four Noble Truths and understanding of the four physical and four mental causes of suffering are the principle teachings of the Dharma. The root of all problems and sufferings is from our discontent with what we have at the present moment and the need to always seek for more. It is this desire that clouds our mind to pursue more in spite of whether we need it or not. The four physical and four mental causes of suffering are the realities of life. King Suddhodana implored his son Siddhartha not to leave the royal kingdom and would grant him anything he wished to change his mind. Prince Siddhartha asked his father to grant him four requests so he would not have to leave in search of a solution to the cycles of suffering in life:

1) To live in permanent youth and not age
2) To have constant good health without any sicknesses
3) To have eternal life without any death
4) To live in perpetual joy without any sorrows

Naturally, King Suddhodana did not have the ability to fulfill these requests, which became the focus and preface to Prince Siddhartha's search for the ultimate realization of life's true nature. The physical sufferings of birth, old age, sickness, and death are the ordinary four stages of life. They do not necessarily follow in this order. Some people pass away in their youth from accidents. Some people pass away without any sicknesses. At least with human birth, we can estimate the arrival of a newborn at eight to nine months. The cause, timing, and place of our death, in addition to the illnesses we develop and when we develop them, are the five unpredictable occurrences. Death is a destination that everyone will arrive at. The only difference is how we live and travel along the way. Once we take that last breath is the first type of death. The second type of death is when we practice to transform from an old, bad habit to a new, good habit. An example is to change from an inebriated person to a sober one. So with this type of death, our life is made anew and persists in other people's hearts and lives with remembrance of our merits even after our physical death. The practice in Buddhism sees death only

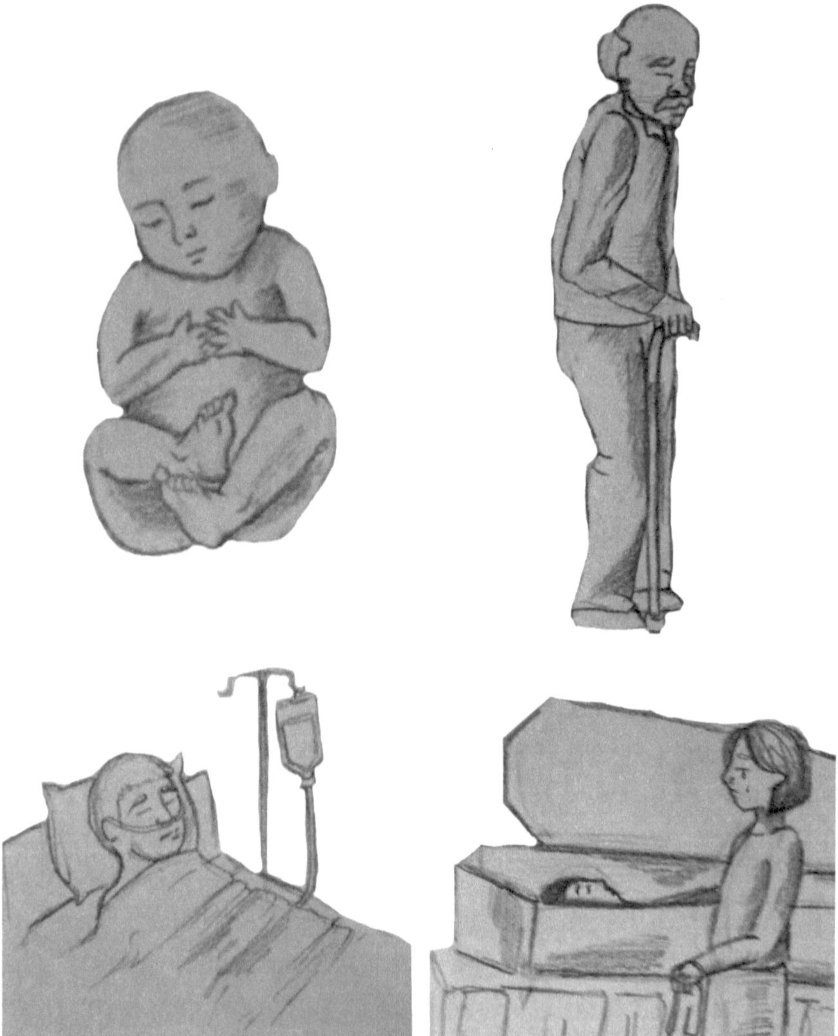

The four stages of life

as the end of the physical form, the body, as it is impermanent. However, there is still a continuation of our grandparents and parents in us and our presence in our children and grandchildren. We cannot change much of the physical sufferings, but we can develop the mental fortitude to grieve with composure. Mental suffering is more difficult to treat, but it can be alleviated through practice. Remember, the four mental sufferings are due to: distance from our loved ones, proximity to those whom we dislike, not able to have what we want, and attachment to the fluctuating nature of our Five Aggregates. We should practice such that although our body is in pain, we still have the mental aptitude to think of the positives and appreciate the rest of our body that is still functioning. We can still see a beautiful flower, hear an upbeat music, and taste a delectable meal. As for not being near our loved ones, being close to those whom we dislike, or not getting what we want, the doctrine of Cause and Condition helps us to understand that sometimes we have no control over these occurrences because all the right conditions have to be sufficient for events to arise. We should enjoy and appreciate what we do have, instead of lingering on what we do not have. Our sensory inputs can be a source of our mental fatigue. We see, hear, smell, taste, and feel things we dislike or fall in love with. This causes us to be fixated on the objects of our experience, resulting in mental unrest. Thus, the Buddha teaches ways to calm our mind, have gratitude, be content with what we have, and practice non-attachment.

The Vehicle of Cause and Condition is the second of the Lesser Vehicle to practice toward enlightenment. This is when life's events awaken us to the noble truths, such as the death of a friend that causes us to realize that life is fragile and subject to change, thus revealing the doctrine of impermanence. It is through contemplation of the twelve interlinked factors of Cause and Condition that allows us to understand the series of conditions leading to our vicious life cycle. It teaches us that when conditions are sufficient, an object, action, or event comes into existence, and conversely. This law reminds us that we can work to change our conditions by cultivating insight that leads towards the great vow and then wisdom, rather than beginning with delusion that inevitably takes us back through the life cycle of rebirths. Once we understand and accept the laws of the universe and the normal course of life, we can take pleasure or endure each phenomenon as it arises and be at peace as we experience and celebrate a well-lived life.

In summary, these Five Vehicles of study and practice emphasize the conviction to augment our wholesome acts and lessen our unwholesome acts. They outline a multi-step approach to practice where we can steadily progress towards cultivating compassion, building merits, and achieving wisdom to have harmony in our life and interactions with others. The volume of information in this chapter may be overwhelming at first, so it should be reread and studied until we can absorb and deeply understand the teachings that the Buddha has laid out for us. Practicing moral conduct allows us to create happiness for our family and peace for the world. Doing so will bring us the happiness and joy that we all seek.

Chapter 19

The Practice

We should utilize the symbols that Buddhism conveys to better understand and reinforce the teachings and practice. An important objective and goal in Buddhism is to apply the knowledge we learn and put it into practice. To practice is to adjust, fix, and transform. Through practice, we can improve and make anew the conditions of our body, mind, and karma. Practice can be carried out formally and informally. In the formal practice with traditional rituals, we study the Dharma and honor the Buddha as our teacher by reciting Sutras, chanting mantras, as well as praying and paying homage to the Buddha. Informally, we apply the Dharma teachings to our daily life by exercising meditation and refining our thoughts, speech, and actions with mindfulness to improve our negative habitual energy. Studying without practice is not satisfactory or meaningful, which can lead to false views. Practice without studying can result in delusions. We should study the Dharma teachings in order to practice towards enlightenment. Buddhism has a paramount of teachings for us to learn, but it is not until we implement the teachings into our daily practice that we can achieve the ultimate comprehension of our studies.

The rituals and activities at the temple are formal practices. They are methods to help concentrate and purify our mind. One of the activities is to read the Sutras. The Sutras can be enigmatic, but with persistent reading, we will commit them to memory, be able to recite and understand them, and remember to apply the teachings in our daily life. When we chant mantras and recite Sutras, our eyes are fixed on the words, our speech flows in the rhythm of the sentences, our ears are tuned into the utterances, and our bodies are in one position. Once our mind is concentrated in one activity, it becomes settled and calm. Another ritual to calm our mind is to pray and pay homage to the Buddha at the altar. On doing this, we are remembering the Buddha's ten merits, vows, and Muni characteristics of compassion, patience, harmony, and purity. We remember the Buddha's merits and study his vows so we can apply them to our practice. The formal bowing and praying to the Buddha statue help to remind us of our innate Buddha-nature. In the absence of the Buddha statue, we can take refuge in the five objects of reverence that represent the presence of the Buddha and his teachings:

1) The Kasaya robe
2) The Bodhi tree
3) The lotus
4) The stupa
5) The Dharma Wheel

The five objects of reverence: the Buddha statue and Kasaya robe, Bodhi tree, lotus flower, stupa, and Dharma Wheel

Objects are used to remind us of persons or things in their absence. The Kasaya robe was worn by the Buddha and is currently worn by the monastics. The Bodhi tree provided a place of rest and shade and is the last location where Prince Siddhartha meditated and finally attained enlightenment, after practicing for seven weeks. The lotus is a symbolic flower representing purity and achievements over all difficulties. The stupa is a religious shrine containing relics of the Buddha. The Dharma Wheel encompasses the Four Noble Truths, the Noble Eightfold Path, and the propagation of his teachings. There are other ways to remember the Buddha besides reflecting on the objects of reverence and the Buddha's statue. We can recite the Buddha's name in a loud or soft tone of voice. We can recollect the Buddha and direct our thoughts to his characters and vows. We can apply his teachings with mindfulness meditation via sitting, walking, breathing, and counting the prayer beads. Lastly, we wholeheartedly have our mind and body in unison to continuously internalize the Buddha's vows and what he represents. The practice of remembrance is an important tool to utilize when we are faced with problems and mental distress. We can take refuge in the Buddha and his teachings wherever we are. Besides remembering the Buddha, there are nine other subjects of remembrance. They are: the Dharma, the Sangha, the precepts, the heaven, generosity, forgiveness and non-attachment, breathing meditation, impermanence, and demise. Taking refuge in these subjects gives us comfort, helps to calm our mind, and allows us to handle troubling issues with a gentle composure. The Dharma, the Sangha, the precepts, the heaven, generosity, and breathing meditation give us support and serenity. Forgiveness and non-attachment help us to release and let go. Impermanence and demise remind us to accept the true nature of life and realize that our problems are minuscule in light of the big picture. These rituals and activities at the temple are traditional practices that seem mundane to our new generation because they may not understand the meanings behind the activities. Nevertheless, these activities have symbolic significance to enhance our understanding and lead us to purity and tranquility. The practice yields a concentrated mind where we humbly praise, bow, and think of the Buddha as we recite the Sutras. They are important practices for the Sangha to reinforce the respect and remembrance of the Buddha and his teachings.

Praying is an important practice in our life. It provides an outlet during times of distress when we pray to a higher being to help relieve our suffering and provide guidance. The clasping of the hands together is symbolic of a prayer. A prayer requires two processes for it to come to fruition. We pray to request a wish to come true. But with this prayer, we need to commit to perform the actions needed in order to receive blessings. There are three important steps in a prayer:

1) To read and listen to the teachings
2) To recite, internalize, remember, and reflect
3) To practice the teachings and apply them to our life

Listening to the sermons and reciting the Sutras are the first step in a prayer. The second step is to memorize and internalize the Sutras so that we know and feel the meanings in our mind and body when we recite them. Lastly, we can reflect on what is learned so we can practice and apply it to our life. In other words, we can only put into practice the things we understand and remember. Let's say we ask someone to get a pen, and he or she agrees but completely forgets upon returning back from another room. In this case, he or she heard the request, but did not put it into practice or carry out the task because he or she did not take note to remember. We cannot carry out tasks that we do not remember. It does not mean that we do not want to do them; it is because we do not pay attention and concentrate to remember them. When we are not able to remember, we are not able to complete any tasks. In school, if we need to pass a math exam, we must remember how to solve the math problem in order to perform it on the date of the exam. Likewise, when we use the prayer beads to recite repeatedly "Nam Mô A Di Đà Phật" (homage to the Amitabha Buddha), this is only the first step. In the second step, we have to understand and remember what the Amitabha Buddha represents. The Amitabha Buddha has three immeasurable characteristics of radiant light, merit, and longevity. When we greet one another with the phrase "Homage to the Amitabha Buddha," we are wishing upon our friend the light of wisdom to practice so as to yield meritorious deeds and create an everlasting impact and presence in the hearts and lives of people. The Vietnamese prayer "Nam Mô Bổn Sư Thích Ca Mâu Ni Phật" (homage to my original teacher Shakyamuni Buddha) is widely heard and chanted at the temple. It is recited so automatically that we may not recognize its meaning. It means taking refuge in the original teacher who is a sage in the Shakya family lineage, embodying the Muni characteristics of compassion, patience, harmony, and purity. As with any prayer, we must internalize its meaning in order to develop, practice, and apply the nature of compassion, tranquility, and patience in our everyday life. When we recite a prayer, we first have to read and listen to the teachings, then reflect and memorize, and lastly practice and apply the teachings to our daily life.

As part of formal practice, every practitioner aims to arrive at Amitabha Buddha's Western Pure Land in spirit at the end of his or her life or in the mental state of this life. It is a place of unparalleled happiness and paramount beauty with a lotus pond covered with seven precious jewels. This destination and practice are a belief as described in the Mahayana school of Buddhism. The Amitabha Buddha represents the purity and serenity we want throughout and at the end of our life. The description of this heavenly destination is symbolic of the state of mind we want to achieve in this life. Practitioners strive to purify their body, speech, and mind to elicit exquisite beauty in character and appearance that is similarly seen in the Amitabha Buddha, Western Pure Land, and lotuses. This beauty is radiated internally and externally by applying the core practice of morality, concentration, and wisdom to overcome the ten roots of affliction, which are:

1) Greed
2) Anger
3) Delusion
4) Pride
5) Skepticism
6) Wrong view
7) One-sided view
8) Wrong view of self
9) Attachment to our view
10) Attachment to misperceptions of how the precepts should be practiced

It is only when we recognize and experience the afflictions of our current life that we want to pursue liberation to the Pure Land. The Buddha describes impurities in our life that contribute to these afflictions. Impurity has several meanings. It can mean dirty and not clean, unstable, things done and used in the wrong way, or the changes and outcomes that are not exactly what we want or think. There are five impurities to be aware of:

1) Impurity of the world
2) Impurity of our view
3) Impurity of living beings
4) Impurity of our life span
5) Impurity of afflictions

In the impurity of the world, there are natural disasters and man's infliction of terrorism that cause disturbances to our living environment. In the impurity of our view, our false views can cause us to act improperly, such as using our parents' hard-earned money to buy drugs rather than purchasing a nutritious meal. The five faulty views that we have are listed under numbers six through ten in the ten roots of affliction. All living beings have a physical body that is naturally impure; we have to brush our teeth, shampoo our hair, and wash our body as part of our daily cleansing regimen. We have nine main orifices where our waste products are excreted: two eyes, two ears, two nostrils, the mouth, urethra, and anal opening. We have positive and negative feelings of love and hate, generosity and jealousy, and equanimity and discrimination. Our life span is impure and is shortened due to the defilements of our environment and body. The impurity of afflictions is contributed by our negative seeds of desire, delusion, and doubt. Our practice should be focused on transforming ourselves to a state of purity and serenity with right view and wisdom. Just as there are many impure states and destinations, there are many other Pure Lands such as the Eastern Pure Land presided over by the Medicine Buddha. On the other hand, the Western Pure Land is governed by the Amitabha Buddha; it is where there are no physical or mental sufferings. It has eight counterparts to contrast with the eight physical and mental sufferings in the worldly life. They are as follows:

1) Birth from lotus – physical birth
2) Eternal beauty – old age
3) Liberation – sickness
4) Longevity – death
5) Collective groups of practitioners in harmony – distance from our loved ones
6) Collective virtuous minds – proximity to those whom we dislike
7) All wishes achieved – not able to have what we want
8) Purity and serenity of the mind and body – attachment to the fluctuating nature of our Five Aggregates.

When there is a physical body, it is prone to the natural course of birth, old age, sickness, and death. Mental sickness arises from attachments to our nature of the self and not having things to our satisfaction. We need to have the benevolent foundations of the mind, sufficient blessings, and the right Causes and Conditions to arrive at the Western Pure Land. With understanding of the Dharma teachings, our Dharma body works with mindfulness in joy and happiness, without complaint or sorrow and, in essence, reaches the pure and serene state of the Western Pure Land. In the Western Pure Land, we will not be stricken by the four physical sufferings or four mental sufferings. The Western Pure Land provides supreme bliss from the purity of the lotus, perfect beauty, liberation, and eternal life. The Western Pure Land has an enlightened Dharma body of practitioners with virtuous minds, which results in achievement of all aspirations and purity of the mind and body. We can arrive at the Western Pure Land in this lifetime and upon a fortunate rebirth. All we need is to have faith that there is such a state and place, and commit to practice towards it.

Besides formal practice, studying the Dharma teachings and applying the practice to our daily life are emphasized in the contemporary practice of Engaged Buddhism. As practitioners, believing in the Buddha as our teacher is the first step, but we must study and learn his teachings and apply them to our daily life. Engaged Buddhism emerged to apply the core teachings of the Buddha and assimilate within different cultures and modern society so practitioners can understand and relate to the teachings more easily. The three important steps in the practice are: listening, contemplating, and practicing. We first need to listen and learn. Before we accept and believe in the teachings, we need to contemplate to make sure they make sense and are correct and benevolent, before carrying out the actions. Buddhism teaches us how to live and treat others so we can have harmony in our life. The Dharma directs our practice toward three goals:

1) To elevate to the highest level
2) To do benevolent things
3) To liberate ourselves from afflictions

We take refuge in the Dharma teachings so our mind can be directed to the highest level and prevent us from heading toward the nadir. Not only do we aim to the highest level, we need to encourage our friends and family to do the same. As we practice and transform toward the highest level, we steer toward virtuous activities. When we practice in the right path, we achieve the right happiness. And as we do good things, our mind will be at peace and liberated from the worries of retributions or strife from others. Being liberated means to arrive at a state of serenity and purity. Liberation is attained when we are able to resolve problems, overcome afflictions, and prevent them from tying us down. Anything that causes sorrow or disturbs our mind is an affliction. It can be as small as a dissatisfaction with the food that is served at a restaurant. If our dish comes out with garlic and onions after we have told the server to omit them, we should just pick out the garlic and onions, instead of being upset and preoccupied by the server's mistake. This is an example of how we can resolve the matter, so we can enjoy the meal without ruining a pleasant evening with our family. Liberation is a process to unfold restraints and transcend limitations. The restraints and limitations are our attachments and the binding knots they cause in our mental state. The three types of liberation are:

1) Liberation from a situation
2) Liberation of the mind
3) Liberation fulfilled to completion

Sometimes we are in a liberated situation, but do not experience liberation because we cannot recognize our blessings. We see that living in a house with an air conditioner, in a safe neighborhood, with all family members healthy and present to eat together every evening are ordinary occasions. We do not appreciate what we have until an unusual event occurs that disrupts our regular routine, such as a family member's absence due to an illness or uncomfortable heat when the air conditioner malfunctions. Often, we create more misery for ourselves by wishing that we were in a bigger house and in a fancier neighborhood, as we are not aware of the state of liberation that we do have. Liberation does not only exist in a certain location or situation, but can be experienced when our state of mind is completely content and satisfied despite the circumstances; this subsequently gives rise to internal peace and happiness. We can feel liberated even when we are in prison. When we live in a restrictive and suppressive condition, we can achieve liberation through mindfulness of appreciation and acceptance. Despite our situation and environment, we have to accept and be at peace in order to achieve liberation of the mind. We have to be mindful to realize our attainment of liberation in order to have the liberation fulfilled to completion. Liberation is achieved when we "cross over to the other shore." For the Dharma teachings to be more meaningful, we need to apply them to our daily practice to achieve liberation.

To practice Buddhism means to diligently and mindfully update our life and understanding with the intent of rectifying our mistakes to do better. We practice to cultivate and bring forth from a nonexistent virtuous deed to a good deed, from a good deed to a better deed, and from a better deed to the best deed. On the other hand, we also practice to decrease an extreme shortcoming to a lesser state of shortcoming, from a lesser state to a minimal state, and from a minimal state to the extinction of our shortcoming. One of the ways to reinforce these virtuous deeds is to commit to study the Dharma teachings. The Buddha's teachings are summarized into three main objectives:

1) To avoid malevolence
2) To develop benevolence
3) To purify and calm the mind

This is emphasized in the Four True Endeavors that are part of the Thirty-Seven Paths to Enlightenment. The Four True Endeavors encourage us to develop benevolent activities that have not arisen yet, nurture existing benevolent ones, and prevent malevolent activities from arising while eliminating existing malevolent ones. Malevolence is any act that diminishes happiness, compassion, and loving-kindness to ourselves and others. It includes feelings of hatred and fear, as well as thoughts of delusion and excessive desires, which cause the loss of peace of mind. Malevolence increases our afflictions and decreases our blessings and merits. Malevolence is any actions that result in gain for ourselves and harm for others. At times, an act that looks malevolent may actually be benevolent, such as pushing a person aside to prevent him or her from being run over by oncoming traffic. Benevolence is any act that promotes welfare to ourselves and others. We can perform the virtuous deeds ourselves or support others in the tasks. It is said that we receive the same blessings as the person carrying out the benevolent actions when we support him or her in the virtuous acts. This is because we release our negative seeds of selfishness while the person who performs the benevolent actions releases the mind of greed. Both minds manifest and unite in harmony. Besides our actions, benevolence and malevolence are also carried out when we support or take pleasure in observing the respective actions that stem from them. For example, we develop malevolence when we hurt someone, give support when a person hurts someone, or feel happy when observing a person hurts someone. The important practice is to recognize actions as benevolent or malevolent, commit to imitate the benevolent behaviors, and not adopt the malevolent ones. For example, if we see our friends helping their parents clean their house, we should emulate this positive act. Conversely, if we see our friends drinking to the point of intoxication, we should not perform this negative act and recognize that we should not adopt it either. This way, we can advance in our practice and prevent regression. There are four rules that guide us to reinforce this virtuous practice. The first is to engage in activities that benefit us and others. The second is not to engage in activities that benefit us but harm others. On the other hand, we should not engage in activities that benefit others but harm us. And definitely, we should not engage in activities that harm us and others. Purifying the mind is the third objective in our practice. When we purify the mind, we in turn purify the three processes that create karma: our thought, speech, and action. Karma is seen in the doctrine of Cause and Effect. Because of this action, this event manifests. Our thoughts lead to what we say in our speech and is subsequently carried out in our actions. We own our karma as a result of our thoughts, speech, and actions, as this is the law of Cause and Effect. If we have benevolent thoughts, loving and kind speech, and compassionate actions, we will have happiness and peace. If we have malevolent thoughts, harsh speech, and ill-natured actions, we will have misery and unrest. When we have ill thoughts of someone we dislike, we speak unkind words of them and exhibit acts of malice. In return, we cannot expect the other person to treat us differently. There are five ways to mindfully practice to lessen malevolent and increase benevolent acts:

> 1) The first is to think and apply benevolence rather than malevolence, direct our mind toward the positives, and ward off malevolence. An example is when we see an obstacle of a tree stump; instead of brooding over it,

we should divert our path to the nice surrounding flowers.
2) The second way is to think of the consequences of the malevolent acts that will deter us, such as the possibility of developing lung cancer from tobacco smoking.
3) The third way is to try our best to forget and dismiss the malevolent acts. An example is to remove all alcohol beverages from the house when we know we have an addiction to alcohol.
4) The fourth way is to block the malevolent acts from arising or progressively lessen them toward elimination. An example is to recognize our addiction to gambling and either stop going to the casino altogether or not go as often until we can stop completely.
5) The fifth and last way is to use our utmost energy to stop the malevolent acts. This is seen in a father who has the compassion to immediately stop smoking due to his daughter's severe lung illness.

As such, the Buddha teaches many ways to improve our character flaws so we can mindfully adjust our thoughts, speech, and actions to practice towards a change for the better.

Buddhism is a way of life that entails the practice of continuous adjustments and transformations to improve our thoughts, speech, and actions from worse to good, good to better, and better to best. In other words, the practice is aimed toward the cultivation of our karma. Because our wrongdoings arise from thoughts originating from our mind, the thoughts or intentions of wrongdoing have to be eliminated from our

The practice is aimed toward the cultivation of our karma: our thoughts, speech, and actions.

mind. Our thoughts lead to our speech and actions. Our mouth is another source of our karma. It is where words are produced and food is consumed. If we are not mindful, the words we say can be hurtful to others, and the food we consume can be harmful to our body. Buddhism holds us responsible and accountable for each of our actions. We need to be aware of the path that we are traveling and how we are navigating along the path, so we can adjust our route accordingly. There are four paths in our life, similar to the cyclic phase of the moon. There is the path from darkness to brightness, and vice versa, the path from brightness to darkness. There are paths where we just maintain the course without changing. They are the path from darkness to darkness and the path from brightness to brightness. Prince Siddhartha took the path from darkness to brightness. With the help of his attendant Channa, he left the royal palace on his white horse Kanthaka in the middle of the night in search of finding liberation, peace, and happiness. Channa questioned the Prince regarding leaving in the middle of the night when people are in deep sleep. The Prince replied that because people are in deep sleep, he has to awaken to lead them out of delusion. We need to aim toward the path to brightness and further maintain the ultimate path from brightness to brightness. Our goal in the practice is to transform our negative to positive karma of thoughts, speech, and actions. If we perform a wrong act, the person whose feelings were hurt can forgive us, but no one can fix or make it right for us except ourselves.

We have to recognize what we are deficient in so we can work to make things better. The person who knows how to transform his or her karma can practice to change from suffering to happiness and maintain that state of happiness. Those who do not know how to practice can cause their happiness to turn into suffering and keep their suffering status quo. We can improve our karma by developing thoughts of the Buddha, speaking virtuously like the Buddha, and performing the vows of the Buddha.

Practice is important and necessary. Studying without practicing is similar to reading about our prescription medication but not taking the medication. To practice is to skillfully augment and fine tune the status quo to improve. We change the filter of the air conditioner vent to get cleaner air, fix our car when it breaks down, and maintain our landscape when the weeds are overgrown. We buy new clothes when trends change, a new refrigerator when it breaks down, and a new cell phone when the latest model comes out. Why would we not want to fix or transform our character flaws? The four important steps of practice are:

1) To stop and recognize the problem
2) To reflect and contemplate the problem
3) To understand the problem
4) To adjust and transform ourselves towards improvement

If we recognize our feelings of anger as a source of discomfort to ourselves and uneasiness to others, a small change in how we express ourselves or withhold our reactive action can bring happiness to everyone. We also do not want to have an attitude of complacency and disregard our problems. For example, if we have committed to stop drinking but inadvertently ordered a drink during a social function, we should stop, acknowledge our habitual drinking disorder, and not take any more sips of the drink. Just because we have already ordered the drink does not mean we should go ahead and drink it up. To heal our ailment, we need to recognize and fix our imperfect habitual actions and energy. If we turn onto the wrong path, we should not keep on going. Instead, we should turn around and get back on the right track. Likewise, if we are disappointed with a poor grade on a test, we recognize that continuing to get poor grades will not allow us to get a good job. We need to reflect and contemplate why we made the poor grade. Did we not study enough and party too much on the week of the test? Did we not keep up with our studies and cram to study for the test? Once we understand the problem and realize that we did not spend enough time studying, then we can adjust and spend one more hour a day to study for that course. When we detect a problem, we should address it immediately, as a small problem will quickly become a much bigger problem. Just as a boat with a small hole will sink slowly and subtly, it will unexpectedly become submerged under water when it reaches a critical water volume. So we need to be attentive and recognize our problem, contemplate and reflect to understand it, and adjust to transform. This is the way to practice in order to improve.

The practice of Buddhism targets to transform the three things that are prone to sickness in all beings, namely our karma, body, and mind. Karma is the law that governs our future life status based on our past and present actions. It is somewhat similar to destiny but is instead a direct result of our actions. For example, the blessings or misfortunes that occur in this life are the result of our past deeds. Negative karma can be treated with repentance and establishing merits. This way, we target the old karma and create a more positive, new karma. The second object prone to illness is our body. Physical sickness can develop from changes in the weather, lack of sleep, or a reaction to spoiled food. It can be treated with medications and rest. Mental sickness, such as fear, depression, or anger, is harder to treat. Mental sickness can be treated with psychological counseling and supplemented with the Dharma teachings in order to develop the wisdom to understand and accept the true nature of things. Among the three objects that can develop sickness, our karma is the main one that we should practice to transform, adjust, and improve for our eternal life.

In our life, we must practice generosity and provide services in order to build up positive karmic energy and blessings for our future life. We can complement and enhance our blessings by developing the four qualities of compassion, generosity, patience, and the ability to transform and teach others. Other ways to augment our blessings include explaining and teaching any ambiguity of the Dharma teachings and life's lessons, supporting everyone in the practice, and aiming toward the supreme path of enlightenment. Blessings are fortunate conditions that we can enjoy as a result of our past virtuous deeds. Blessings are important to have so we can increase the likelihood to encounter good teachers, supportive friends, and peaceful surrounding conditions. There are two types of blessings: forms and formless. The blessings that we are able to see and touch, such as our house and car, manifest in forms. The blessings that are formless appear in the exchange of ideas among friends, knowledge learned from the Dharma teachings, or experience gained in a vocation. The blessings seen in forms are subject to the laws of impermanence and, therefore, can be lost. The blessings that are formless are more enduring. An example of a blessing in form is a stethoscope that is owned by a physician. The blessing that is formless is the physician's ability and skills to diagnosis and treat an illness even when the stethoscope is lost or stolen. Another example is our recipe book that may be misplaced, but we still remember and have an idea on how to cook a certain dish. At times, we may not have the blessings to enjoy our blessings. We may have blessings of a delicious meal but may not have sufficient blessings to eat it due to a toothache or stomachache. Our blessings are everything we have, from a healthy tooth to a luxurious sports car. The question is, do we have the wisdom to recognize and appreciate what we have? Oftentimes, we are dissatisfied because we are fixated on what we do not have and dream of things to pursue. We do not appreciate the blessings we do have until problems arise or when our blessings are used up. We do not appreciate our teeth and feet until we are not able to eat or walk because of pain. Hence, we need to use our wisdom to recognize the blessings that we do have. The Buddha teaches that we should enjoy the blessings we currently have and also replenish them by using our blessings to create more blessings. An example is when we donate our hair to make wigs for cancer patients. Or we can use our car and time to pick up a nearby friend to go to the temple with us. The blessings that we have are similar to the monies we have in our savings account. Our earned blessings are deposited into our savings account when we do good deeds.

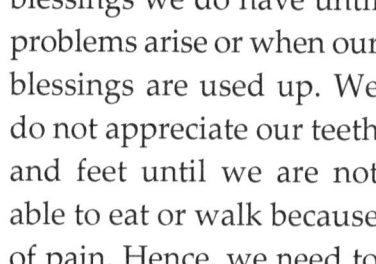

We must use our blessings to generate more blessings.

As we enjoy the blessings, we are spending the monies in our savings account. The misfortunes that we have are our debts that we have incurred in the past or our past life due to our unkind actions. We should not be upset over our misfortunes, but be glad that we are paying off our debts. There are three ways we can cultivate more blessings:

1) Provide service, gratitude, and respect for all beings in the world
2) Abide in moral disciplines
3) Act in accordance to the vow of a Bodhisattva

The first way is to develop filial piety toward our parents and gratitude toward our teachers. We should respect one another and persons of authority and nurture our children physically and mentally. The second way is to take refuge in the Three Jewels, live and abide by the Five Precepts, and follow the paths of the Five Vehicles. These moral disciplines guide us to prevent malevolence and act in benevolence, resulting in increased blessings. The third way is to promote the mind of enlightenment, and develop acts of virtue like the Bodhisattvas by deeds of great compassion to transform ourselves and others. The ensuing five blessings we will receive from our practice are good health, longevity, wealth, luxury, and a peaceful death. With good health, we can have a long life. If we have wealth, we can live a luxurious life. We are wealthy when we can recognize that we have enough. The person who feels content living in a small house is able to feel wealthy. A wealthy person who is discontent living in a big house with debt feels poor. We tend to feel that we do not have enough and, therefore, do not feel satisfied or happy. We are constantly wanting to have more, as we tend to be dissatisfied with our current status. We say we will be happy when we graduate from college. Once we obtain a college degree, we have a new goal to get a good job. Then, we seek a lifetime companion to establish a family, and so on and so forth. Pursuing a moving target of happiness in life is endless. According to the Zen Buddhist statement: "There is no way to happiness. Happiness is the way, the here and now, in the present moment." It is when we practice to feel gratitude and satisfaction, and focus our goal upon serving others and accumulating merits, then we will have the blessings and peace throughout and at the end of our life.

One of the vital practices in Buddhism is cultivating our body and mind to create peace for the body and intrinsic joy for the mind. We need to constantly adjust our body and character, and regulate our minds and thoughts. This is similar to taking the car to an auto shop where the body of the car is transformed with a new coat of paint, and the engine is fixed with new parts. Following the Five Precepts, particularly the first three, is a way to cultivate our physical body. Our goal is to regulate our bodily actions and fine-tune each posture of sitting, standing, walking, and talking to foster the righteous habitual actions and energies. We do this by choosing to preserve life, practice generosity, build faithful relationships, speak loving-kindness, and consume healthy nutriments for the mind and body. If our body is slouched, we adjust it to be more upright. Our body is a Bodhi tree. We have to treat our body like a sacred Bodhi tree by caring for and nourishing it, so we can utilize it as a vehicle to practice, just like a raft is used to cross to the other shore. The physical body is made up of the four great elements of earth, water, wind, and fire. It gives us the physical appearance of being tall, short, beautiful, or ugly. We need to exercise to maintain good health for our physical body. We need clear vision to read and study the Dharma teachings, intact hearing to listen to the sermons and practice deep listening, and a strong breath to recite the Sutras and speak words of wisdom. There are two other types of body besides the physical body: the working body and the Dharma body. When we perform a particular role in life, we have the working body. We work to benefit ourselves and serve others. We serve in the role of a parent when we take care of our children. We are members of the Sangha when we participate in the activities of the temple. We work as a dishwasher when we wash dishes. Through the working body, we aim to do things that are good for ourselves and for the welfare of people and our community. The Dharma body is the ultimate body that we want to pursue to have. This body always work with mindfulness, in joy and happiness, and without complaint or sorrow. The Dharma body is the enlightened body that is omnipresent and everlasting. Although the physical body is limited in capability and longevity, it can work and create unlimited and everlasting benefits through the working and Dharma body. It is through diligence and practice that we can develop the Dharma body.

The Buddha realized the importance of nurturing the physical body to support his practice after he fainted due to the severe deprivation of his body; he was subsequently revived when Sujata offered a bowl of rice milk to him. In the fifth precept, the Buddha teaches us to be mindful of what we intake for our body and mind so that it provides nourishment rather than harm. It is worthwhile to mention here that the reason practitioners commit to a vegetarian diet is not mainly because of health reasons but out of compassion for animal beings. This practice evolved from the Mahayana school, as the monastics from the Theravada school and those practicing during the time period of the Buddha consumed whatever was offered during the alms round. The Buddha classifies four types of nutriments for our body and mind:

1) The edible food
2) The sensory impression
3) Our aspirations
4) Our consciousness

The primary purpose of eating is for us to live, so we should choose nutritious food for the well-being of our body and mind and not food that will adversely alter them. This includes the food we eat, the books we read, the shows we watch, and the music we listen to. The first two nutriments involve the physical body. The edible food entails masticating, swallowing, and digesting the food. We should choose foods that are healthy and avoid foods that are harmful for the body. The second way we intake nutriment is through our sensory organs. We can see, smell, feel, and taste the food. At times, after a full day of cooking, we feel full from consuming through our senses. The last two nutriments feed our mind. The third nutriment is our positive aspirations and goals. They are a form of food and energy to give us strength and determination to overcome any hindrances and continue our endeavors to achieve our goals until the endpoint. It is important to set goals that are benevolent rather than malevolent, as they can supply and support our mind in a positive manner. The fourth nutriment is from our feelings, emotions, and thoughts that are developed from what we see, hear, smell, taste, and contact. If we choose to hold on to our dislikes of a person or event, this consciousness adversely feeds our mind to hold hatred and resentment. If we retain pleasant feelings and thoughts, this positive consciousness reinforces good nutrition for our mind. This is why the Buddha encourages us to deliberately choose what we feed our sensory consciousness. We should read and listen to the Dharma teachings to decrease and transform our negative karma to bring peace and joy to our body, mind, and community, instead of engaging in non-purposeful gossips and entertainment that can cause feelings of afflictions, jealousy, and hatred. The sound of the Dharma teachings is similar to the beautiful chirping sound of the birds that feed into our sensory consciousness. Thus, it is essential to take care of both our body and mind by performing virtuous acts and regulating what we consume.

Cultivating the mind is important, as the status of the body follows our mental attitude. If our mind is stricken by anguish and grief, our physical body will follow suit and manifest ailments such as stomach discomfort or body fatigue and achiness. Our mind is a large reflective mirror. If we can recognize when the emotion of jealousy surfaces, we can work on being happy for the other person for their success. If we find ourselves being selfish and not sharing, we should work on developing compassion and loving-kindness. The state of our mind can be reflected in our dreams. One of the reasons why we dream, whether it is pleasant or unpleasant, is that our mind is not at peace. The dream does not mean that we have a mental condition. We may be physically tired or have constant thoughts of the subject matter surfacing from our store consciousness. Our karma can remind us of our thoughts, speech, and bodily actions in our deep sleep. The dream may be an indication from the demons or heavenly beings. We may be traveling down the wrong path in life, and the dreams are awakening and redirecting us. The mind is more difficult to exercise, as it is influenced by temptations of defilements. Our mind has the inherent property of exquisite brilliance, similar to that of a clean mirror. But over time, our mind can accumulate layers of afflictions, similar to a mirror collecting layers of dust. This naturally radiant mind is our Buddha-nature. An attempt to clean the mirror by blowing off dust is inadequate, as we have to use special chemicals and apply enough pressure to thoroughly wipe off the dust with a cloth. Likewise, we have to use a specific proper method to cultivate our mind. Through practice, we can recognize and understand our state of mind so we can train and purify it. There are four types of mind and their opposites that we need to be aware of:

1) The right mind and the wrong mind
2) The true mind and the false mind
3) The immense mind and the minuscule mind
4) The wholesome mind and the partial mind

The mind can be like a messy house where we need to tidy up one area at a time. Recognizing the paired features of the mind will help distinguish the mind we want to use and the mind we want to disregard in our practice. We want to develop our mind so that it remains righteous and true and continues to grow immensely and wholeheartedly. We want to avoid the mind that has wrong and false thoughts and one with a small and partial view of things. There are also five minds of the Bodhisattva that we should develop:

1) The mind of enlightenment
2) The mind of filial devotion
3) The mind of compassion
4) The mind of reverence
5) The mind of truthfulness

Each state of mind is interconnected. The presence of one is dependent on the other. When we have an enlightened mind, it follows that we will be mindful to apply the virtues of devotion, compassion, reverence, and truthfulness towards everyone. Of the different types of mind, developing the four immeasurable minds consisting of loving-kindness, compassion, sympathetic joy, and equanimity is the most powerful and essential practice that will bring happiness and serenity in our life.

The mind of enlightenment is important to cultivate so we can use it to see clearly and make prudent decisions. There are five components needed to illuminate the mind and maintain its glow, similar to the parts of a kerosene lamp needed to maintain the light. The five components are faith, compassion, mindfulness, upholding the Five Precepts, and meritorious deeds. Faith is the flaming light. Compassion is the oil that fuels the blaze. Mindfulness is the container of the kerosene lamp. Commitment to the Five Precepts is the tube that expels the smoke to maintain the glow. Meritorious deeds radiate like the halo of light. Faith, compassion, mindfulness, commitment to uphold the Five Precepts, and meritorious deeds are all necessary components to illuminate the mind and promote wisdom. It is important to keep the light of enlightenment attained from the Dharma studies bright so we can continue our clear, correct path. When our mind is clear, we can avoid committing faults, just as it is easier to avoid stepping on a prickling thorn in daylight rather than in darkness. Illuminating the mind will help to develop the seven cherished jewels in a practitioner consisting of:

212 *The Symbolisms in Buddhism*

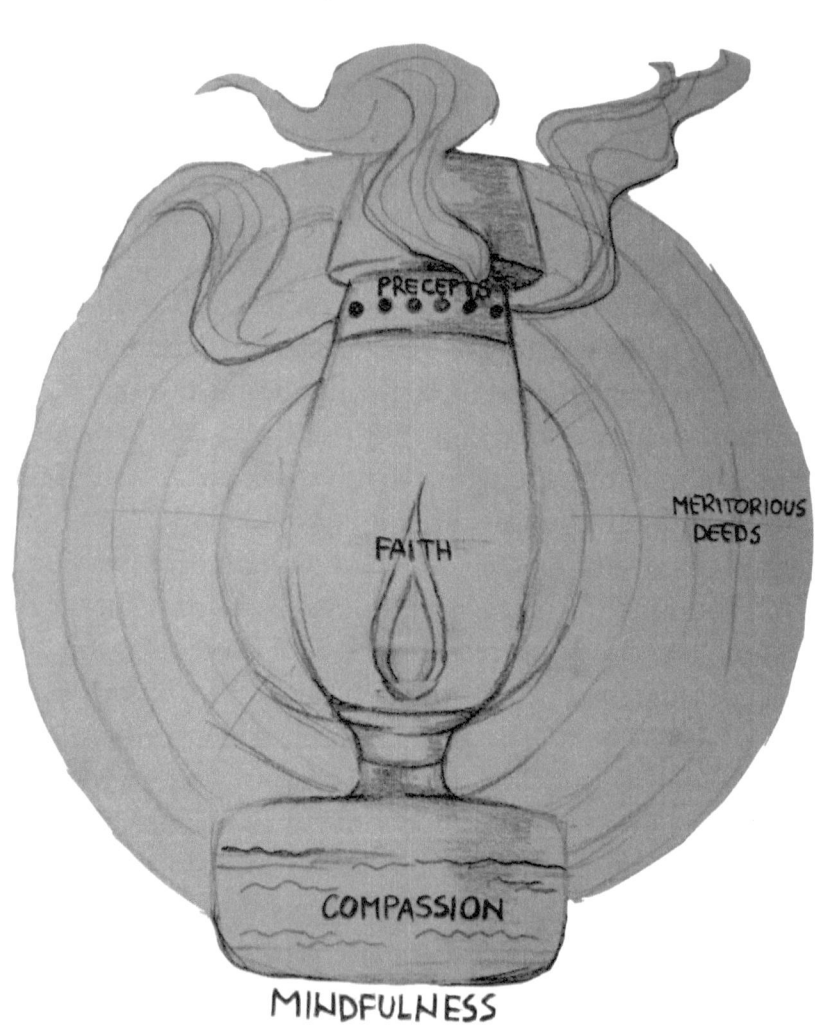

The kerosene lamp's analogy to the illumination of the mind

1) Faith
2) Morality
3) Repentance with self
4) Repentance with others
5) Deep listening
6) Generosity and release of attachments
7) Wisdom

Unlike the seven jewels of the worldly person (gold, silver, lapis lazuli, crystal, nacre [mother of pearl], red pearl, and carnelian), the seven jewels of a practitioner will perpetually flourish as we foster them. Our initial belief in any study is eventually transformed into faith as we diligently study and practice. Upholding the precepts is the basis and foundation of every practitioner and, when reinforced, will yield a multitude of happiness and blessings to our life. Repentance to oneself and others will relieve us from built-up faults and cleanse our mind and heart. Deep listening will allow us to be patient and joyful as we will not be quick to react with unregulated emotions and words. Our generosity will strengthen as we give without an emotional attachment or expectation. Ultimately, our wisdom will magnify as we nurture to practice all these qualities. Transforming the mind will result in a change in the bodily form and character. Just as a miner who pans for gold or a water filter that traps unwanted chemicals, we need to lessen and weed out our afflictions and wrong views in order to purify our mind and body. Both the body and mind need to work together as one, and we cannot foster one without the other. In order to achieve a successful practice, we need to establish and shape the temple within us before we can build the temple externally.

One of the best ways to reinforce our practice is through meditation and mindfulness. To meditate is to have deep thoughts, reflections, and contemplation over an activity in the present moment. The practice of meditation purifies the mind and, in return, results in clear thoughts for deep reflection. So when we are mindful, we are fully and completely aware of each current thought, speech, and action of our life. Through meditation, we restore our inner peace by calming our thoughts. Our unsettled mind is similar to a glass of water that becomes opaque when powder is stirred into it. But when left undisturbed, the water becomes clear and transparent as the powder settles to the bottom. When settled and calmed, our mind can think clearly, make rational decisions, and conduct ourselves with integrity. The two main steps in meditation are:

1) To stop our current thoughts, speech, and actions as we adjust our physical body and settle our mind
2) To contemplate and reflect

We first need to stop what we are doing and then return back to ourselves. When we speak of meditation, everyone may envision the practitioner in a seated lotus position with eyes closed. On the contrary, we can meditate in different postures and during any activities. We can engage in meditation while eating, breathing, sitting, walking, standing, or lying down. The four postures we should emulate into practice are to sit like a bell, walk like a peacock, stand like a pine tree, and lie down on the right side curved like an archery bow. The bell represents the solid pose of sitting meditation. The peacock walks majestically with its broad open fan of feathers. The pine tree is as straight and upright as the incense and its fragrance.

The four postures: the bell, peacock, pine tree, and archery bow

The archery bow is curved in a shallow semi-circle, resembling the right-sided recumbent position of the Buddha at Nirvana. In sitting meditation, we first stop our rambling thoughts and actions; we then straighten our posture and clothing. Our back is upright, both shoulders are relaxed, and hands are resting on our lap or knees. Next, we focus and follow our breath so we can calm our mind. Regulating our breath in turn helps to modulate our body and mind, resulting in a slower heart rate and softening of our intense emotions. Our breath is like a strong rope that anchors our mind to the present moment, similar to how a boat is anchored to the dock. This seated meditative pose portrays a beautiful image of our practice to transform ourselves. During a meal, we can practice meditation by eating in silence. While eating, we focus on the savory taste of the food as we chew it down to its chemical constituents. We develop a feeling of gratitude toward the farmer who grew the crops, and all the conditions of the sun, water, and soil that made it possible to yield the fruits and vegetables for us to eat, enjoy, and nourish our body. Another common practice prior to a meal is to meditate on the Five Contemplations to show appreciation and awareness of the food that we are eating. The main points in recitation of the Five Contemplations are as follows:

1) The food that we have is a gift from the earth, sky, and much loving, hard work of others.
2) We vow to eat in mindfulness and with gratitude to be deserving of the food we receive.
3) We vow to be mindful to transform our unskillful actions, especially to practice eating in moderation.
4) We vow to consume in a manner to minimize harm to animal beings, preserve our Mother Earth, and prevent

any harm that can cause damage to the environment and climate.
5) We vow to mindfully consume food that will provide us the strength to serve others and promote the communal and collective bond in the Sangha.

Despite the different postures and activities that can be engaged in meditation, the sitting meditation is the best practice since our body is stationary and not distracted by movements or activities; this allows our five sensory organs and mind to settle more easily. From practice, our mind will be calm and clear. This noble silence is characteristic of a practitioner, in contrast to the quietness of a person who is angry.

The practice of meditation has many benefits. It can help us develop insight and clarity in all situations. This clarity of mind develops the concentration needed to help us in all difficult situations; it allows us to have right view, make proper decisions, and solve problems. In return, concentration is used to continue our meditation practice. Meditation helps to cultivate our five sensory organs to form righteous sensory consciousness. It also regulates our mental formations (actions) and promotes diligence in our body and mind. The purpose of meditation is not to empty the problems occupying our mind but to attain serenity and purity of the mind so we can think clearly, attain wisdom, and carry out skillful and wholesome acts.

Besides focusing on our breath to calm the mind, there is another aspect of meditation where the objects of our focus are the body, feelings, mind, and phenomena. These are the Four Mindfulness Foundations. It is the first of the seven categories that contain four out of the Thirty-Seven Elements in the Path to Enlightenment. When we meditate on the body, we are aware of our bodily actions, positions, and postures. When we meditate on our feelings, we are aware of our sentiments. When we meditate on our mind, we are aware of the state of our thoughts. When we meditate on the phenomena, we understand the reasons for their existence and extinction. As we meditate, we see that the body is impure, the feelings as a cause for our distress, the mind in constant flux, and the phenomena of the universe is unreal. This helps us to understand the true nature of life. It helps us not to be fixated and attached to a new diagnosis of our illness or remain down with our temporary feelings of sadness. It helps us to recognize the changes in our state of mind and let go of unpleasant phenomena, as they are without a true self. The focus on these four elements of the body, feelings, mind, and phenomena helps us to be mindful of our existence and surrounding nature.

Meditation will help us to develop mindfulness. Mindfulness is the key and heart of our practice as it is emphasized in the Noble Eightfold Path, the Four Practices to achieve Transcendental Power, the Five Roots and Five Powers of Practice, and the Seven Elements of Enlightenment. Mindfulness is the constant awareness of our thoughts, speech, and actions. The emphasis is on the practice in the present moment. This awareness helps us to assess whether our thoughts, speech, and actions are appropriate and wholesome. Mindfulness helps to regulate our unskilled habitual actions and energies to prevent the development of negative karma. The four acts of conduct we should mindfully work on are walking, speaking, taking actions, and choosing the appropriate words to speak. We should walk gently with every step, unhurriedly and silently, without creating a sound. We should speak in a soft tone of voice. We should always act righteously. And we should use words that are pleasant and kind. Before speaking or acting, we have to determine whether our intended speech or action will bring happiness or sadness to others. If it brings sadness, we should refrain from speaking and acting. If it brings joy, we should wholeheartedly speak and act accordingly. We have two main periods in a day, each day. The morning time is the start of a new day, representing a new beginning in each twenty-four hours for us to start fresh, begin anew, and correct the mistakes we made yesterday. It is a time when the sun rises in the east and we open our eyes to interact with the world. The night time is the end of the day when we settle our mind and rest our body, reflect on our day's activities to determine what we have accomplished or failed, and contemplate on how we can improve the next day. It is a time when the sun sets in the west, and we close our eyes to rest our six senses. The continual awareness of the present moment will refine our impending speech and action to promote peace and harmonious interaction with others. From awareness, we can then adjust to effect purposeful, loving speech and kind actions.

One of the initial steps in purifying the mind is to recognize our current state of mind; is it thinking with proper or wrong view, or thoughts of equality or discrimination? Secondly, we need to be aware of the ten roots of our vices that can grow and negatively affect our mind. To review, the ten roots are:

1) Greed
2) Anger
3) Delusion
4) Pride
5) Skepticism
6) Wrong view

220 *The Symbolisms in Buddhism*

The three poisons

7) One-sided view
8) Wrong view of self
9) Attachment to our view
10) Attachment to misperceptions of how the precepts should be practiced

These ten roots lead us to think, speak, and act inappropriately and unkindly and are the sources of our suffering. They can cloud and disrupt the mind, and these are what we need to purify.

Of the ten roots, the Buddha labels the first three as the "three poisons," "three poisonous snakes," or "mara." Snakes can kill us instantaneously. Greed, hatred, and delusion kill us over many lifetimes. They can cause us to suffer day by day, month by month, and all year long. We remain in delusion if we let these distressing feelings go unchecked. In Vietnamese, the word "ma" literally means "ghost" and is derived from the Sanskrit word "mara." Mara is interpreted as anything that disrupts our peace and happiness, creates obstacles, and conquers our mind such that our merits and wisdom are eliminated, and we no longer have control over our actions. Mara can mean delusion, as it is the opposite of enlightenment. Mara is classified into four types:

1) Mara of our Five Aggregates (form, feeling, perception, mental formation, and consciousness)
2) Celestial mara
3) Mara of affliction
4) Mara of demise

Our Five Aggregates and discriminatory consciousness can cover and hinder our awakened mind. The celestial mara can skillfully instigate, provoke, and persuade us to do non-virtuous acts based on our weaknesses. The mara of affliction and demise can disrupt our ordinary life. In general, mara can be anything that goes against our wishes.

Greed, anger, and delusion are three of the ten roots that are most commonly discussed as the sources of our suffering and problems. The three poisons are described to correlate with the three great natural disasters of the world. Namely, they are deluge, fire, and whirlwind. A heavy flood can drown us like our greed. A fire can be as heated as our anger. The fires of the world are present in the three poisons and the three realms comprising of cravings, forms, and non-forms. A whirlwind is a strong movement of wind that can wrap us into a state of delusion. The more greed we have, the more we develop hatred. The more deluded we are, the more these poisons dominate our mind.

The first root, greed, is excessive craving; this craving can be for something good or bad. It is normal for us to have a feeling of want for the ordinary necessities of life, such as clothing to keep us warm, water for our thirst, and food for our hunger. However, we have to recognize whether our excessive desire is benevolent or malevolent. If we have an intense desire to work and study hard to attain a doctorate degree, we do not want to extinguish this aspiration but modulate it so we do not get burnout. When our desire exceeds what we need or our capability to obtain it, this then turns into greed that is malevolent, creating negative karma with our thoughts, speech, and actions to satisfy our excessive wants. When we desire for more, such as a bigger house or a fancier car, is when we are chasing after a moving target and become dissatisfied with what we do not have or the incapability to attain. We start thinking slyly of ways to get a promotion to make more money, degrading our colleagues, and acting differently in front of our supervisors. Showing gratitude and acceptance is one of the mindfulness practices that helps us be content with what we do have and can offset our cravings.

Anger and hatred, the second root, are uncomfortable emotions that arise when we do not have what we want or perceive something that is not to our satisfaction. There are different stages of anger and hatred, as they ignite from within even before the heated emotion manifests to be seen. The uneasiness starts to brew within us the second an activity or a comment is not satisfactory to us. Once it builds up and becomes too intense to remain inside, it manifests outward into our physical appearance with an angry face with eyes opened wide, loud harsh speech, and stomping in our gait. One of our goals in practice is to lessen our anger and prevent it from being imprinted in our mind. We should subdue our anger and forgive at ease, similar to how words easily disappear on an undulating body of water. When we require some encouragement and time to let go of our anger, it is like words that get slowly washed away from the ground. Attachment to our anger and inability to forgive create the anger that is like words carved onto rocks. The times when we are in delusion can lead to misunderstanding, and this can lead to anger. We can easily get angry when we find our teenager not finished with his or her chores before leaving the house. But once we realize that the reason is to drive a friend to the doctor, we then understand and calm down. The emotions of anger and hatred are difficult to control; practicing to subdue them will give us great satisfaction and peace.

The third root, delusion, is the inability to understand or see clearly the true nature of life. Delusion can lead to ignorance, but this ignorance does not equate to stupidity.

Ignorance is the inability to see right from wrong. The root of our suffering is due to delusion and, therefore, results in acts of greed and hatred. It is said that we are in a state of the underworld when we suffer and have conditions of greed, anger, and delusion. We then need to take refuge in Kshitigarbha Bodhisattva's vow, utilize his circular jewel to illuminate onto our suffering for us to see the way out, and rely on his staff to stabilize and lead us out from the state of the underworld. The Buddha understands that we sometimes live in delusion and act without thinking. This then creates cycles of bad karma and a negative feedback loop that increases greed and anger. Therefore, we should use wisdom to find the actual causes of our suffering and the right path to alleviate them. The emphasis of the practice is to transform greed, hatred, and delusion to morality, concentration, and wisdom.

The fourth to tenth roots are just as important to acknowledge in order to transform our karma. Pride and skepticism, the fourth and fifth roots, can cause conflicts and misunderstandings. Instead, we need to develop a mind of humility and faith. We need to know the art of living, respect elders and authorities while yielding to the young, and sense when to give or take in our relationships. We need to have faith in the teachings, ourselves, and others. This faith will enable us to complete our committed tasks.

The roots numbered six to ten fall under the five faulty views. The Buddha talks at great length on faulty views because they are a great source of conflicts in life. As such, he placed the Right View as the first treatment in the Noble Eightfold Path. As with any problems the Buddha points out, he always provides an answer for them. The five faulty views consist of the following:

1) Wrong view
2) One-sided view
3) Wrong view of self
4) Attachment to our view
5) Attachment to false views of how the precepts should be practiced

We have to recognize the right view in order to see any wrong view. To avoid conflicts, we should be open and flexible to see others' point of view, rather than be restricted to our narrow-minded point of view. When we learn of a recipe on how to prepare and cook tofu, we should not think that our way is the best way and should try others' suggestions. We tend to view our body as real and experience significant distress when we develop a terminal illness. The doctrine of non-reality teaches the concept of non-self, stating that our physical body is not real. Remember, our body is made up of the four great elements consisting of earth, water, wind, and fire, which will be decomposed and returned back to earth upon our passing. We should practice non-attachment, as fixation on our view is a source of craving that causes suffering. Sometimes, adhering strictly on the precepts can cause a hindrance in our practice, such as living with roaches and rats that roam our home because the first precept dictates us to not harm living creatures. As such, the rodents can be hazardous to our health. The precepts should not be viewed as a restriction on our life, but as a set of rules to follow in order to create happiness and avoid any future predicaments. If we study but do not practice, we steer toward the wrong view. If we practice but do not study, we increase our ignorance. So, we have to both study and practice to develop the right view and wisdom to see the ten roots of our vices in order to transform them.

The faulty views may be due to the type of vision that we use. There are five types of visual faculties that differ depending on how things are viewed, and we should develop the last four that are not of the worldly person. The five visual faculties are:

1) The eye and what it sees
2) The holy and divine vision
3) The vision of wisdom
4) The vision of the Dharma
5) The vision of enlightenment

With our eyes, we can recognize an object through our visual consciousness and see things as they are. The naked eye has the ordinary vision to see the immediate front and lateral views but not what is behind or afar. We can see places that are lit but not things in darkness. Because of this narrow vision, we look with the eyes of prejudice and hatred, which can impede right views and result in wrong views. The ordinary eye sees a flower as is, and we miss it when it decomposes. Likewise, it sees the wrinkles and gray hair as is, and this causes us to become discontent with our age-related changes. But with the holy and divine vision, we understand the true nature of things, and that anything that has matter in form is subject to change. We see the true nature of the flower and know that its beauty is only temporary. With diligence and practice, we can use our eyes to attain divine vision, which is capable of seeing in front, back, inside, outside, and within. With this vision, we hold back eliciting a negative emotional response so we can investigate further to understand the true nature of the situation. When our son does not finish cleaning the house for tonight's party, we calmly talk with him to understand the reasons before getting upset and punishing him. He may have had an important test to study for or a project to finish. The third visual faculty, the vision of wisdom, allows us to see clearly the karmic effects of actions and their consequences. If we see the rice is uncooked when we are prepared to eat, we do not get easily upset as we are able to reflect and recall that there was an electricity outage several hours before. Furthermore, if we see a person who lives a righteous life but continues to have misfortunes, we can deduce that this is due to his or her previous malevolent, karmic actions, as the current good deeds have not yet ripened to bring the expected blessings. We can use the vision of wisdom to practice and overcome any negative and wrong views. We see the presence of the flower is not real, as it is only a representation of different constituents of elements combined. Therefore, we accept and understand the course of the flower's lifecycle—to enjoy the flower when it is in bloom and recycle as compost back to the earth when it decomposes. Thus, we need to be mindful to use physical objects appropriately in the present moment to achieve their purpose, and enjoy them so that we will not have any regrets when they later change or decompose. Fourthly, the vision of the Dharma allows us to know the meanings and symbolisms of objects and written texts, and see that the existence and extinction of things are due to a combination of favorable and unfavorable conditions. We see the beautiful flower as a culmination of rain water, sunshine, and soil that provided nourishment for its seed to sprout and grow. We also recognize that the flower will become compost in the next few days when conditions are no longer sufficient to maintain it. With the Dharma vision, we see that all phenomena are only a vehicle, a convenient means to lead us to our goal. For example, a special retreat titled

"Sowing the Seeds to be Ordained" centers upon this theme and features the activity of putting on the holy Kasaya robe. This robe serves as a special vehicle to attract practitioners to attend and simulate living the life of an ordained person. Lastly, the vision of enlightenment encompasses all four types of vision and can see everything as it is. We use the enlightened vision to help us see all types of vision with a non-attached view. Once we learn all the teachings, put them into practice, and eliminate all illusions, we develop the vision of enlightenment. The Buddha points out the different types of visual faculties and encourages us to develop the ones that can see the true nature of all phenomena.

There are Five Roots of Practice that are essential to cultivate to counter the ten roots of our vices. They are described as the benevolent foundations and core characteristics needed for us to achieve the practice. The Five Roots of Practice are:

1) Faith
2) Effort
3) Mindfulness
4) Meditative concentration
5) Wisdom

In every practice, we have to start with faith in the teaching. In life, we must believe in something, as this helps us commit to furthering our studies. When we first learn of a topic, we develop a belief. This initial belief is then transformed to faith after contemplation and reflection, resulting in a deep belief with mindfulness and understanding that propels us to action. There are six important things to believe in:

1) Ourselves and others
2) The Cause and Effect
3) The symbolic forms and their representation of the teachings

The belief in ourselves will help us reinforce a positive attitude. If we are taking a hard chemistry class, we are more likely to do well if we have the confidence that we have the potential to do well. This increases our self-esteem, and we will have more motivation to study, resulting in passing the class with a higher grade. The belief in other people will help build relationships. We should share our friends' joy when they express pride in their son's intention to purchase a car for them. Instead of questioning them with skepticism, congratulate them for having raised such a dedicated son. Even if their son does not carry through with the purchase, his intention to buy a car for his parents is something to be respected. In addition, our belief in a friend who has transformed for the better, such as becoming sober from alcoholism, will give him or her the strength and reinforcement to continue abstinence. As each person supports one another in the practice, the power of the group becomes stronger and results in the overall strengthening of the belief and dedication to the practice. The third and fourth belief, the Cause and Effect, is infallible. Even if we do not believe in this doctrine, we still live with its truth. The fruit tree flower blooms, then yields the fruit. If we do not study hard for a test, we will not do well. A malicious act will result in negative consequences, and conversely. The fifth and sixth belief is in the symbolic forms and their representation of the teachings. In life, if we look deeply enough at why we act a certain way or what an object stands for, we would understand its nature more clearly. If our son gives us a gift on Mother's Day, his action represents that he is thinking of us and loves us. Other symbolic forms are the flower and light. The flower represents impermanence. The light represents wisdom. Each action and figure has meanings that represent a teaching. In summary, faith is our greatest asset. It is the light that shines into our mind to create an outward radiance. This faith comprises a clear, complete understanding, which then leads to the effort needed to accomplish our practice.

The second Root of Practice, effort, is one of the most important characteristics to cultivate as it is included here and mentioned in the Vehicle of the Bodhisattva. Effort is the diligence needed in order to achieve the other four Roots: faith, mindfulness, concentration, and wisdom. We need effort to maintain the perseverance for continued practice. Unlike the teaching of contentment, effort requires us not to be satisfied with the results of our work but continue to strive to do more and better. We have to expend energy and persistence to decorate our enlightened mind, remember and apply the Buddha's teachings, and consistently live and work zealously. Effort gives us the strength to anchor ourselves at our current level of practice so we do not slip backwards. It helps us to move forward easier when we are mentally and physically ready. With diligence, we can spark the fires of a practitioner with right concentration, meditative concentration, and a firm and unshakeable practice.

The third Root of Practice, mindfulness, is the complete awareness of our feelings, perceptions, and actions in the present moment. We have to be mindful of the Three Jewels and the precepts as well as fostering generosity and virtuous acts. When we are aware, we are able to understand, and this will reflect itself in proper actions, speech and thoughts. We are then able to choose the appropriate time and place to speak and act to prevent havoc in relationships. Mindfulness is the heart of Buddhists' practice that can be achieved through meditation.

The fourth Root of Practice, concentration, is the ability to focus on one object or event, leading to the clarity of the mind and wisdom to make proper decisions. Practicing mindfulness leads to concentration and, vice versa, concentration is required to practice mindfulness. Just because we are physically present during the day does not mean that our mind is settled in the present moment. All day long, we are exposed to the natural inclinations of attachment and provocative aggravation through our five senses. As we practice to bring our mind to a state of serenity through concentration and mindfulness practice, we are able to develop insight toward attaining the wisdom needed to transform our negative habits into positive, virtuous ones.

The fifth Root of practice is wisdom. Practicing mindfulness, developing meditative concentration, and attaining wisdom are the three essential principles to cultivate for every practitioner. At times, the three practices are referred to as morality, concentration, and wisdom. Here, mindfulness of the precepts represents morality, as being aware of each of our actions will guide us to perform the right deeds. The mudra of the three mountains is a form to remind us to develop mindfulness, concentration, and wisdom in order to be as solid and sturdy as the three mountains. It is a symbolic seal of the hand involving the index finger, fifth finger, and thumb that is used to raise our bowl of food in prayer prior to a meal. The bowl needs to be raised above the level of the eye to display respect. When we practice the three tenets of mindfulness, concentration, and wisdom, the result is an unparalleled radiant light from our Buddha-nature that is transmitted to an outward beautiful character.

The mudra of the three mountains

Among the Five Roots of Practice, the Roots of effort, concentration, and wisdom overlap with the practice of the Vehicle of the Bodhisattva. In addition, the Roots of effort, mindfulness, and concentration are included as the treatments in the third pillar of the Noble Eightfold Path. All Five Roots of Practice are essential qualities, as they are in the core doctrine and path of studies in Buddhism. They are all important to cultivate in order to achieve a successful practice.

The Five Roots of Practice are needed to yield the correlating Five Powers for our use in daily life. Both the Five Roots and the resultant Five Powers are part of the Thirty-Seven Paths to Enlightenment. The Powers of faith, effort, mindfulness, meditative concentration, and wisdom are the results we want to attain to ward off the five negatives that can impede our practice. The five negatives are distrust, laziness, aggravation, anger, and resentment. We have to be aware of these impediments during our practice to prevent and halt them from developing. When we are misinformed or misled, it is hard to regain our deep belief. Laziness is the lack of drive to work and hinders our diligence needed to succeed, both mentally and physically. When our mind is disturbed or aggravated, we are not able to be aware and mindful of our thoughts, speech, and actions. Anger is an escalated emotion that disrupts our ability to concentrate and settle our mind. Resentment is an ill-will feeling that makes us act in ignorance and impedes the wisdom needed to carry out our activities. We have to recognize these negative habits so that we can prevent them from hindering the cultivation of our Five Roots and Five Powers of Practice.

Once we establish the foundations of the teachings, we should execute them in our daily practice. The important steps are:

1) To believe
2) To commit
3) To act

As discussed, we need to believe in the studies and what we are doing in order to commit and carry out the practice. When we believe, we will have the diligence to commit to the task. Once we make the commitment, we will act on it. We carry through the task either by doing it ourselves or enlisting others to help. Once done, we attain the results of happiness and liberation. This series of events is an example of the law of Cause and Effect. Only we ourselves can accomplish this task; no one can do it for us. We can learn how to cook by watching others and gathering recipes, but it is not until we actually cook can we master the concept. In the process, we want to prevent the thoughts of regression in our commitment, action, and resultant effect from arising. These three factors are linked together and have a domino effect. If we do not continue forward with our commitment, we will not perform the action and, therefore, will not have any positive results. We recognize this so we can develop the diligence to work hard and prevent regression. If we make the commitment, we need to act on it, and only then the results will ensue.

One of the reasons we practice is to alleviate our sorrow and create peace and joy in our life. Pain and sorrow are the sources of our suffering which are due to our wrong views, misunderstandings, and excessive wants. The seven methods to mitigate our pain and suffering are:

1) To develop knowledge of right view
2) To support and safeguard our six senses
3) To utilize supportive conveniences to lessen our discomfort

4) To endure and accept the true nature
5) To deter from troublesome situations
6) To expeditiously eliminate greed, hatred, and delusion
7) To practice earnestly

We need to have the right view so we can see clearly and accurately which path in life leads to peace and joy and which will not. We want to mindfully guard and regulate our six sensory organs that are constantly receiving external stimuli, causing us to react unconsciously. Our six sensory organs are similar to the windows of a house in which dirt and debris will be blown through, if we do not close them during a storm. The sensory inputs cause seven types of emotions consisting of joy, anger, happiness, sadness, love, hate, and cravings that create a disturbance in our mind. We should use supportive measures to ease our discomfort. When we are hot, we use the fan to cool ourselves. When we are cold, we put on a jacket to warm ourselves. When there is a difficult situation, we need to practice patience to endure, accept, and work through the problem at hand. An example is when we are taking a difficult class that requires our diligence and stamina to study hard to earn a good grade. We should recognize the three poisons that lead to unskillful actions, so we can immediately eliminate and prevent from committing them again. The Buddha cannot save us from the results of our actions. He helps us by pointing out the causes of subsequent problems and teaches us to preemptively avoid committing actions that will lead to unfortunate predicaments. Lastly, we need to practice earnestly in order to achieve the mind of enlightenment. We can try our best to practice, but there are events and things in our life that are inevitable. That is when we should embrace the conditions, whether they are positive or negative. But when they are no longer in our life, we should let them go readily without excessive lingering over the heartaches.

Our attachments to external conditions and our egocentric characters both contribute to our afflictions. Our egocentric nature impairs our views. There are four egocentric characters that can cause us problems:

1) Our delusion
2) Our view
3) Our pride
4) Our self-love

We tend to have a delusion of the self, thinking that we know everything and are the best in what we do. We get disappointed when we do not receive first prize in a competition and realize that there is someone better than us. We have a tendency to see that our view is always correct. This can create conflicts with our friends and family. Our pride can cause a barrier for us to associate with people of different levels and prevent us from admitting our faults. Lastly, our self-love reinforces our ego and creates conditions of selfishness. We become easily insulted with the perceived or actual criticisms toward us; this can easily create discord among our friends and family. Practicing non-attachment to external conditions and our ego is one the most important skills to achieve, which will help us adapt to the constant changes in conditions of our life.

Aside from showing us ways to alleviate our problems, the Buddha teaches us to cultivate peace and joy through several steps involving our body, speech, and mind. The first is to steer ourselves away from people or places that cause problems and sufferings. When we are faced with adversities in life, we should talk with our friends or go to the temple or church for comfort instead of resorting to alcohol, gambling, or other unhealthy places to escape. In fact, the Buddha outlines the conditions that determine when we should stay or leave a place. If a place provides food to eat but does not allow us to study or practice, we should not stay. If a place allows us to study and practice but does not provide food, we can try to stay. On the other hand, we should definitely stay in a place that provides food and allows us to study and practice. However, we should leave a place that neither provides food nor the ability for us to study and practice. The second way to cultivate peace and joy is to regulate our speech so we do not blame or degrade others. This is the karma of speech. The words we use, our tone of voice, and how we communicate can bring peace and joy to others if we do it with loving-kindness. The third way is to tame our mind to prevent thoughts of hatred, jealousy, or rivalry. This is the karma of thoughts and mind. Pleasant and kind thoughts will generate virtuous speech and actions that will give joy to others and ourselves. The fourth way is to commit to the practice of creating blessings and helping to liberate others. The Buddha distinguishes the happiness of the worldly life from the intrinsic joy that he encourages us to pursue. This joy has a deeper meaning than just the elation from the events that suit us with personal satisfaction. This joy is from our deep contemplation, understanding, empathy, and acceptance of a situation. For example, we are really happy when Thầy accepts our invitation to speak at our retreat and has arrived safely. However, we should not be upset if he is not able to give a talk due to a sore throat. When we understand and accept the conditions, we can still be content and happy with Thầy's presence and determination to show up. We can also experience internal joy by developing concentration and mindfulness and committing to the four immeasurable minds of loving-kindness, compassion, joy, and equanimity. When we are able to bring happiness and alleviate suffering for others, forgive and not be attached to others' unkind words or actions, we will have internal joy. In addition, we have internal joy when we are mindful of our actions and are able to develop the concentration to know right from wrong to adjust our actions accordingly. Learning and recognizing our emotions will help us understand to release sorrow and foster the seed of intrinsic joy.

The Buddha placed much emphasis on the practices that will create harmony in our life and the community. One of the ways is to have a positive view of tolerance, acceptance, and gratitude in order to have harmony in life. When our children do or say inappropriate things, instead of yelling at them and getting angry, take the opportunity to teach them when they are still receptive to listening to us. When they reach adulthood and are ready to leave home, the golden opportunity to instill additional teachings will have passed, and we should be grateful for the eighteen years that we had to raise and mold them into the person they are presently. Another way to create harmony is to take refuge in a deeper meaning rather than the superficial form in our interactions with others. There are four ways to do this:

1) Take refuge in the teaching and not the person's actions.
2) Take refuge in the meaning but not the words.
3) Take refuge in the wisdom but not the opinion.
4) Take refuge in the revelation of the complete meaning but not the partial meaning.

It is easier to preach to others on the philosophy of what and how things should be done but is more difficult to carry out this advice. We should focus on the teaching, rather than condemn others when they do not do what they preach. At times, our friend may be expressing an apology, but the words and tone of voice used do not seem sincere. We should focus on the intent of his or her apology, rather than on the words that were used and how they were delivered. We should take refuge in the wisdom but not the opinion. We may consider the altar to be scarcely decorated, but we should focus on the effort required to display and maintain the altar and understand that this sparseness may be due to a small operating budget. This way, we direct our attention to understand the situation rather than fixating on our negative opinions. When we invite ten monastics to perform a ceremony at the temple but only five show up, we should not be in contempt and feel let down. We should look at the big picture that some monastics did show up to carry out and support the Sangha in the ceremony. This is taking refuge in the whole entire meaning rather than having a narrow point of view. There are six other ways to develop harmony within our Sangha, home, and workplace. We want to practice together to develop the following:

1) Harmony of the community body
2) Harmony of speech
3) Harmony of collective thoughts of the mind
4) Harmony of collective sharing of perceptions
5) Harmony of collective practice of the precepts
6) Harmony of collective benefits and achievements

Harmony of the community body manifests when we share the environment and space that are present and available. When the meditation hall is small and the gathering is crowded, we should have an open heart to share the cramped sitting space and not mind the heat and stuffiness of the air. Harmony of speech occurs when we speak in accord and refrain from disputes. We should speak gently and respectfully so that our words will bring joy to one another, rather than creating conflicts. Harmony of the mind appears when we resolve our differing opinions in a group setting to foster a common goal. Harmony of perception is seen when we work together to share our viewpoints to promote understanding, as we all see things differently at different angles. Harmony in the precepts exists when we strive to support and remind each other to practice and follow the precepts. Harmony of collective benefits is achieved when we share knowledge, exchange services, and support one another to promote everyone's well-being to achieve a happy, fulfilling life. We can apply these six collective practices to make any gathering amicable, resulting in a deeper, more meaningful connection for everyone. We should set aside our viewpoints that place emphasis on ourselves and our opinions and work toward a common goal for the benefit of the community. Understanding the deeper meaning of things and applying these six collective practices will result in tranquility and harmony for ourselves and others.

In the course of any practice, there may be obstacles along the way. It is important to recognize these obstacles so we can acknowledge, manage, and overcome them instead of allowing them to subdue us. These obstacles are considered an impediment or a cover. There are two types of obstacles, internal and external. Internal obstacles are harder to remove because they are something we need to recognize from within and resolve on our own. External obstacles can be removed more easily with outside help or by dodging them, such as removing a big rock on the road or evading from the person we dislike. Other examples of external obstacles are lack of transportation to go to the temple or unavailability of the Sutras. Whether internal or external, the obstacles need to be recognized so we can practice to overcome them.

There are external circumstances that can cause internal strife, as external obstacles can become internal obstacles. We frequently are faced with the four pairs of gusts of wind consisting of gain and loss, praise and blame, honor and dishonor, and happiness and sorrow. They cause us to react and disrupt our peace of mind. Gain and loss go hand-in-hand. When we win, we may lose the comradery of our competitor. When we lose, we develop restlessness and worry. Praise and blame either make us happy or sad. They disturb our mind as we need to evaluate whether the praise is accurate or false. When we are blamed, we should not get upset too easily as we need to assess whether it is true or not. If the critique is true, we should happily receive it as feedback to improve ourselves. If it is false, we should not be preoccupied with the false claim. Honor and dishonor are similar to love and hate. The key is not to be attached to others' disposition toward us, as it is beyond our control. Happiness and sorrow are emotions that are ephemeral and come and go. The external events and occurrences elicit emotions that are inevitable reactions from our sensory inputs. Just as we are careful to wear a hat and jacket on a cold windy day, we should act mindfully to these gusts of wind in life so they do not overpower us. The Buddha points out these four pairs of sentiments so we can train our mind to be solid as a mountain and not allow them to agitate our mental state.

Internal obstacles are harder to overcome as they originate from within. An example is when we get upset upon hearing the person's name that we dislike. This is because we have difficulty letting go of our hatred. There are five hindrances that put a covering over our innate Buddha-nature and inhibit our progress:

1) Desire
2) Ill will
3) Mental lethargy and physical laziness
4) Mental unrest and physical restlessness
5) Skepticism and doubt

Desire can be good or bad. We want to cultivate the benevolent aspirations and suppress the malevolent cravings. Ill will is the hatred present in one of the three poisons. Lethargy and laziness work against the effort we need to put into our practice. The causes of our laziness can be attributed to the eight conditions of being too hot, too cold, too hungry, too full, too sleepy, too tired, too much good food, or too little good food. Worry and restlessness are states of uneasiness. Skepticism and doubt interfere with our ability to trust and believe in others and can hinder our faith in the teachings. All these characteristics have a negative energy that does not promote refinement of our character or development of wisdom. We should recognize when they arise in us so we can practice to overcome them.

The Buddha points out other types of obstacles that seem to be external but are related to our karma. The five obstacles are:

1) Afflictions
2) Karma
3) Unfavorable birth circumstances
4) Inaccessibility of the Dharma teachings
5) Inability to have complete knowledge and understanding of the teachings

Afflictions are things that cause sorrow or disrupt our mental state. There are four types of afflictions, which are described as powerful as a strong water current that can carry our well-being downstream. They are the water current of our cravings, possessions, fixated views, and delusions. The cravings for things we do not need, our discriminatory Five Aggregates and the three poisons that we own, our fixated views, and our misunderstanding of the teachings all disrupt our peace and decrease our wholesome roots. The second obstacle, negative karma, is the retributions from our past and present habitual actions. We cannot change our past actions resulting in unwholesome karma, but must accept and face them with our mental strength to continue along our determined path. An example is taking care of an illness we have that interferes with our ability to study or work. The third obstacle is to be born into an unfavorable environment. The circumstances that we are born in and our predestined path are factors that we cannot control, which can either facilitate or impede our practice. If we are born in a less fortunate household, we may have hardship due to lack of resources and time to practice. The fourth obstacle is not having access to the Dharma teachings. The unavailability of a nearby temple, Sangha, or a monastic teacher hinders the opportunity to learn. The fifth obstacle is our inability to fully grasp the understanding and practice of the teachings. Our fixation and attachment of our perceived understanding of the teaching can cause a barrier to practice. An example is being committed to eat as a vegetarian so as to practice compassion for the animals; we can create more hassle for our family if we purchase a whole other set of dishes, pots, and pans to avoid contamination with meat products. This will increase the amount of time and energy spent dishwashing. Having a fixed viewpoint can create mental inflexibility as well as negative karmic action and energy. This can be seen in the three interrelated impediment of our viewpoint, impediment of our sorrow, and impediment of our karma. When we only see our viewpoint, we are not able to be open-minded and see others' points of view. This can cause conflict, resulting in irritation and disruption of our mind; consequently, it causes us to think, speak, and act unkindly. We should be aware that the negative karma of our thoughts, speech, and actions can hinder our practice, so we need to be mindful to improve.

Obstacles can cause an impasse or a regression in our practice. It is important to recognize when they arise so we can change course. The five signs of regression manifest in the following ways:

1) The wilting of our flower with our frowning face
2) An odor in our sweat
3) A blurring of our radiant light
4) Mental confusion
5) The mind not being at peace

It is important to study and apply the Dharma teachings for our practice, but not become attached to them, as they can become one of our obstacles and cause our practice to relapse. We use the surrounding manifestations and forms as means to accomplish the practice and arrive at the ultimate goal of liberation. The Dharma teachings are just one of the instruments to get there; they are not the goal that we need to hold onto. Just as a raft is used to cross the shore, we leave the raft behind once we have crossed. Similarly, when we resort to chewing gum to stop smoking, we should not become addicted to chewing gum once we stop smoking. Despite the obstacles, we should see them as an opportunity to learn, reflect, and practice instead of a barrier to overcome.

There are four different types of energy we can utilize to fuel our practice. They are physical energy, mental energy, energy from wisdom, and energy from the path of study. Mental energy can prevail and continue as our source of energy when physical energy is exhausted. When practiced with mindfulness, mental energy is much more invigorating and robust than physical energy. The energy from our mind propels our internal energy to manifest in outward appearance such that the state of our thoughts and mind are seen in our body and actions. We should use this energy to practice with much effort to overcome obstacles so there is no regression in our practice. The energy of wisdom provides an incessant light to shine and reinforces the energy from the path of study. With these energies, we can strive to develop the Transcendental Power needed for us to achieve any goals to our utmost satisfaction. Zeal, diligence, mindfulness, and contemplation are the four practices needed to achieve this power. When we have passion and put effort toward our goals, apply constant awareness of our thoughts, speech, and actions, and reflect deeply, we will develop this power to attain the fulfillment of our set goals. As discussed, these four practices are part of the Thirty-Seven Paths to Enlightenment. Our accomplishments in the practice can also generate a different set of Six

Transcendental Powers that penetrate to provide a clear comprehension of our faculties through the supernatural component of our sixth senses. These Six Transcendental Powers are:

1) The power of divine vision
2) The power of divine hearing
3) The power of claircognizance
4) The power of supernatural movement
5) The power of clairvoyance
6) The ultimate power to end all defilements

The power of divine vision allows us to view things clearly with compassion and nondiscrimination. The power of divine hearing allows us to listen deeply with compassion. The power of claircognizance allows us to understand and experience another person's feelings and thoughts; this allows us to provide emotional support and prevent us from reacting to the other person's actions and words. The power of supernatural movement allows us to come and go with ease and freedom. Hence, we can be in the same room and proceed with the same activities in the presence of someone whom we dislike. The power of clairvoyance allows us to know the person's past, present, and future circumstances so we can understand and empathize with their current situation. The ultimate transcendental power is to understand and eradicate all afflictions and comprehensively possess all other five powers. Despite the magnificence of these energies and powers, they cannot supersede the karma that we build up over our lifetime, which will naturally and timely prevail according to the law of Cause and Effect.

The Buddha's life and teachings are closely connected to nature. He describes the practitioner in an analogy with the elements of nature in several ways. The practitioner has five powerful energies similar to the properties of the fire. These five powerful energies are used to initiate, maintain, and propagate our studies and practice in addition to overcoming obstacles. The five energies are:

1) The energy of wisdom to extinguish all afflictions
2) The energy to eradicate any sorrow without discrimination
3) The energy of diligence and effort to continuously practice
4) The energy of compassion to empathize and support others in need
5) The energy of wisdom to shine in situations of ignorance and wrong views

Just like a fire that burns everything without discrimination, a practitioner uses the fiery energy of wisdom to get rid of all things that disturb his or her peace of mind, whether pleasant or unpleasant. Just like a fire is made when it is cold, a practitioner applies the fiery energy of diligence and effort to offset laziness. Just like a fire that provides heat for many purposes, the practitioner provides the fiery warmth of compassion for those in need. Just like a fire that shines in a place of darkness, the practitioner uses the fiery energy of wisdom to shine through ignorance and wrong-held views. We have to distinguish and use these energetic fires of the practitioner, rather than the fire within our untamed mind associated with the three poisons and the three realms of cravings, forms, and non-forms. The practitioner also has strengths comparable to rain water. The rain can form a strong current to wash the dirt from all surfaces. Similarly, a practitioner can use the wisdom attained to untangle afflictions. The rain cools the earth. The practitioner trains to cool and calm the mind from the heat of anger in order to give rise to well-being. The rain flourishes green foliage. The practitioner fosters deep belief to promote diligence toward three accomplishments: to become a person of high merit, to be in the heavenly sphere, and to have the ultimate happiness of Nirvana in this lifetime. The rain causes the plant's roots to bind tightly to the soil so its flowers and leaves can thrive and blossom. The practitioner anchors his or her practice in the Dharma teachings to develop the ultimate wisdom. The rain fills up all the crevices and holes of the earth, then overflows on the surface ground. This is similar to the practitioner who absorbs the words of the Sutras in all facets of his or her mind. In essence, the practitioner should practice with the energy of the fire and nourish his or her progress like the rainfall.

As with any activity or practice, it is always better to have a friend to go along with for mutual support. The three things we want to have abundantly are good friends who know and understand us, the ability to listen and learn the Dharma teachings, and an open heart to give generously. There are three types of good friends who know and understand us. The first is a friend who is an advisor to remind, lead, and encourage us in the study and practice. The second is a friend who studies and practices together with us in the same path. The third is a friend who supports us with their time, service, and assistance, such as by offering us a ride to the temple or lending a robe to wear. One of the powerful practices to provide support to our friends and loved ones is to offer our presence. This can be done through the practice of deep listening, where we give our undivided attention, listen without interruption, and understand what is being communicated. The Buddha distinguishes between listening and hearing, and points out the four circumstances for both:

1) There is no hearing; there is no listening.
2) There is hearing; there is no listening.
3) There is hearing; there is listening.
4) There is no hearing; there is listening.

In the first instance, we neither hear sounds or words nor listen to or comprehend what is being said. In the second instance, we hear the sounds and words but do not listen to or comprehend the message. In the third instance, we hear the sounds and words, and listen to and comprehend the message. In the fourth instance, we do not hear the sounds or words but can listen and comprehend through our enlightened mind. This is when we know our friends and loved ones so well that we understand their concerns without them being expressed to us. Hearing is just the initial step, but not until we actually listen can we be mindfully present and understand to offer support. And it is through understanding that we may give our true love. Besides deep listening, we want to promote encouragement and prevent regression of the practice. Even when our friends cannot attend events at the temple or when they are busy helping to prepare a meal for the Sangha, we can share what we learn from the Dharma talk and transfer our merits in prayer to them. Praying to transfer merits is an expression of generosity, support, and remembrance of our friends in the practice. It is an act of sharing the blessings that we have and granting others to receive what they do not yet have. The initial step is to reflect inward and assess what we have before transferring our merits to others. We can transfer our merits with four techniques. The first is through the transfer of our knowledge on the symbolic forms and the noble teachings. We study to understand the symbolic forms and their representations of the teachings, so we can share this knowledge with others. An example is the flower as the symbol that represents the teaching of impermanence. Secondly, we can develop merits for others through the doctrine of Cause and Effect. We invest money and expend the effort to build a Sangha and temple and subsequently provide a peaceful place for future generations to practice. Thirdly, we can transfer our merits of the minuscule matter toward bigger goals. Oftentimes, we have to suppress our disagreement regarding an issue and go along with the idea held by the majority of the group in order to maintain harmony. This is a way to avoid a small conflict so we can direct our efforts towards a bigger cause. Fourthly, we can direct the merits to ourselves and others. When we transfer our merits of offering, support, and remembrance to others, we are also doing it for ourselves and thus receive the same benefit. The result is a strong and unified Sangha among friends of the practice.

It is equally important to nourish and support the novice Bodhisattvas who are newcomers to the temple, as well as the seasoned Bodhisattvas in our Sangha. For new practitioners, we can introduce and sow the seed of the Dharma teachings to open their mind and pique their interest to look further into the practice. We want to make sure they feel welcomed and find happiness in the practice and continue to make progress. We should not take for granted that this small deed will not amount up to anything, as a new practitioner may become a great teacher one day. Every little good deed adds up to a great deed, just as every small bad deed constitutes a large malevolent deed. If we pick up a broken glass off the street, this can prevent a bicycle from getting a flat tire or a person from cutting his or her foot. If we lie about turning off the heater in our room, this may result in igniting a fire in our absence. Other things we should not take lightly are a small snake, a young monastic, a small fire, and a young prince. A small snake has enough venom to kill. A young monastic can become a venerable teacher one day. A small fire can burn down the entire forest. A young prince can become a king and world leader. The Buddha always encourages us to practice with a collective mind and body. He emphasizes the practice of the four immeasurable minds to strengthen and build a bond in any relationship. We can apply the four immeasurable minds comprised of loving-kindness, compassion, joy, and equanimity to overcome any conflicts or perceived ill will. They are essential for us to develop the comradery needed to nourish the brotherhood and sisterhood in the Sangha. We want to live so that people celebrate as we are born crying as a newborn, and people cry as we pass away rejoicing in our fulfilled life. Having friends in the practice is important, and we should not underestimate how much we can help others by doing what we can to support and encourage one another in the practice.

The Buddha classifies and characterizes different types of friends and people so we can be aware of, understand, and develop tolerance in our interactions with them. There are four types of friends:

1) A friend like a flower
2) A friend like a scale
3) A friend like the earth
4) A friend like the mountain

A friend who is like a flower holds a beautiful and dear relationship with us when our life is in bloom but forsakes us when we wither away. A friend who is like a scale always keeps track of the relationship so it is balanced in terms of giving and receiving. A friend like the earth is someone whom we can rely on to listen and empathize, just as the ground absorbs anything and everything that we pour onto it. A friend like the mountain pervades his or her goodness and brilliance on us, just like the snowcap of a mountain shining its reflection onto a vulture's wings. The Buddha points this out so we can clearly choose the type of friend to associate with and strive to become the type of friend we want to be for others. There are also different types of people that mirror the different stages of ripening in fruits. There are fruits that are unripe on the exterior but are ripe on the inside. Similarly, a person may not be physically appealing but has a good heart. There are fruits that are ripe on the exterior but are unripe on the inside. Likewise, a person who is physically attractive may not possess a kind heart. There are fruits that are unripe on the exterior and interior, just as there are people who are both ugly on the outside and inside. And of course, there are fruits that are ripe both on the exterior and interior, just as there are people who are attractive both on the outside and inside. Not everyone is born with complete attributes. We may not be attractive on the outside but our nice and kind personality constitutes our internal beauty. The Buddha points out the different types of people so we can be aware of and mindful in interacting with them. This way, we know how to help and support them in the practice of developing internal beauty with compassion and wisdom. The Buddha further classifies four characteristics of a person:

1) The person who talks without doing
2) The person who does not talk but takes action
3) The person who talks and takes action
4) The person who neither talks nor does anything

We use mindfulness and wisdom to recognize each person's character in order to help us interact with others. If we know that our friend likes to talk but does not carry out commitments, we should not put much confidence in relying on him or her. This will prevent us from being let down or angry when he or she fails to follow through. We can rely on friends who carry out their commitments, whether they talk or not. And we should definitely not rely on those who neither express their intentions nor put any effort on the required task. There are many different facets of people and understanding their characters will help prevent disappointments and unrealistic expectations in our interactions with them.

The Buddha recognizes that our human nature has flaws. That is why he emphasizes the practice to improve and transform. One of the practices that is important in most religions is the act of repentance. There are several processes to carry out the act of repentance. We can implement our penitence through our thoughts and expression of remorse and by the formal ritual of bowing to the Buddha at the altar. The initial step in fixing any problem is to first recognize that there is a problem. There are two steps in the act of repentance of faults we have committed, whether intentionally or unintentionally. The first is to acknowledge and admit our faults in order to release the built-up guilt we have from our errors. The second step, which is the most important, is to repent by vowing not to commit these wrong actions again. Faults originate from our mind. Therefore, our mind has to repent. Once the mind is awakened, the cause of the faults will be eliminated. When we are able to see our faults as wrong, malevolent, and undesirable, we will not commit them again. The faults are then dismissed, and the mind will be pure and at peace. It is then that we view our wrongdoings as a lesson rather than as faults. In addition to repenting with our mind, we can repent with our body in form. At the altar, we bow and direct our concentrated mind to the Buddha who serves as the witness of our true remorse. With each bow, we vow to change and make a commitment to not repeat the wrongdoings. This ritual serves as a reinforcement for us to carry out our pledge for repentance. The final step for us is to keep this promise and continue our practice.

Some people may think that we must be at the temple, a special place, or in a particular condition in order to practice. With the hectic schedules that many of us have, it would be difficult and impractical to require this. Many people practice and study during their daily commute in the car. We can practice at home, at work, or at the temple. We can practice in the morning, afternoon, or evening. We can practice by ourselves or while interacting with families and friends. We can practice during times of happiness, sorrow, or stress. We should try our best to practice depending on our situation, time availability, capability, and health. If it is late at night, we should respect our family members and not recite the Sutras loudly, which would disturb their sleep. If we have low back pain and cannot sit on the ground to meditate, we can sit on a chair. We should adjust the rituals so everyone can be at ease. The most important goal in our practice is for us to diligently apply and practice the Buddha's teachings. The temple is a place that provides support and a foundation for us to turn to and where the Sangha reassures and reinforces our practice. We then should take this renewed strength and knowledge to practice in other places where we spend most of our time, whether at home, work, or with friends. It is emphasized that when we practice, we should not desert our role in life as a parent, spouse, or coworker. If we decide to be a vegetarian, we should not forget to cook a balanced meal for our growing children. When we sign up for a ten-day retreat at the temple, we should make arrangements to take care of our family at home and businesses at work during our absence. Our practice will result in an improvement for ourselves and our relationships with others. It will also influence a positive change in others. So we must start practicing and not wait until we are ready, as there is never a right time.

The sequence of events in our life is a pilgrimage. A pilgrimage is a journey where we can design our path in accordance with the right Dharma path. We do not have to travel very far to go on a pilgrimage, as we can do this anywhere in our daily life. This can be carried out through these four practices:

1) Commitment to charity
2) Words of kindness
3) Beneficial acts of virtue
4) Collective service

Each one of us has the responsibility to add fragrance to this world. We all should strive to practice charity, loving speech, virtuous acts, and harmonious collective service to impart the fragrant incense upon our life. The Buddha emphasizes for us to provide service to others and our community. It is important to provide service with an enlightened mind and energy so we are not steered in the wrong direction. We give in order to share with others. We speak words of kindness so others will never forget. We carry out acts of virtue to create benefits for everyone. We work together to achieve a common goal. We want to practice such that we can elicit the four attractions of a practitioner, namely with mindfulness in speech, tone of voice, actions, and generosity. From practice, we develop the five qualities of the strongest person who has right view, faith, wisdom, compassion, and harmony within the community. We want to be the high-level person who actually practices from what has been learned and not the average person who only remembers to practice every now and then. We certainly do not want to be the below average person who does not understand and, therefore, ridicules the teachings and does not practice at all. We should strive to develop the merits of wisdom, the Dharma body, and liberation to apply to and subdue the different six flavors (sour, spicy, bitter, sweet, salty, and bland) that our life experiences provide. Each flavor has its own lesson and distinct taste. When we mindfully use wisdom to carry out the actions of our Dharma body, we will be free of attachments and achieve liberation. This way, we can decorate our body, speech, and mind as well as our Sangha and environment. If we can do all of this, we will have an extraordinary life pilgrimage.

Our life's path should parallel our religious path. Our life can be compared to that of a mountain climber who accumulates precious gemstones, which he or she picks up along the way. Toward the end of the climb, the mountain climber has something to show from the expedition. Our lives can be lived similarly, such that we work to accumulate meaningful accomplishments in our daily journey. Life events and experiences are our precious gemstones, as they help us gain wisdom and strengthen our character. We can do this by utilizing our Buddha-nature to view the true nature of things. There are four volitional acts that, if carried out with the practice of mindfulness, will help us achieve our goals and overcome our difficulties in life:

1) Understand and concede to our karmic retributions
2) Enjoy our earned blessings and work to replete them
3) Refrain from excessive conditional requests and expectations
4) Implement each action with benevolence, generosity, and purity

The first volitional act is to understand and concede to our karmic retributions. When we have this attitude regarding all things that come our way, we are more likely to be untroubled. Anything that is not to our satisfaction is difficult to accept. From developing a terminal illness to not marrying the perfect spouse, we get depressed and complain of our unfortunate plight. The person who does not reflect in order to understand can easily feel suffering when experiencing this untoward situation. On the other hand, the person who is enlightened in this situation can be at peace with acceptance after contemplation and understanding. There is a reason for things that come to us in this life. We have no one else to blame as this is due to karma and the law of Cause and Effect. Our past negative actions result in retributions that we have to repay in this present moment. When we understand and accept the karmic retributions, we can rejoice that we are paying down our debts. When we accept this, our mind becomes at ease and content without the reactive sadness that usually and naturally occurs. The second volitional act is to enjoy our earned blessings and augment our virtues. We should recognize our blessings and enjoy them, but also continue to work on generating more to prevent their depletion. These blessings can be presented as a successful career or a happy, healthy family. We should use our blessings to augment our virtues by helping more people, performing acts of charity, and replenishing the merits of blessings. This can be compared to using seeds from the last fruit eaten to plant another fruit tree, or else there will be no more fruits in the future for us to enjoy. Whether there is any suffering or joy that comes our way in life, instead of reflexively becoming depressed or elated, we should understand and accept that it is either a retribution or blessing that has resulted from our previous actions. The third act of practice is to refrain from excessive wishing and expecting for more. When we desire for more than what we need, we are in delusion. Because we are in delusion, we continue to wish for more. The things we wish for are neither real nor permanent. When our wish is achieved, we are happy; but when our wish is not achieved, we are disappointed. Our temperament is dependent on an unknown outcome. We should strive and work to achieve our aspirations, then learn to live with gratitude and be fulfilled with what we have, so our body and mind will be at peace. The fourth volitional act is to carry out each action with benevolence, generosity, and purity. If we apply this, we can then perform the other three volitional acts more readily. We will not be sad to accept the karmic retributions. We will understand to accept the conditions that come our way. And we can live with what we have and not constantly seek for more, once we have done our best. Each act encompasses the other acts. It is important to remember that the mountain climber who gathers precious gemstones along the path should simultaneously let go of worthless rocks to prevent buildup of a heavy baggage. As we accrue the blessings from our virtuous acts, we should eliminate the unrighteous ones to avoid being bogged down by the accumulated attachments along our life's path. All our actions should be carried out joyfully and sincerely for the betterment of ourselves and our community. Whether walking, standing, laying, or sitting, we can practice mindfully to implement these four volitional acts.

Buddhism is the quintessential practice of compassion and wisdom. In other words, it is the practice of love and understanding. At the temple, the sound of the bell and drum awakens us to elicit our compassion and wisdom, respectively. Compassion is to give joy to others and lessen others' suffering. Compassion is the practitioner's love expressed through words or actions that are nondiscriminatory, without expectation of reciprocity from the receiver or possessiveness of the giver. Wisdom is making good judgment based on our knowledge, reflection, and experience. Compassion and wisdom are the two essential characteristics to cultivate for our body and mind. It is through compassion that we are able to do all things. And it is by wisdom that we may implement virtuous actions with mindfulness.

Buddhism is the quintessential practice of compassion and wisdom.

Compassion is the key factor to generate the qualities of generosity, patience, and the ability to transform and teach others. It is with compassion that we can share and give wholeheartedly. It is with compassion that we can develop the endurance needed to be patient and overcome all difficulties. It is with compassion that we can resolve any difficulties and help liberate others. Developing the mindful and enlightened mind is important within our practice of compassion and virtuous deeds. We can stray down the wrong path and act in delusion if we do not apply wisdom in our activities. We should strive to develop the perfect wisdom,

Prajna, that will help us transcend all sufferings and attachments. We want to develop this wisdom of listening, contemplation, and achievement through practice so we can be on the right path. We can also assess a situation by observing, listening, questioning, and concluding. These are the four steps taken by a physician, mechanic, or anyone with a problem before reacting and making a decision. When our children slam the door and are not talking to one another, we can see and hear that they are upset. Before we react and get upset ourselves, we need to question them on what transpired and understand the situation. Once we understand why one child is upset with the other regarding a broken promise, we can practice forgiveness and work on keeping promises. When we do not understand, misunderstanding arises. When we can understand, love will surface. We cannot offer our love without understanding. The more we understand our loved ones, the more we can give our true love. Developing compassion will increase our wisdom and having wisdom will increase our compassion. With each practice, we can develop morality, concentration, and wisdom. At a gathering around a big table, if someone does not serve us a dish near him or her, and we reciprocate the behavior, this is considered an ordinary phenomenon. We should not emulate this behavior in our life. That person may not want to be impolite and reach over across the table or may have a painful wrist that cannot support the heavy dish. Instead, we should use the enlightened phenomenon to efface the ordinary phenomenon and offer that person the dish that is near us. This is the right way to treat others. Besides the ordinary phenomenon, there are abnormal and extraordinary phenomena. The abnormal phenomenon is when a person performs ill will towards another without any instigation. On the other hand, the extraordinary phenomenon is when a person reacts with goodwill towards another even though he or she is treated with ill will. The Buddha performs the extraordinary phenomena and encourages us to do the same. From contemplation, we realize what the right way is and use wisdom to perform what is right. From this wisdom, we have the awareness to know how to act, when to act, and whom to address our actions towards. The enlightened phenomena transcend all worldly phenomena. Establishing compassion and wisdom in our everyday practice will establish the paragon that we should live.

The reason we practice Buddhism is to cultivate compassion, wisdom, and mental purity. When we do this, we are transforming our karma in body, speech, and mind. In return, we can recognize the true nature and reality of our life, subdue our fear of the unknown, and give joy and lessen suffering to our friends and family. Whether we practice formally or informally, the end result is to purify and pacify our mind. Because when the mind is pure and calm, without any contaminants or agitation, we can see clearly what is right or wrong, and subsequently act in mindfulness and awareness to avoid malevolence and perform benevolence. The Buddha has turned the Dharma Wheel in motion after his Enlightenment to propagate his teachings. We can also turn the Dharma Wheel in motion to advance in our studies by the following four practices:

1) Residing in a place of well-being, such as the temple
2) Relying on good friends
3) Committing to true vows
4) Cultivating the benevolent foundations of practice

Following this training will help us overcome the hindrances in our path of study and practice. The Buddha came into this world to reveal the noble truths of impermanence, non-self, Cause and Condition, Cause and Effect, and the pairing of happiness and suffering in life. While the Buddha reveals and preaches the noble truths to us, he cannot change the Cause and Effect, grant us wisdom, practice for us, or liberate us without sufficient conditions. His purpose is to show us how to cultivate blessings and live a virtuous life so we can internalize and practice the teachings in order to transform our karma and achieve enlightenment. He cautions us to practice his teachings with mindfulness and in the right path so the results do not rebound. This is similarly compared to an incorrect method of catching a snake whereby snatching its tail results in the head of the snake turning around to bite us. The Buddha encourages us not to accept his teachings at face value; instead, he urges us to evaluate and contemplate the teachings to determine and verify their absolute truths, by acknowledging the relative truths that we experience in life. Even though the relative truths are conditional and are not real, we have to reflect on life's events so we can see and accept the absolute truths. Understanding the absolute truth will enable us to attain a state of peace and happiness. From this, we will have faith in the Buddha as the Enlightened teacher whose teachings will lead us to awakening and enlightenment and guide us to live a happy life. We need to study continuously and practice diligently to create a meaningful life so that when all is said and done, we can comfortably reminisce upon each segment of our well-lived life full of merits and virtues.

Chapter 20

Significance of the Numbers

There are many numbers referenced throughout the Dharma teachings that help to elucidate the symbolisms in Buddhism. The following sections outline the teachings, topics, and concepts that apply this numerology to define, describe, and quantify their meanings. This serves to categorize the topics and facilitate the study and memorization of the teachings. As we read through the outline of number systems, we should reflect back upon what we have learned in prior chapters and review the teachings.

The number 1

The Buddha is the World-Honored One. His one-time presence in this world is to reveal and teach us the teachings so we can acknowledge and realize the practice to help us cross over to the shore of liberation in ten different directions. The Buddha's one teaching benefits innumerable beings. And the one right path is the Path to Enlightenment.

One teaching and path represents and encompasses all the others. One Bodhisattva represents all the other Great Bodhisattvas. Morality, concentration, and wisdom can comprehensively be represented by each one by itself. The Bodhidharma carries one shoe, which symbolizes a pair of opposites and the extremes of states contained in one.

The practice is to develop one concentrated mind. One concentrated mind is achieved when we humbly bow, praise, and think of the Buddha as we recite the Sutras.

The number 2

The number 2 has pairs of teachings that complement one another. There are fewer in numbers compared to the contents of the other numbers.

The Buddha had 2 significant meals in his lifetime:
1. The rice milk offered by Sujata revived the Buddha from the deterioration of his health due to the extreme practice of physical deprivation.
2. The unintentional offering of the poisoned mushroom that led to the Buddha's demise at the age of eighty.

There are 2 types of truths:
1. Relative truth
2. Absolute truth

The 2 opposing words are just one state. The presence of the 2 extremes is related and within each other.

There are 2 main periods in a day:
　　1. Morning time
　　2. Night time

There are 2 non-realities:
　　1. Our physical body
　　2. All forms and phenomena in the universe

The main 2 goals to cultivate in the practice are:
　　1. Compassion
　　2. Wisdom

There are 2 magnificent qualities to develop from the teachings:
　　1. Our blessings
　　2. Our wisdom

There are 2 methods to cultivate wisdom:
　　1. Listening, contemplation, practice
　　2. Morality, concentration, wisdom

The worldly life possesses 2 types of fire:
　　1. The three poisons: greed, hatred, and delusion
　　2. The three realms of cravings, forms, and non-forms

There are 2 types of karma:
　　1. Old karma
　　2. New karma

There are 2 types of silence:
1. Noble silence of a practitioner
2. Silence from anger

The number 3

The number 3 is an important number as it represents achievement and completion of a project or goal. An auctioneer normally calls out 3 times in a set announcement of "going once, going twice, sold," before settling and closing a bid. In Buddhism, there are formalities carried out 3 times in rituals such as bowing at the altar, chanting a Sutra phrase, and questioning a practitioner's decision to leave home to enter the monastery. Performing these rituals 3 times confirms our commitment to our decision, promise, and action to stay on course and carry out tasks to completion and perfection.

Buddhist practitioners take refuge in the 3 Jewels:
1. The Buddha
2. The Dharma
3. The Sangha

There are 3 categories of the Three Jewels:
1. The Three Jewels of the worldly life
2. The Three Jewels of the ordained life
3. The Three Jewels present in everyone

The Vesak celebration commemorates 3 important events in the Buddha's life:
1. The birth of the Buddha
2. His Enlightenment
3. Nirvana

There are 3 distinctive attributes of the Buddha:
- 1. Compassion
- 2. Enlightenment
- 3. Invincibility

There is a Buddha in each of the 3 time spans:
- 1. Amitabha Buddha is the past Buddha.
- 2. Shakyamuni Buddha is the present-day historical Buddha.
- 3. Maitreya, "the Happy Buddha," is the future Buddha.

The Amitabha Buddha has 3 characteristics:
- 1. Immeasurable radiant light
- 2. Immeasurable meritorious deeds
- 3. Immeasurable longevity

The Bodhisattva has 3 key attributes:
- 1. Truth
- 2. Virtue
- 3. Beauty

The Bodhisattva vows to do 3 things:
- 1. Uphold the precepts and avoid malevolent acts
- 2. Do benevolent work
- 3. Liberate others

There are 3 things that Prince Siddhartha relinquished upon leaving home in search of enlightenment:
- 1. His wealth and possessions
- 2. His family, wife (Princess Yasodhara), and son (Rahula)
- 3. His royal status and kingdom

The monastics give up 3 things upon renunciation of the ordinary life:
1. Their family to enter into their new Sangha family
2. The afflictions of the world
3. The three realms consisting of cravings, forms, and non-forms

There are 3 conditions upon entering the monastic life:
1. Live in the house of compassion, the temple
2. Wear the wardrobe of patience, the Kasaya robe
3. Sit on a pedestal that is ingrained in the Dharma teaching of Conditioned Genesis and non-reality

Bhikkus and Bhikkunis are male and female monastics who commit to do the following 3 roles:
1. Avoid performing any malevolent acts
2. Avert all afflictions
3. Live as a mendicant

Samanera and Samaneri are novice monks and nuns who have 3 characteristic roles:
1. To eliminate malevolence and perform benevolence
2. To diligently study and practice
3. To pursue purity and serenity

There are 3 types of practitioners who study the Dharma teachings:
1. The high-level person who actually practices from what has been learned
2. The average person who practices every now and then based on what he or she remembers

3. The below average person who does not understand and, therefore, ridicules the teachings and does not practice at all

There are 3 levels of practitioners:
   1. Superior
   2. Intermediate
   3. Inferior

There are 3 fires in a practitioner:
   1. The fire of right concentration
   2. The fire of meditative concentration
   3. The fire of unshakeable strength in the practice

There are 3 ways we must practice:
   1. Practice continuously through the obstacles
   2. Practice with joy despite any circumstances
   3. Practice nonstop

There are 3 types of body:
   1. The physical body
   2. The working body
   3. The Dharma body

There are 3 types of enlightenment:
   1. The absence of enlightenment
   2. The enlightenment upon a distressing experience
   3. The continuous and complete enlightenment

There are 3 aspects of enlightenment:
   1. Self-enlightenment
   2. Cultivation of enlightenment for others
   3. The supreme and complete enlightenment

There are 3 stages of enlightenment:
1. Our innate enlightenment
2. Our initial enlightenment
3. Our complete and perfect enlightenment

There are 3 methods of how we process knowledge that is learned and wisdom attained:
1. Unretainable
2. Inside out
3. Vast and monumental

There are 3 important practices required to attain wisdom:
1. Listen and learn
2. Contemplate and reflect
3. Practice

There are 3 types of wisdom:
1. The wisdom of listening
2. The wisdom of contemplation
3. The wisdom of practice

Prajna is the perfectly wonderful and completely understanding great wisdom attained from 3 characteristic practices:
1. Learning through listening
2. Contemplation and reflection
3. Achievement through practice

There are 3 essential practices that comprise the wisdom of an achieved practitioner:
1. Morality/ Mindfulness
2. Concentration
3. Wisdom

There are 3 elements of practice:
1. Believe
2. Commit
3. Perform

There are 3 ways to develop the perfect endeavor:
1. Wear a coat of armor for diligence
2. Work steadily and continuously toward benevolence
3. Always strive to do better and not remain content with the status quo

There are 3 acts of merits to practice to subdue the six different flavors that our life experiences provide:
1. The merits of wisdom
2. The merits of the Dharma body
3. The merits of liberation

The Dharma directs our practice toward 3 goals:
1. To elevate to the highest level
2. To do benevolent things
3. To liberate ourselves from afflictions

There are 3 types of liberation:
1. Liberation from a situation
2. Liberation of the mind
3. Liberation fulfilled to completion

Of the ten ways to practice the virtues of patience, the following are the 3 main ways:
1. Patience with every person
2. Patience in all situations and circumstances
3. The natural inclination for patience

There are 3 types of good friends who know and understand us:
>   1. An advisor who reminds, leads, and encourages us in the study and practice
>   2. A companion who studies and practices with us in the same path
>   3. A supporter who provides time, service, and assistance

There are 3 faithful offerings:
>   1. Material possessions
>   2. The Dharma teachings
>   3. The actions of fearlessness

There are 3 ways to provide faithful offerings:
>   1. Magnanimous giving
>   2. Reciprocal giving
>   3. Respectful giving

The 3 bows remind us to:
>   1. Pay homage to the Buddha, Dharma, and Sangha
>   2. Pursue toward mindfulness, concentration, and wisdom
>   3. Overcome greed, hatred, and delusion

There are 3 ways to cultivate blessings:
>   1. Provide service, gratitude, and respect for all beings in the world
>   2. Abide in moral disciplines
>   3. Act in accordance to the vow of a Bodhisattva

There are 3 ways that we can carry out wrong doings:
1. Self-commit the faults
2. Encourage others to commit the faults
3. Take delight to watch others commit the faults

There are 3 things that we can retrogress in:
1. Our commitment
2. Our actions
3. The end result

There are 3 realms in the universe:
1. The realm of cravings
2. The realm of forms
3. The realm of non-forms

The 3 karma are created by our:
1. Body
2. Speech
3. Mind

There are 3 habitual energies that give rise to karma:
1. Our actions
2. Our speech
3. Our thoughts

There are 3 karmic concepts in the practice:
1. The karmic action
2. The karmic Cause
3. The karmic Effect

There are 3 impediments that hinder our practice:
1. The impediment of hardship and affliction
2. The impediment of karmic action and energy
3. The resultant impediment

There are 3 interrelated impediments:
1. Impediment of our viewpoint
2. Impediment of our sorrow
3. Impediment of our karma

There are 3 types of illnesses in all living beings:
1. The body
2. The mind
3. The karma

There are 3 types of suffering:
1. The suffering of suffering
2. The external suffering
3. The acts of suffering

There are 3 sources of suffering:
1. From ourselves
2. From natural disasters such as earthquakes and hurricanes
3. From society creating prejudice and conflicts

The 3 poisons are the 3 common causes of suffering:
1. Greed
2. Hatred
3. Delusion

There are 3 great natural disasters that correlate with the 3 poisons:
1. A deluge
2. A fire
3. A whirlwind

The realms of the animal world, hungry ghost world, and underworld correlate with the 3 tragedies in the world:
1. Assassinations
2. Flood
3. Fire

There are 3 ways anger can be imprinted:
1. Anger like words drawn in the water
2. Anger like words written on the ground
3. Anger like words chiseled onto rocks

There are 3 main objectives in the Buddha's teachings:
1. To avoid malevolence
2. To develop benevolence
3. To purify and calm the mind

The number 4

Many topics under "the number 4" category convey a lot of the commonsensical aspects of life but are not obvious to us in our realm of delusion. It is when things are pointed out that we have the realization of their presence.

Prince Siddhartha saw the 4 Sights that provoked him to renunciate the worldly life and find the solution to end the vicious cycle of life's suffering:
1. Old age
2. Sickness
3. Death
4. An ascetic

Prince Siddhartha asked his father, King Suddhodana, to grant him 4 requests so he would not have to leave the royal kingdom in search of a solution for the cycles of suffering in life:
1. To live in permanent youth and not age
2. To have constant good health without any sicknesses
3. To have eternal life without any death
4. To live in perpetual joy without any sorrows

The Buddha's life can be summarized in 4 important events on the lunar calendar:
1. His birth, April 8
2. His renunciation, February 8
3. His Enlightenment, December 8
4. His Nirvana, February 15

There are 4 holy places that are marked by the distinguished events in the Buddha's life. They are pilgrimage sites where we should visit, if given the opportunity:
1. Birthplace: Lumbini Grove in Nepal
2. Place of Enlightenment: Bodhgaya, India
3. Place of the First Sermon: Deer Park in Sarnath, India
4. Place of Nirvana: the Sala Forest at Kusinara, India

There are 4 qualities of Nirvana:
1. Permanence
2. Inner peace and joy
3. Liberation
4. Purity

There are 4 reasons the Buddha came into this world:
1. To reveal the Noble Truths
2. To show us the path
3. To awaken us to practice
4. For us to internalize the teachings and practice

The "Muni" in Shakyamuni embodies 4 qualities:
1. Compassion
2. Patience
3. Harmony
4. Purity

The Buddha has compassion for all living beings that are categorized in 4 different types of births:
1. Live births (humans and mammals)
2. Birth from eggs (chickens and ducks)
3. Birth in the soil (ants and worms)
4. Birth through metamorphosis (cocoons and butterflies)

There are 4 ways the Buddha preaches his sermons:
1. True speech
2. Gentle speech
3. Loving speech
4. Avoidance of false speech

The 4 characteristic hallmarks of the Buddha's teachings, the Dharma Seals, are:
1. Impermanence
2. Tribulation
3. Non-reality and non-self
4. Nirvana

There are 4 elements of the Dharma light:
1. The Dharma teaching
2. The noble and absolute truth
3. The mindfulness practice
4. The benevolent result

There are 4 pairs of teaching points in the Dharma:
1. The Cause and Effect
2. The symbolic forms and their representation of the teachings
3. The minuscule and grandeur
4. Self-reliance and reliance on others

There are 4 elements in the Dharma Wheel that need to be set in motion to counter the eight misfortunate conditions interfering with Dharma studies:
1. Residing in a place of well-being, such as the temple
2. Relying on good friends
3. Committing to true vows
4. Cultivating the benevolent foundations of practice

There are 4 Noble Truths:
1. There is suffering in life.
2. The cause of suffering is our craving.
3. There is a solution to end suffering.

4. The Noble Eightfold Path is the guide for us to live a happy life and lessen sufferings.

There are 4 physical sufferings that parallel with the 4 stages of life:
   1. Birth
   2. Old age
   3. Sickness
   4. Death

There are 4 mental sufferings:
   1. Separation from our loved ones
   2. Proximity to people whom we dislike
   3. Not able to get what we want
   4. Attachment to the fluctuating nature of our Five Aggregates

There are 4 types of Mara:
   1. Mara of our Five Aggregates
   2. Celestial mara
   3. Mara of affliction
   4. Mara of demise

There are 4 water currents of afflictions:
   1. The water current of cravings
   2. The water current of possessions
   3. The water current of fixated views
   4. The water current of delusions

Impermanence applies to 4 objects in life:
   1. Our flesh and body
   2. Our mind

3. Our situation and circumstances
4. All phenomena

There are 4 things the Buddha cannot change or do:
1. Our Cause and Effect
2. Grant us wisdom
3. Practice for us
4. Liberate us without sufficient conditions

There are 4 types of members in the assembly who listen to the Dharma:
1. The member who queries in order to clarify any ambiguity concerning the Dharma
2. The member who supports and develops the Dharma for transmission
3. The member who receives and understands the Dharma
4. The member who does not yet have sufficient conditions to receive and understand the Dharma

There are 4 types of person who are ordained:
1. The person who is ordained in the physical body but not in the mind
2. The person who is not ordained in the physical body but is ordained in the mind
3. The person who is neither ordained in the physical body nor the mind
4. The person who is ordained in the physical body and the mind

There are 4 basic life necessities to provide offerings to the monastics:
1. Shelter
2. Nutriments

3. Clothing
4. Medications

The novice Bodhisattva has to develop 4 qualities in order to commit to the study and practice:
1. A stable and solid practice
2. Purity in the body and mind
3. Boundless deeds
4. A direction toward the supreme level of enlightenment

There are 4 pairs of the state of mind:
1. The right mind and the wrong mind
2. The true mind and the false mind
3. The immense mind and the minuscule mind
4. The wholesome mind and the partial mind

There are 4 immeasurable minds:
1. Loving-kindness
2. Compassion
3. Sympathetic joy
4. Equanimity

There are 4 types of wisdom:
1. The wisdom of clear reflection
2. The wisdom of impartiality
3. The wisdom of deep contemplation
4. The wisdom of perfect achievement

There are 4 levels of enlightenment:
1. The absence of enlightenment
2. The partial enlightenment
3. The complete and perfect enlightenment
4. The collective enlightenment of the Sangha

There are 4 paths in our life, similar to the cyclic phase of the moon:
1. The path from darkness to brightness
2. The path from brightness to darkness
3. The path from darkness to darkness
4. The path from brightness to brightness

There are 4 types of lights:
1. Light from the fire
2. Light from the moon
3. Light from the sun
4. Light of wisdom

There are 4 kinds of nutriments:
1. The edible food
2. The sensory impression
3. Our aspirations
4. Our consciousness

There are 4 Holy Paths to pursue beyond the Six Paths of existence:
1. The realm of the Hearer
2. The realm of awakening from Cause and Condition
3. The realm of the Bodhisattva
4. The realm of the Buddha

There are 4 fortunate conditions that are difficult to have in life:
1. To be reborn into the realm of human life
2. To be able to live peacefully through the entire duration of our normal lifespan

3. To be able to listen and understand the miracle of the Dharma
4. To be able to encounter the holy and divine person

There are 4 great elements that make up our body:
1. Earth
2. Water
3. Wind
4. Fire

There are 4 attractions of a practitioner:
1. Mindfulness in speech
2. Mindfulness in tone of voice
3. Mindfulness in actions
4. Mindfulness in generosity

There are 4 endeavors needed to truly achieve in our practice:
1. A stable and strong endeavor
2. A pure endeavor
3. A boundless endeavor
4. A supreme endeavor

There are 4 True Endeavors to develop in life:
1. If a benevolent activity has not arisen, cultivate it so it will materialize.
2. If a benevolent activity has already arisen, cultivate it so it will be enhanced.
3. If a malevolent activity has not arisen, prevent it from appearing.
4. If a malevolent activity has already arisen, extinguish it.

There are 4 types of energy to fuel our practice:
1. Physical energy
2. Mental energy
3. Energy from wisdom
4. Energy from the path of study

There are 4 practices we take refuge in:
1. Take refuge in the teaching and not the person's actions.
2. Take refuge in the meaning but not the words.
3. Take refuge in the wisdom but not the opinion.
4. Take refuge in the revelation of the entire meaning but not the partial meaning.

There are 4 four main acts of practice:
1. Listen to the Dharma teachings
2. Chant and recite the Dharma Sutras
3. Pay homage to the Buddha
4. Meditate to achieve mindfulness, concentration, and wisdom

There are 4 Practices required to develop the Transcendental Power for us to achieve our aspirations to the greatest satisfaction:
1. Zeal
2. Diligence
3. Mindfulness
4. Contemplation

There are 4 rules that guide us to reinforce the practice of benevolence and avoid malevolence:
1. Engage in activities that benefit us and others
2. Not to engage in activities that benefit us but harm others

3. Not to engage in activities that benefit others but harm us
4. Not to engage in activities that harm us and others

There are 4 ways to cultivate peace and joy:
1. Steer ourselves from people or places that cause problems and sufferings
2. Regulate our speech so we do not blame or degrade others
3. Tame our mind to prevent thoughts of hatred, jealousy, or rivalry
4. Commit to the practice of creating blessings and helping to liberate others

There are 4 practices to develop intrinsic joy:
1. Deep contemplation
2. Understanding
3. Empathy
4. Acceptance of the situation

There are 4 main objects of contemplation in the Foundations of Mindfulness:
1. Our body
2. Our feelings
3. Our mind
4. All phenomena

There are 4 benefits in the practice of meditation:
1. To develop insight and clarity in all situations
2. To cultivate our five sensory organs to form righteous sensory consciousness
3. To regulate and transform our mental formations
4. To promote diligence in our body and mind

There are 4 activities in the pilgrimage of our life:
1. Commitment to charity
2. Words of kindness
3. Beneficial acts of virtue
4. Collective service

There are 4 volitional acts to mindfully apply in difficult situations:
1. Understand and concede to our karmic retributions
2. Enjoy our earned blessings and work to replete them
3. Refrain from excessive conditional requests and expectations
4. Implement each action with benevolence, generosity, and purity

There are 4 acts of conduct to mindfully work on to exhibit purity and serenity:
1. Walking
2. Speaking
3. Our actions
4. The words we use

There are 4 postures we should emulate in our practice:
1. Sit like a bell
2. Walk like a peacock
3. Stand like a pine tree
4. Lie down on the right side curved like an archery bow

There are 4 circumstances in hearing and listening:
1. There is no hearing; there is no listening.
2. There is hearing; there is no listening.
3. There is hearing; there is listening.
4. There is no hearing; there is listening.

There are 4 ways to assess a situation:
1. Observe
2. Listen
3. Question
4. Conclude

There are 4 conditions that determine when we should stay or leave a place:
1. If a place provides food to eat but does not allow us to study or practice, we should not stay.
2. If a place does not provide food but allows us to study and practice, we can try to stay.
3. If a place provides food and allows us to study and practice, we should definitely stay.
4. If a place neither provides food nor the ability for us to study and practice, we should leave.

There are 4 ways we can transfer our merits to another practitioner:
1. The symbolic forms and their representation of the teachings
2. The Cause and Effect
3. The minuscule and big objectives
4. Ourselves and others

There are 4 types of people who have different ways to transform their karma:
1. A person who has suffering, then experiences joy
2. A person who has happiness, then experiences suffering
3. A person who has suffering and continues to suffer
4. A person who has happiness and continues to enjoy happiness

There are 4 characteristics of a person:
1. The person who talks without doing
2. The person who does not talk but takes action
3. The person who talks and takes action
4. The person who neither talks nor does anything

There are 4 types of fruits that mirror the different types of people:
1. The exterior is unripe, but the inside is ripe; a person may not be physically appealing but has a good heart
2. The exterior is ripe, but the inside is unripe; a person who is physically attractive but does not possess a kind heart
3. The exterior is unripe, and the inside is unripe; there are people who are both ugly on the outside and inside
4. The exterior is ripe, and the inside is ripe; there are people who are attractive both on the outside and inside

There are 4 egocentric characters that can cause us problems:
1. Our delusion
2. Our view
3. Our pride
4. Our self-love

There are 4 types of friends:
1. A friend like a flower
2. A friend like a scale
3. A friend like the earth
4. A friend like the mountain

There are 4 things that we should not take lightly:
1. A small snake
2. A young monastic
3. A small fire
4. A young prince

There are 4 tangible assets:
1. House and real estate
2. Money
3. Jewelry
4. Land

The Number 5

The number 5 is symbolic in many of the Buddha's teachings and traditions.

There were 5 ascetic friends present at the First Sermon.
The Buddha gave his First Sermon to his 5 ascetic friends at Deer Park in Sarnath, India. They practiced and trained with him in the early years before his Enlightenment, at a time when they focused on the extreme practice of austerity.

There are 5 practices in the remembrance of the Buddha:
1. Recite the Buddha's name
2. Reflect on the Buddha's statue in form
3. Think of the Buddha, his character, and vow
4. Meditate by sitting, walking, breathing, and counting prayer beads as we think of the Buddha
5. Internalize the Buddha's vows and what he represents in both our body and mind

There are 5 objects of reverence representing the presence of the Buddha and his teachings:
   1. The Buddha statue or Kasaya robe
   2. The Bodhi tree
   3. The lotus
   4. The stupa
   5. The Dharma Wheel

The Happy Buddha has 5 playful children surrounding him, representing our 5 sensory organs and their senses.

There are 5 colors in the Buddhist flag:
   1. Blue
   2. Yellow
   3. Red
   4. White
   5. Orange

There are 5 purposes of a Sutra:
   1. To give our life happiness and a bright future
   2. To reveal the true nature of life and universe
   3. To direct us to a noble straight path
   4. To serve like a strong water current to carry us out from the crevices of life's hindrances and afflictions
   5. To connect each Dharma teaching like a garland of flowers

There are 5 benefits derived from listening to the Dharma:
   1. It provides the teachings that we have not yet heard.
   2. It provides the understanding of the things that we have not yet understood.

3. It resolves any doubt or knowledge that are not regarded with right view.
4. It provides clarity and right view so we can develop purity and tranquility of our karma.
5. It provides the wisdom that we all seek.

There are 5 reasons a word cannot be translated:
1. A word that has multiple meanings and excluding some of its meanings would not accurately depict the entire meaning of the word
2. A word that is holy and sacred
3. A name of a person
4. The object or item is nonexistent in a place of inhabitant
5. A word that is mystical

There are 5 basic moralities in the Five Mindfulness Trainings and the Five Precepts:
1. Respect and preserve life and avoid harming living beings
2. Give generously and avoid taking from others
3. Build faithful relationships and avoid unfaithfulness
4. Speak kind, truthful words and avoid malevolent, deceptive speech
5. Be mindful of healthy consumption and avoid the intake of unhealthy food and harmful exposures to the body and mind (e.g., alcohol, drugs, and violent movies)

There are 5 Vehicles that carry the Dharma teachings for us to practice:
1. The Vehicle for the Worldly Person
2. The Vehicle of the Heavenly Being (Ten Benevolent Practices to train the three karma)

3. The Vehicle of the Bodhisattva (6 paramitas)
   4. The Vehicle of the Hearer
   5. The Vehicle of the doctrine of Cause and Condition

The 5 Roots of Practice are the foundations to achieve in order to yield the 5 Powers:
   1. Faith
   2. Effort
   3. Mindfulness
   4. Meditative concentration
   5. Wisdom

There are 5 negatives that impede the 5 Roots of Practice:
   1. Distrust
   2. Laziness
   3. Aggravation
   4. Anger
   5. Resentment

There are 5 fragrant natures of the incense:
   1. Morality
   2. Concentration
   3. Wisdom
   4. Liberation
   5. Liberation from our fixated view and understanding

There are 5 ways to mindfully lessen malevolent and increase benevolent acts:
   1. Think and apply benevolence rather than malevolence, direct our mind toward the positives, and ward off malevolence
   2. Think of the consequences of the malevolent acts

3. Try our best to forget and dismiss the malevolent acts
4. Block the malevolent acts from arising or progressively lessen them toward elimination
5. Use our utmost energy to stop the malevolent acts

There are 5 Contemplations to meditate on prior to a meal:
1. The food that we have is a gift from the earth, sky, and much loving, hard work of others.
2. We vow to eat in mindfulness and with gratitude to be deserving of the food that we receive.
3. We vow to be mindful to transform our unskillful actions, especially to practice eating in moderation.
4. We vow to consume in a manner to minimize harm to animal beings, preserve our Mother Earth, and prevent any harm that can cause damage to the environment and climate.
5. We vow to mindfully consume food to provide us the strength in order to serve others and promote the communal and collective bond in the Sangha.

There are 5 blessings we can earn to have in our life:
1. Health
2. Longevity
3. Wealth
4. Luxury
5. A peaceful death

There are 5 minds of a Bodhisattva:
1. The mind of enlightenment
2. The mind of filial devotion
3. The mind of compassion
4. The mind of reverence
5. The mind of truthfulness

There are 5 components needed to illuminate the mind and maintain its glow. They are an analogy to a kerosene lamp that maintains the light:
1. Faith is the flaming light.
2. Compassion is the oil that fuels the blaze.
3. Mindfulness is the container of the kerosene lamp.
4. Commitment to the 5 Precepts is the tube that expels the smoke to maintain the glow.
5. Meritorious deeds radiate like the halo of light.

There are 5 reasons why we dream:
1. Physically tired
2. Constant thoughts
3. Previous karma
4. Disturbance from the demons
5. Reminder from the heavenly body

The strongest person possesses these 5 qualities:
1. Right view
2. Faith
3. Wisdom
4. Compassion
5. Harmony within the community

The practitioner has 5 powerful energies similar to the properties of the fire:
1. The energy of wisdom to extinguish all afflictions
2. The energy to eradicate any sorrow without discrimination
3. The energy of diligence and effort to continuously practice
4. The energy of compassion to empathize and support others in need

5. The energy of wisdom to shine in situations of ignorance and wrong views

The practitioner has 5 strengths comparable to the rain:
1. The rain can form a strong current to wash the dirt from all surfaces. Similarly, a practitioner can use the wisdom attained to untangle the afflictions.
2. The rain cools the earth. The practitioner trains to cool and calm the mind from the heat of anger in order to give rise to well-being.
3. The rain flourishes green foliage. The practitioner fosters deep belief to promote diligence toward three accomplishments:
   a. Become a person of high merit, like the Bodhi tree
   b. To be in the heavenly sphere
   c. To have the ultimate happiness of Nirvana in this lifetime
4. The rain causes the plant's roots to bind tightly to the soil so its flowers and leaves can thrive and blossom. The practitioner anchors his or her practice in the Dharma teachings to develop the ultimate wisdom.
5. The rain fills up all the crevices and holes of the earth, then overflows on the surface ground. The practitioner absorbs the words of the Sutra in all facets of his or her mind.

There are 5 skandhas or Aggregates that constitute our mental and physical existence:
1. Form, including the five sensory organs and senses
2. Feeling
3. Perception
4. Mental formation
5. Consciousness

There are 5 types of visual faculties:
1. The eye and what it sees
2. The holy and divine vision
3. The vision of wisdom
4. The vision of the Dharma
5. The vision of enlightenment

There are 5 faulty views:
1. Wrong view
2. One-sided view
3. Wrong view of self
4. Attachment to our view
5. Attachment to false views of how the precepts should be practiced

There are 5 impediments that hinder our progress:
1. Desire
2. Ill will
3. Mental lethargy and physical laziness
4. Mental unrest and physical restlessness
5. Skepticism and doubt

There are 5 obstacles related to our karma that we should be aware of:
1. Afflictions
2. Negative karma
3. Unfavorable birth circumstances
4. Inaccessibility of the Dharma teachings
5. Inability to have complete knowledge and understanding of the teachings

There are 5 impurities:
1. Impurity of the world
2. Impurity of our view
3. Impurity of living beings
4. Impurity of our life span
5. Impurity of the afflictions

There are 5 signs of regression in our practice:
1. The wilting of our flower with our frowning face
2. An odor in our sweat
3. A blurring of our radiant light
4. Mental confusion
5. The mind is not at peace

There are 5 features of an object that can cause afflictions if we are not awakened to see their true nature:
1. Its form or figure
2. Its designated name
3. Its distinguishing characteristics
4. Its true nature
5. Its purpose

There are 5 objects of cravings:
1. Wealth
2. Beauty
3. Fame
4. Pleasure in delicacy
5. Oversleeping

Our estate will eventually return back to their 5 true homes:
1. Washed away by water
2. Burned by fire
3. Stolen by thieves

4. Confiscated by the government
5. Squandered by future generations

Our material possessions should be allocated into these 5 areas:
1. Daily expenses and miscellaneous use
2. Savings
3. Investment
4. Gift for dear friends and family
5. Charity

There are 5 intellectual categories of knowledge that everyone wants to have:
1. Knowledge of the Dharma teachings
2. Knowledge of fluency in multiple languages
3. Knowledge of vocations and STEM courses (science, technology, engineering, and math)
4. Knowledge of medical science and medications
5. Knowledge of the worldly life

There are 5 signs of aging:
1. Change in physical beauty
2. Decline in physical function
3. Decrease in respiratory capacity
4. Lessening of appetite
5. Shortening of longevity

There are 5 events we cannot predict:
1. The illnesses we will have
2. The time we develop the illnesses
3. The cause of our death
4. The time and place of our death
5. The realm we will be born into

The number 6

The number 6, although few in numbers, holds important aspects of the teachings.

Prince Siddhartha endured 6 years of an austere practice before attaining enlightenment.

There are 6 offerings at the altar for the Buddha:
1. Incense
2. Trays of fruits
3. Vases of flowers
4. A pair of lights
5. A pair of cups of water
6. White rice

Each written discourse in the Sutras has 6 descriptions to validate that the Buddha's sermons took place:
1. "Thus have I heard" appears at the beginning of every Sutra to attest that the scriptures were recorded exactly the way they were heard from the Buddha's sermons
2. "Thus have I heard" is an attestation that the sermons were heard by Ananda
3. An announcement that the Buddha was the speaker of the sermons
4. An announcement of the time period of the sermon
5. A description of the location of the sermon
6. A description of the number of members and attendants present

The Sutra has 6 powerful insights that shine upon the practitioner:
1. To direct us to the right path
2. To serve as an aid and convenience to transmit the teachings
3. To reveal the infallible truth
4. To entice the practitioner to study and practice
5. To increase our blessings
6. To provide the rules of moral conduct

There are 6 syllables in the *Om Mani Padme Hum* mantra.
Om is a sacred phonetic word, often used as the beginning word of mantras.
Mani literally means gem. We should take refuge in our innate, shining Buddha-nature to live a fulfilling life.
Padme is the lotus flower. The lotus flower can bloom from the mud. Likewise, we can rise above the difficulties in life to achieve strength and wisdom.
Hum means stable and not inclined to change or move.

This Sanskrit mantra unveils the radiant truth, to evoke our innate Buddha-nature to practice and transform our mind to a state of purity and serenity, despite the ever-changing conditions in life.

There are 6 types of faith to cultivate:
1. Faith in ourselves
2. Faith in others
3. Faith in the Cause
4. Faith in the Effect
5. Faith in the symbolic form, deed, and activity
6. Faith in the symbolic representation of the teachings

There are 6 paramitas in the Vehicle of the Bodhisattva to achieve our practice to perfection and completion:
1. Generosity
2. Upholding the precepts
3. Patience
4. Effort
5. Meditative concentration
6. Wisdom

There are 6 foundations of collective practice to realize harmony within a Sangha:
1. Harmony of the community body
2. Harmony of speech
3. Harmony of collective thoughts of the mind
4. Harmony of collective sharing of perceptions
5. Harmony of collective practice of the precepts
6. Harmony of collective benefits and achievements

There are 6 Transcendental Powers that penetrate to provide a clear comprehension of our faculties through the supernatural component of our sixth senses:
1. Power of divine vision
2. Power of divine hearing
3. Power of claircognizance
4. Power of supernatural movement
5. Power of clairvoyance
6. The ultimate power to end all defilements

There are 6 Paths of existence in the cycles of rebirth of life:
1. The heaven realm
2. The asura realm
3. The human realm
4. The underworld

5. The hungry ghost world
6. The animal world

All man-made objects are transient in nature, similar to the ephemeral state of the following 6 forms:
1. A dream
2. An inauthentic object
3. A foam
4. A blinking light
5. A shadow
6. A dew on grass

There are 6 sensory organs and their corresponding objects:
1. Eyes – form
2. Ears – sound
3. Nose – smell
4. Mouth – taste
5. Body – contact and touch
6. Mind – mind consciousness

There are 6 flavors that our life experiences provide:
1. Sour
2. Spicy
3. Bitter
4. Sweet
5. Salty
6. Bland

The Number 7

The representations in the number 7, although fewer in quantity than other numbers, have to be mentioned as they have much significance. Just as the 7 musical notes that make up the melody of a song, the number 7 in Buddhism exemplifies the Buddha's valiant nature to accomplish all tasks and overcome all difficulties.

The Buddha took 7 steps onto 7 blooming lotuses at birth.

The 7 steps represent the 7 elements comprising this universe:
1. Earth
2. Water
3. Wind
4. Fire
5. View
6. Consciousness
7. Emptiness or space

The 7 steps also represent the four cardinal directions of north, south, east, west and the three eras of past, present, and future.

There are 7 topics of teachings that comprise the Thirty-Seven Paths to Enlightenment. They are the expanded version of the Noble Eightfold Path:
1. The Four Mindfulness Foundations
2. The Four True Endeavors
3. The Four Practices to achieve Transcendental Power
4. The Five Roots or Foundations of Practice
5. The Five Powers
6. The Seven Elements of Enlightenment
7. The Noble Eightfold Path

There are 7 Elements of practice to attain Enlightenment:
1. Mindfulness
2. Right determination
3. Right effort
4. Serenity
5. Joy
6. Concentration
7. Equanimity

The Buddha attained enlightenment after 7 weeks of sitting meditation under the Bodhi tree. There are 7 past Buddhas, with the Shakyamuni Buddha being the seventh.

The Buddha has 7 types of disciples:
1. Layman
2. Laywoman
3. Samanera (novice monk)
4. Samaneri (novice nun)
5. Siksamana (novice nun observing the precepts)
6. Bhikku (male monastic)
7. Bhikkuni (female monastic)

There are 7 practices needed to cultivate the mind of enlightenment to perfection and completion:
1. Peacefully reside in the compassionate character of the Bodhisattva
2. Take refuge in the mind of enlightenment
3. Consistently exhibit compassion and generosity
4. Establish merits and virtues in our designated vocation
5. Be skilled and mindful in the nature of all phenomena
6. Direct toward the supreme level of enlightenment

7. Develop purity in character to overcome afflictions and impediments

The 7 jewels of the worldly person are impermanent and will deteriorate over time:
1. Gold
2. Silver
3. Lapis lazuli
4. Crystal
5. Nacre (mother of pearl)
6. Red Pearl
7. Carnelian

The 7 cherished jewels of a practitioner will perpetually flourish when cultivated:
1. Faith
2. Morality
3. Repentance with self
4. Repentance with others
5. Deep listening
6. Generosity and release of attachments
7. Wisdom

There are 7 methods to mitigate our pain and suffering:
1. Develop knowledge of right view
2. Support and safeguard our six senses
3. Utilize supportive conveniences to lessen our discomfort
4. Endure and accept the true nature
5. Deter from troublesome situations
6. Expeditiously eliminate greed, hatred, and delusion
7. Practice earnestly

There are 7 emotions that stir us from within:
1. Joy
2. Anger
3. Happiness
4. Sadness
5. Love
6. Hate
7. Cravings

The Number 8

We cannot stop at the number 7 and not discuss the number 8 because it includes one of the principal teachings on how to live a happy and peaceful life, the Noble Eightfold Path.

The Noble Eightfold Path outlines 8 important right paths to cultivate to overcome the challenges in life:
1. Right view
2. Right thought
3. Right speech
4. Right action
5. Right livelihood
6. Right effort
7. Right mindfulness
8. Right concentration

There are 8 characteristic stages in the Buddha's life that led to his Enlightenment:
1. Abide in a heavenly realm in preparation for descent into the world
2. Enter the right side of his mother, Queen Maya, to stay for a 10 month pregnancy, rather than the typical 9 months and 10 days
3. Emerge into the world from Queen Maya's right side in Lumbini Garden
4. Renunciate the worldly life along the river Anoma, after viewing the Four Sights
5. Overcome the seductions of evil spirits and not succumb to life's diversion
6. Attain Enlightenment under the Bodhi tree
7. Set the Dharma Wheel in motion to share his teachings with others
8. Attain Nirvana

There are 8 unfortunate conditions that make it difficult to encounter the Buddha and Dharma teachings:
1. To be born in the dark place of the underworld realm
2. To be born in the hungry ghost realm
3. To be born in the animal realm
4. To be born in the heaven realm
5. To be born in a bountiful and pleasant residence
6. To be born with a deficiency of the sense faculties: blind, mute, deaf, and dumb
7. To be born with too much of the worldly intelligence
8. To be born before or after the Buddha

There are 8 gusts of wind that can disrupt our peace:
1. Gain
2. Loss
3. Praise
4. Blame
5. Honor
6. Dishonor
7. Happiness
8. Sorrow

The causes of our laziness can be attributed to the 8 conditions of:
1. Too hot
2. Too cold
3. Too hungry
4. Too full
5. Too sleepy
6. Too tired
7. Too much good food
8. Too little good food

Of the ten attributes of the lotus, the following 8 are unique that symbolize a teaching:
1. Remains pure despite its impure environment
2. Purifies its dirty surroundings
3. Emerges at the right time and place (patience)
4. The flower and leaf have separate stems (purposeful)
5. The flower and fruit coexist (Cause and Effect)
6. All parts can be cooked into a dish (fruitful)
7. The leaves are water repellent (non-attachment)
8. The stem is hollow (detachment)

Conclusion

Symbolisms use forms to represent a character and personality so we can associate with life's experiences. Although Buddhism does not recognize physical forms as real, it presents statues and figures for us to relate to the understanding of the Dharma teachings and life's phenomena. At the temple, musical instruments and their sounds, colors, statues and figures, fruits and flowers serve as decorations and provide subtle teachings. Because we are attracted to physical beauty and take pleasure in listening to melodic sounds, we are enticed by these attractions to learn more about the teachings. The Buddha statues and Dharma phenomena are the external representations that serve as vehicles to remind us to turn within our innate Buddha-nature and practice toward the virtuous path with a focused goal to achieve wisdom and serenity. All forms and phenomena that are ubiquitous in our daily life serve as Dharma teachings. Enjoy them in the present moment, recognize their true nature, and learn from the lessons they provide. Do not become attached to them, but practice letting go, whether they are good or bad, as they only manifest under sufficient conditions. Buddhism is a path to attain purity, mindfulness, and wisdom so we can see the true nature of all forms and our Five Aggregates that act on those forms to make up our existence. Upon learning the teachings of the noble truths, we have to practice to receive beneficial results. We need to practice continuously through the obstacles, practice with joy despite any circumstances, and practice nonstop. When we reflect, we can see more clearly the conditions in ourselves and others so we can cultivate a harmonious life together. When our body and mind are at peace and joyful, we develop the deep concentration needed to decorate our enlightened mind. From this understanding, we can preclude from living in delusion and manage any transpiring circumstances in life with graceful composure and equanimity. The symbolisms in Buddhism are immense, and we can use this knowledge as a stepping stone in our initial study to delve deeper into the practice. And this is how we can further our learning and practice in Buddhism.

Deep prayers that these meritorious deeds
Directly permeate to everyone and every place
To each practitioner and sentient being
So all will wholeheartedly achieve the path of enlightenment.

References

Bài Giảng Thầy Thích Pháp Hòa. (2018, September 27). *Bài giảng 10 năm trước của Thầy Thích Pháp Hòa được nhiều người tìm nghe* [Video File]. Retrieved from https://www.youtube.com/watch?v=EZQiegg4xTA

Hai Loi. (2016, January 16). *Ba Thứ Trí Tuệ - Thích Pháp Hòa* [Video File]. Retrieved from https://www.youtube.com/watch?v=jSsk5tfvf2A&t=2889s

He Is Risen Tabernacle. (2014, March 20). *Myles Munroe - Prayer & Fasting In The Kingdom (2014)**Final Sermon Series*** [Video File]. Retrieved from https://www.youtube.com/watch?v=LGkAq-2jIdY&feature=youtu.be

Hoang Phap. (2015, July 3). *T.T Thích Pháp Hòa " Tôn Kính Pháp Bảo" tại Hiển Như Tịnh Thất 7/2/2015* [Video File]. Retrieved from https://www.youtube.com/watch?v=BJBGDZ2J8Qg&feature=youtu.be

Học Phật Bước Đầu. (2018, December 7). *Thầy Pháp Hòa || "Bi Trí Dũng" là Tam Bảo Bất Biên (hay lắm)* [Video File]. Retrieved from https://www.youtube.com/watch?v=hb4gawp3ay4

Mai Trọng Nghĩa. (2015, June 16). *Trả Lời Vấn Đáp Rất Hay Thầy Thích Pháp Hòa TrucLam mp3,2014* [Video File]. Retrieved from https://www.youtube.com/watch?v=yO5gYXhWDS8&feature=youtu.be

Pháp thoại Thích Pháp Hòa. (2018, September 9). *3 cách HÀNH XỬ trong đời sống - Thầy Pháp Hòa (nên nghe 2018)* [Video File]. Retrieved from https://www.youtube.com/watch?v=8UmPMDeG5q8&t=2707s

Pháp thoại Thích Pháp Hòa. (2018, December 29). *5 chướng ngại Ở ĐỜI - Thầy Thích Pháp Hòa (rất tuyệt vời)* [Video File]. Retrieved from https://www.youtube.com/watch?v=Er67DXQvZaU&feature=youtu.be

Pháp thoại Thích Pháp Hòa. (2017, December 20). *Bí quyết để gia đình luôn HẠNH PHÚC – Thầy Thích Pháp Hòa (quá ý nghĩa)* [Video File]. Retrieved from https://www.youtube.com/watch?v=jYUiIGVl97I&feature=youtu.be

Pháp thoại Thích Pháp Hòa. (2019, February 10). *Cách xa lìa CHƯỚNG NGẠI - Thầy Thích Pháp Hòa (xuất bản 01.2019)* [Video File]. Retrieved from https://www.youtube.com/watch?v=429eSzAh_t4&feature=youtu.be

Pháp thoại Thích Pháp Hòa. (2018, October 15). *ĐỜI KHỔ LẮM biết nương tựa vào đâu Thầy Pháp Hòa (rất Bổ Ích)* [Video File]. Retrieved from https://www.youtube.com/watch?v=iHQ0cM3G-ug&feature=youtu.be

Pháp thoại Thích Pháp Hòa. (2018, February 7). *Hiểu thế nào về HẠNH YÊU THƯƠNG Thầy Thích Pháp Hòa (rất bổ ích)* [Video File]. Retrieved from https://www.youtube.com/watch?v=DO10RDKE7tA&feature=youtu.be

Pháp thoại Thích Pháp Hòa. (2018, July 30). *Học cách RÈN LUYỆN tâm - Thích Pháp Hòa (hay quá)* [Video File]. Retrieved from https://www.youtube.com/watch?v=n6dx5_jRWU&feature=youtu.be

Pháp thoại Thích Pháp Hòa. (2018, January 30). *HỌC PHẬT để chuyển hóa CHÍNH MÌNH – Thầy Thích Pháp Hòa (cực hay)* [Video File]. Retrieved from https://www.youtube.com/watch?v=UG7oOSHLNro&feature=youtu.be

Pháp thoại Thích Pháp Hòa. (2017, December 18). *LÒNG NGƯỜI KHÓ LƯỜNG - Thầy Thích Pháp Hòa (quá hay và ý nghĩa)* [Video File]. Retrieved from https://www.youtube.com/watch?v=UnFUiDaN_2I&feature=youtu.be

Pháp thoại Thích Pháp Hòa. (2018, November 18). *Nên Hiểu Để Mà TU - Thầy Pháp Hòa (tuyệt vời)* [Video File]. Retrieved from https://www.youtube.com/watch?v=jetQ05FWhcA&feature=youtu.be

Pháp thoại Thích Pháp Hòa. (2018, March 26). *NGƯỜI BIẾT CHUYỂN NGHIỆP - Thầy Thích Pháp Hòa (hay quá 2018)* [Video File]. Retrieved from https://www.youtube.com/watch?v=gttF8xbDMK4&feature=youtu.be

Pháp thoại Thích Pháp Hòa. (2018, August 7). *Những điều CẦN BIẾT ĐỂ SỐNG – Thích Pháp Hòa (hay quá – vui quá)* [Video File]. Retrieved from https://www.youtube.com/watch?v=lp0egtF4XjU&feature=youtu.be

Pháp thoại Thích Pháp Hòa. (2018, January 29). *PHÁP QUANG - Thầy Thích Pháp Hòa (cực hay)* [Video File]. Retrieved from https://www.youtube.com/watch?v=Q5ebipjGjik&feature=youtu.be

Pháp thoại Thích Pháp Hòa. (2017, December 13). *PHƯỚC NÀO LỚN NHẤT - Thầy Thích Pháp Hòa (quá hay 2017)* [Video File]. Retrieved from https://www.youtube.com/watch?v=lUObT-oOOds&feature=youtu.be

Pháp thoại Thích Pháp Hòa. (2018, March 17). *SỐ và NGHIỆP của mỗi người như thế nào? Thầy Thích Pháp Hòa (quá hay 2018)* [Video File]. Retrieved from https://www.youtube.com/watch?v=m6-JFOKM8UU&feature=youtu.be

Pháp thoại Thích Pháp Hòa. (2018, August 19). *SỐNG ĐƠN GIẢN khó hay dễ - Thầy Thích Pháp hòa (mới nhất 2018)* [Video File]. Retrieved from https://www.youtube.com/watch?v=F9rs6qnJTCs&feature=youtu.be

Pháp thoại Thích Pháp Hòa. (2018, April 10). *Vấn đáp - Làm sao để VƯỢT CHƯỚNG NGẠI trong cuộc sống – Thầy Thích Pháp Hòa (quá tuyệt vời 2018)* [Video File]. Retrieved from https://www.youtube.com/watch?v=kekEr86S69E&feature=youtu.be

Pháp thoại Thích Pháp Hòa. (2018, August 1). *Vấn đáp MỚI / Thế nào là TIỂU THỪA và ĐẠI THỪA - Thích Pháp Hòa* [Video File]. Retrieved from https://www.youtube.com/watch?v=NmkbPSkGL6s&feature=youtu.be

Pháp thoại Thích Pháp Hòa. (2018, October 23). *VÔ THƯỜNG - Thích Pháp Hòa (rất ý nghĩa)* [Video File]. Retrieved from https://www.youtube.com/watch?v=ZcSGlTJhEBE&feature=youtu.be

Pháp thoại Thích Pháp Hòa. (2018, November 27). *Vượt qua 8 CHƯỚNG NẠN trong đời sống – Thầy Thích Pháp Hòa (rất tuyệt vời)* [Video File]. Retrieved from https://www.youtube.com/watch?v=7djAC5G56FA&feature=youtu.be

Pháp thoại Thích Pháp Hòa. (2018, February 28). *Ý NGHĨA LỄ PHẬT, QUY Y đầu năm mới – Thầy Thích Pháp Hòa (quá ý nghĩa)* [Video File]. Retrieved from https://www.youtube.com/watch?v=y3NRTHaeGOA&feature=youtu.be

Pháp thoại Thích Pháp Hòa. (2018, November 21). *Ý nghĩa tượng QUAN ÂM BỒ TÁT Thầy Thích Pháp Hòa (nên nghe)* [Video File]. Retrieved from https://www.youtube.com/watch?v=aMWhoGzH1ok

Rahula, Walpola. *What the Buddha Taught*. 2nd ed. London: The Gordon Fraser Gallery Ltd., 1978.

The Soka Gakkai Dictionary of Buddhism. *Soka Gakkai Nichiren Buddhism Library*. (2002). Retrieved from https://www.nichirenlibrary.org/en/dic/toc/

Thông Minh Channel. (2018, November 19). *Nói Dễ Làm Khó ... 16 - 11 - 2018 : Thầy Thích Pháp Hòa* . [Video File]. Retrieved from https://www.youtube.com/watch?v=1XMeJLvrajs&feature=youtu.be

Truc Lam (Thích Pháp Hòa). (2014, January 9). *5 Chướng Của Ngũ Căn - Thầy.Thích Pháp Hòa (Nov.2, 2013)* [Video File]. Retrieved from https://www.youtube.com/watch?v=1Yb0S4kO4K4&feature=youtu.be

Truc Lam (Thích Pháp Hòa). (2018, June 18). *Ai An Tâm Cho Mình ? (Vấn Đáp) - Thầy Thích Pháp Hòa (Ngày 29.4.2018)* [Video File]. Retrieved from https://www.youtube.com/watch?v=g_O3L_-OFXk

Truc Lam (Thích Pháp Hòa). (2019, February 25). *Ai Có Duyên Với Mình (vấn đáp mới) -Thầy Thích Pháp Hòa (Ngày 4.11.2018)* [Video File]. Retrieved from https://www.youtube.com/watch?v=Jj4eFgBW3e8

Truc Lam (Thích Pháp Hòa). (2019, May 17). *Ai Nhấc Được Tảng Đá 1 - Thầy Thích Pháp Hòa (Chùa Hải Đức , Ngày 9.2.2019)* [Video File]. Retrieved from https://www.youtube.com/watch?v=0ktsonnEwQQ

Truc Lam (Thích Pháp Hòa). (2019, January 13). *Ân Nghĩa Hằng Ngày - Thầy Thích Pháp Hòa (Ngày 3.11.2018)* [Video File]. Retrieved from https://www.youtube.com/watch?v=vE0B_78FN_c

Truc Lam (Thích Pháp Hòa). (2014, January 4). *Bài Pháp Đầu Tiên 1 - Thầy. Thích Pháp Hòa (Jan.4, 2014)* [Video File]. Retrieved from https://www.youtube.com/watch?v=yclL9YDZi_8

Truc Lam (Thích Pháp Hòa). (2014, January 5). *Bài Pháp Đầu Tiên 2 - Thầy. Thích Pháp Hòa (Jan.5, 2014)* [Video File]. Retrieved from https://www.youtube.com/watch?v=LvRIA5TFalo

Truc Lam (Thích Pháp Hòa). (2016, October 17). *Bảy Yếu Tố Giác Ngộ - Thầy. Thích Pháp Hòa (May 15, 2016)* [Video File]. Retrieved from https://www.youtube.com/watch?v=Fo_JcctZi2A&feature=youtu.be

Truc Lam (Thích Pháp Hòa). (2019, June 21). *Biết Lo (Vấn Đáp) - Thầy Thích Pháp Hòa (TV Tây Thiên, ngày 20.4.2019)* [Video File]. Retrieved from https://www.youtube.com/watch?v=hYyPRPSW6bA

Truc Lam (Thích Pháp Hòa). (2017, May 22). *Bồ Tát Tại Gia 15 - Thầy. Thích Pháp Hòa (June 25, 2016)* [Video File]. Retrieved from https://www.youtube.com/watch?v=qpbmXj5J8L0&feature=youtu.be

Truc Lam (Thích Pháp Hòa). (2017, March 15). *Bốn Điều Cần Có - Thầy. Thích Pháp Hòa (chùa Hải Đức, May 15, 2016)* [Video File]. Retrieved from https://www.youtube.com/watch?v=U6S0LOigBPI&feature=youtu.be

Truc Lam (Thích Pháp Hòa). (2019, March 6). *Bốn Điều Phước 1 - Thầy Thích Pháp Hòa (Chùa Viên Giác)* [Video File]. Retrieved from https://www.youtube.com/watch?v=CvsDMndZUdI&feature=youtu.be

Truc Lam (Thích Pháp Hòa). (2019, March 8). *Bốn Điều Phước 2 - Thầy Thích Pháp Hòa (Chùa Viên Giác)* [Video File]. Retrieved from https://www.youtube.com/watch?v=lXL68MJh7nk&feature=youtu.be

Truc Lam (Thích Pháp Hòa). (2019, February 15). *Bốn Loại Nhận Thức - Thầy Thích Pháp Hòa (Chùa Quang Minh , Melbourne 3.11.2018)* [Video File]. Retrieved from https://www.youtube.com/watch?v=m4jjgbLlFS4&feature=youtu.be

Truc Lam (Thích Pháp Hòa). (2019, May 10). *Bốn Pháp Hỷ Lạc - Thầy Thích Pháp Hòa (Chùa A Di Đà , Ngày 27.9.2018)* [Video File]. Retrieved from https://www.youtube.com/watch?v=H4D27qa9ImM

Truc Lam (Thích Pháp Hòa). (2018, June 22). *Bốn Thần Túc Thầy Thích Pháp Hòa Chùa Hải Đức , ngày 25 2 2018 1* [Video File]. Retrieved from https://www.youtube.com/watch?v=DFRlgF1wdpM&feature=youtu.be

Truc Lam (Thích Pháp Hòa). (2018, April 18). *Cái Gì Cũng Tội! - Thầy Thích Pháp Hòa (Tư Gia PT Diệu Cẩm 7 Dec. 2017)* [Video File]. Retrieved from https://www.youtube.com/watch?v=LG0bedPgOjI&feature=youtu.be

Truc Lam (Thích Pháp Hòa). (2018, July 27). *Cầu Phước - Thầy Thích Pháp Hòa 29-5-2018 (Chùa Phổ Đức Calgary , 29 5 2018)* [Video File]. Retrieved from https://www.youtube.com/watch?v=djYIaeVGMLs&feature=youtu.be

Truc Lam (Thích Pháp Hòa). (2018, March 28). *Chăm Sóc Đất Tâm 1 - Thầy Thích Pháp Hòa (Heilbronn ngày 20.6.2017)* [Video File]. Retrieved from https://www.youtube.com/watch?v=BgHU1_kGNuQ&feature=youtu.be

Truc Lam (Thích Pháp Hòa). (2015, October 6). *Chí Nguyện Siêu Việt 5 - Thầy Thích Pháp Hòa (Feb 07 , 2015)* [Video File]. Retrieved from https://www.youtube.com/watch?v=j3BdsRTzGLI&feature=youtu.be

Truc Lam (Thích Pháp Hòa). (2015, October 16). *Chí Nguyện Siêu Việt 7 - Thầy Thích Pháp Hòa (March 28 , 2015)* [Video File]. Retrieved from https://www.youtube.com/watch?v=5bKpxqG6n5w&feature=youtu.be

Truc Lam (Thích Pháp Hòa). (2015, November 5). *Chí Nguyện Siêu Việt 8 - Thầy Thích Pháp Hòa (April 04, 2015)* [Video File]. Retrieved from https://www.youtube.com/watch?v=RDoEzappUz8&feature=youtu.be

Truc Lam (Thích Pháp Hòa). (2015, December 27). *Chí Nguyện Siêu Việt 13 - Thầy Thích Pháp Hòa (May 02 , 2015)* [Video File]. Retrieved from https://www.youtube.com/watch?v=RWPYqVeqCik&feature=youtu.be

Truc Lam (Thích Pháp Hòa). (2017, August 14). *Chỗ Nương Tựa 3 (vấn đáp) - Thầy Thích Pháp Hòa (May 20, 2017)* [Video File]. Retrieved from https://www.youtube.com/watch?v=XgiYavirkP0&feature=youtu.be

Truc Lam (Thích Pháp Hòa). (2019, May 13). *Chú Tâm Việc Của Mình - Thầy Thích Pháp Hòa (Tu Viện Trúc Lâm , Ngày 19.1.2019)* [Video File]. Retrieved from https://www.youtube.com/watch?v=wMTk1LBqnLE

Truc Lam (Thích Pháp Hòa). (2015, May 17). *Chuyển Tam Nhiễm Thành Tam Đức - Thầy Thích Pháp Hòa (June 5, 2014)* [Video File]. Retrieved from https://www.youtube.com/watch?v=db9pwVUIiQM&feature=youtu.be

Truc Lam (Thích Pháp Hòa). (2019, February 18). *Cực Khổ - Cực Lạc Thầy Thích Pháp Hòa (Ngày 23.12.2018)* [Video File]. Retrieved from https://www.youtube.com/watch?v=-p8yqNaeKrE&feature=youtu.be

Truc Lam (Thích Pháp Hòa). (2013, February 26). *Đại Bi Thập Chú 1/6 - Thầy. Thích Pháp Hòa (September 1 , 2012)* [Video File]. Retrieved from https://www.youtube.com/watch?v=UqWB2RMnu3M&feature=youtu.be

Truc Lam (Thích Pháp Hòa). (2013, March 4). *Đại Bi Thập Chú 4/6 - Thầy. Thích Pháp Hòa (September 29, 2012)* [Video File]. Retrieved from https://www.youtube.com/watch?v=o3QdVN3o0Hs&feature=youtu.be

Truc Lam (Thích Pháp Hòa). (2015, June 10). *Đấng Mâu Ni Cao Đẹp 1 - Thầy Thích Pháp Hòa giảng tại Chùa Hải Đức Regina* [Video File]. Retrieved from https://www.youtube.com/watch?v=_N9HGB-2cMo&feature=youtu.be

Truc Lam (Thích Pháp Hòa). (2015, June 12). *Đấng Mâu Ni Cao Đẹp 2 - Thầy Thích Pháp Hòa giảng tại Chùa Hải Đức Regina* [Video File]. Retrieved from https://www.youtube.com/watch?v=xxss6ld5OEY&feature=youtu.be

Truc Lam (Thích Pháp Hòa). (2015, June 12). *Đấng Mâu Ni Cao Đẹp 3-Thầy Thích Pháp Hòa giảng tại Chùa Hải Đức Regina* [Video File]. Retrieved from https://www.youtube.com/watch?v=gsDt1rnh04c&feature=youtu.be

Truc Lam (Thích Pháp Hòa). (2013, December 26). *Đẹp Xấu Giàu Nghèo - Thầy Thích Pháp Hòa (Dec.16, 2007)* [Video File]. Retrieved from https://www.youtube.com/watch?v=t3o9gDwQAbQ

Truc Lam (Thích Pháp Hòa). (2019, January 30). *Độ Người Thân - Thầy Thích Pháp Hòa (Chùa Hải Đức , Ngày 18.8.2018)* [Video File]. Retrieved from https://www.youtube.com/watch?v=6jWz8ixEpHM&feature=youtu.be

Truc Lam (Thích Pháp Hòa). (2013, December 30).*Hạnh Phúc Chân Thật - Thầy Thích Pháp Hòa* [Video File]. Retrieved from https://www.youtube.com/watch?v=FBm92-vhpvU&feature=youtu.be

Truc Lam (Thích Pháp Hòa). (2018, August 3). **Hạnh Phúc Được Làm Người** - *Thầy Thích Pháp Hòa (Chùa Giác Lâm , ngày 12.5.2018)* [Video File]. Retrieved from https://www.youtube.com/watch?v=AH_R9ewbIAg&feature=youtu.be

Truc Lam (Thích Pháp Hòa). (2013, December 30). **Hạnh Trẻ Thơ - Thầy. Thích Pháp Hòa** [Video File]. Retrieved from https://www.youtube.com/watch?v=IqpeUUWIrEo&feature=youtu.be

Truc Lam (Thích Pháp Hòa). (2018, December 19). *Hướng Đẹp - Thầy Thích Pháp Hòa (Ngày 23.9.2018)* [Video File]. Retrieved from https://www.youtube.com/watch?v=RqpMWqUnMac&feature=youtu.be

Truc Lam (Thích Pháp Hòa). (2016, April 11). *Hướng Về Kính Lạy - Thầy. Thích Pháp Hòa* [Video File]. Retrieved from https://www.youtube.com/watch?v=23RWffwAglA&feature=youtu.be

Truc Lam (Thích Pháp Hòa). (2019, July 19). *Khó Thay Sống Đời Lành - Thầy Thích Pháp Hòa (Tv, Phổ Đức Calgary AB Ngày 19.5.2019)* [Video File]. Retrieved from https://www.youtube.com/watch?v=fRbu36KprY0

Truc Lam (Thích Pháp Hòa). (2011, March 17). *Kinh Dược Sư - Tỏa Ánh Lưu Ly 2 -Thầy. Thích Pháp Hòa* [Video File]. Retrieved from https://www.youtube.com/watch?v=1IKrny8n-Dw

Truc Lam (Thích Pháp Hòa). (2011, March 18). *Kinh Dược Sư - Tỏa Ánh Lưu Ly 3 -Thầy. Thích Pháp Hòa* [Video File]. Retrieved from https://www.youtube.com/watch?v=BDkIIcqkW8Q

Truc Lam (Thích Pháp Hòa). (2018, November 14). *Làm Đẹp Quốc Độ Của Mình - Thầy Thích Pháp Hòa (TV. Tuệ Viên, Toronto , 1.7.2018)* [Video File]. Retrieved from https://www.youtube.com/watch?v=k32EA_In2uY&feature=youtu.be

Truc Lam (Thích Pháp Hòa). (2018, April 9). *Làm Mới 2 (Vấn Đáp) - Thầy Thích Pháp Hòa (Memorial Hall 24.9.2017)* [Video File]. Retrieved from https://www.youtube.com/watch?v=soQNtgfuiiI&feature=youtu.be

Truc Lam (Thích Pháp Hòa). (2015, February 1). *Lời Cảnh Tỉnh - Thầy. Thích Pháp Hòa (Sep.27, 2014)* [Video File]. Retrieved from https://www.youtube.com/watch?v=lJ6JUW60ph4

Truc Lam (Thích Pháp Hòa). (2018, April 25). *Lục Độ - Thần Thông 1 - Thầy. Thích Pháp Hòa (cực hay 20.10.2017)* [Video File]. Retrieved from https://www.youtube.com/watch?v=i6mZsX_9Ir0&feature=youtu.be

Truc Lam (Thích Pháp Hòa). (2018, April 27). *Lục Độ - Thần Thông 2 Thầy Thích Pháp Hòa (Tu Viện Huyền Quang TX , Ngày 20.10.2017)* [Video File]. Retrieved from https://www.youtube.com/watch?v=b7sxaoFLdaE&feature=youtu.be

Truc Lam (Thích Pháp Hòa). (2011, January 16). *Thầy Thích Pháp Hòa - Lục Thông (January 16, 2011)* [Video File]. Retrieved from https://www.youtube.com/watch?v=lQAtWmVQb6o

Truc Lam (Thích Pháp Hòa). (2015, July 9) *Mồi Đèn Tiếp Lửa - Thầy Thích Pháp Hòa giảng tại Chùa Hải Đức (May 24 , 2015)* [Video File]. Retrieved from https://www.youtube.com/watch?v=5__AqU3R4vY&feature=youtu.be

Truc Lam (Thích Pháp Hòa). (2011, February 11). *Thầy. Thích Pháp Hòa - Mười Hai Duyên Khởi (phần 1)* [Video File]. Retrieved from https://www.youtube.com/watch?v=IJUU3Y9SHk8&feature=youtu.be

Truc Lam (Thích Pháp Hòa). (2011, February 11). *Thầy. Thích Pháp Hòa - Mười Hai Duyên Khởi (phần 2)* [Video File]. Retrieved from https://www.youtube.com/watch?v=41YqZtaXc2s&feature=youtu.be

Truc Lam (Thích Pháp Hòa). (2017, April 26). *Năm Đóa Hoa Lành 1 - Thầy. Thích Pháp Hòa (April 8, 2017)* [Video File]. Retrieved from https://www.youtube.com/watch?v=Jg89JlzVbBc&feature=youtu.be

Truc Lam (Thích Pháp Hòa). (2017, April 28). *Năm Đóa Hoa Lành 2 - Thầy. Thích Pháp Hòa (April 8, 2017)* [Video File]. Retrieved from https://www.youtube.com/watch?v=YhI_4i2H5f8&feature=youtu.be

Truc Lam (Thích Pháp Hòa). (2019, June 5). *Năng Lực Của Kinh - Thầy Thích Pháp Hòa (Chùa Việt Nam Seattle. WA Ngày 30.3.2019)* [Video File]. Retrieved from https://www.youtube.com/watch?v=9GNUonmRJRo

Truc Lam (Thích Pháp Hòa). (2018, November 5). *Nghiệp Và Nguyện (Vấn Đáp) - Thầy Thích Pháp Hòa (Toronto , ngày 1.9.2018)* [Video File]. Retrieved from https://www.youtube.com/watch?v=1Tbu9KtTY_A&feature=youtu.be

Truc Lam (Thích Pháp Hòa). (2018, March 9). *Người Mạnh Nhất - Thầy Thích Pháp Hòa (Chuyến Hoằng Pháp Châu Âu 6.6.2017)* [Video File]. Retrieved from https://www.youtube.com/watch?v=eVcn54SZrxs&feature=youtu.be

Truc Lam (Thích Pháp Hòa). (2018, February 26). *Người Sống Có Ý Thức - Thầy Thích Pháp Hòa (Chuyến Hoằng Pháp Bắc Mỹ 18.10.2017)* [Video File]. Retrieved from https://www.youtube.com/watch?v=fsqPOcuaUZ8&feature=youtu.be

Truc Lam (Thích Pháp Hòa). (2019, July 3). *Người Tỏa Sáng - Thầy Thích Pháp Hòa (Chùa Bảo Quang, TX Ngày 29.4.2019)* [Video File]. Retrieved from https://www.youtube.com/watch?v=CMtQ-cGxZ7k

Truc Lam (Thích Pháp Hòa). (2018, February 7). *Người Trụ Trì - Thầy Thích Pháp Hòa* [Video File]. Retrieved from https://www.youtube.com/watch?v=2k8FaOs5-vU&feature=youtu.be

Truc Lam (Thích Pháp Hòa). (2012, September 28). *Nhân Lành Quả Đẹp 1 - Thầy. Thích Pháp Hòa tại Regina, SK(April 28 , 2012)* [Video File]. Retrieved from https://www.youtube.com/watch?v=e4DWQOrH6_Y&t=2811s

Truc Lam (Thích Pháp Hòa). (2013, October 11). *Nhân Lành Quả Đẹp 2 - Thầy. Thích Pháp Hòa tại Regina, SK (April 29 , 2012)* [Video File]. Retrieved from https://www.youtube.com/watch?v=y7zzK-eVpSc

Truc Lam (Thích Pháp Hòa). (2019, July 15). *Nhị Đế Dung Thông - Thầy Thích Pháp Hòa (Chùa Diệu Đế Pensacola FL Ngày 7.6.2019)* [Video File]. Retrieved from https://www.youtube.com/watch?v=nlpR5WdnfP8

Truc Lam (Thích Pháp Hòa). (2019, June 14). *Như Lai Bát Tướng 1 - Thầy Thích Pháp Hòa (TV Huyền Quang Ngày 24.4.2018)* [Video File]. Retrieved from https://www.youtube.com/watch?v=NmHqLUmqbqI

Truc Lam (Thích Pháp Hòa). (2019, June 19). *Như Lai Bát Tướng 2 - Thầy Thích Pháp Hòa (TV Huyền Quang , TX Ngày 24.4.2019)* [Video File]. Retrieved from https://www.youtube.com/watch?v=cLnkppEp2mc

Truc Lam (Thích Pháp Hòa). (2013, July 27). *Nước Từ Rửa Sạch Oan Khiên 1 - Thầy. Thích Pháp Hòa (Jan. 5, 2013)* [Video File]. Retrieved from https://www.youtube.com/watch?v=k9XDFWBNCUo&feature=youtu.be

Truc Lam (Thích Pháp Hòa). (2018, October 22). *Pháp Hoa Bảy Dụ 1 - Thầy Thích Pháp Hòa (TV Huyền Quang, TX Ngày 6.4.2018)* [Video File]. Retrieved from https://www.youtube.com/watch?v=atdyIx_PAzs&feature=youtu.be

Truc Lam (Thích Pháp Hòa). (2017, May 26). *Phật Có Trong Xe Không? - Thầy. Thích Pháp Hòa (Mar 4, 2017)* [Video File]. Retrieved from https://www.youtube.com/watch?v=cc23GsOU3AE&feature=youtu.be

Truc Lam (Thích Pháp Hòa). (2019, March 1). *Phát Nguyện - Hồi Hướng - Thầy Thích Pháp Hòa (Chùa Viên Giác , Oklahoma 15 11 2018)* [Video File]. Retrieved from https://www.youtube.com/watch?v=QVyoXRqNyGg&feature=youtu.be

Truc Lam (Thích Pháp Hòa). (2014, January 12). *Phương Châm Học Đạo -Thầy. Thích Pháp Hòa - Düsseldorf, Germany (Nov.3, 2013)* [Video File]. Retrieved from https://www.youtube.com/watch?v=WSPzkydSgqA&feature=youtu.be

Truc Lam (Thích Pháp Hòa). (2018, April 11). *Rộng Kết Duyên Lành -Thầy Thích Pháp Hòa (Chuyến Hoằng Pháp Châu Âu , Đức Quốc 22.6.2017)* [Video File]. Retrieved from https://www.youtube.com/watch?v=BUq540RYH7E&feature=youtu.be

Truc Lam (Thích Pháp Hòa). (2018, April 2). *Sống " Hơn " Chân Thật - Thầy Thích Pháp Hòa (Chùa Thập Phương , Bronx NY 26.11.2017)* [Video File]. Retrieved from https://www.youtube.com/watch?v=fDWb03Kv3G8

Truc Lam (Thích Pháp Hòa). (2015, June 28). *Sự Kiện Đời Người - Thầy Thích Pháp Hòa (jun 14 , 2015)* [Video File]. Retrieved from https://www.youtube.com/watch?v=idUjd4ijBcU&feature=youtu.be

Truc Lam (Thích Pháp Hòa). (2012, April 13). *Tài Sản Chân Thật - Thầy Pháp Hòa tại Saskatoon, SK (May.31, 2009)* [Video File]. Retrieved from https://www.youtube.com/watch?v=YFuVA5eaqH4&feature=youtu.be

Truc Lam (Thích Pháp Hòa). (2015, August 24). *Tấm Lòng Cho Nhau (Vấn Đáp) - Thầy Thích Pháp Hòa July 15 , 2015* [Video File]. Retrieved from https://www.youtube.com/watch?v=xzAVdvIWBeQ&feature=youtu.be

Truc Lam (Thích Pháp Hòa). (2018, June 11). *Tham Và Dục (Vấn Đáp) - Thầy Thích Pháp Hòa (Chùa Hải Hội, Winnipeg 20.1.2018)* [Video File]. Retrieved from https://www.youtube.com/watch?v=hBUibqBJk1o&feature=youtu.be

Truc Lam (Thích Pháp Hòa). (2018, November 9). *Thần Thông Không Bằng Đạo Thông - Thầy Thích Pháp Hòa (Ngày 16.9.2018)* [Video File]. Retrieved from https://www.youtube.com/watch?v=Q7c49CMI430

Truc Lam (Thích Pháp Hòa). (2016, April 26). *Thế Gian Tam Phước - Thầy. Thích Pháp Hòa tại Winnepeg,MB (Jun.21, 2009)* [Video File]. Retrieved from https://www.youtube.com/watch?v=C1YQRZBAS84

Truc Lam (Thích Pháp Hòa). (2017, May 18). *Thù Thắng Của Ba La Mật - Thầy Thích Pháp Hòa (Chùa Đông Hưng ngày 28.10.2017)* [Video File]. Retrieved from https://www.youtube.com/watch?v=oS01MyIwIaY&feature=youtu.be

Truc Lam (Thích Pháp Hòa). (2011, January 15). *Thầy Thích Pháp Hòa - Thuyền Tuệ Sang Sông (phần 1/6)* [Video File]. Retrieved from https://www.youtube.com/watch?v=0hFjTux-3Vg&feature=youtu.be

Truc Lam (Thích Pháp Hòa). (2011, January 15). *Thầy Thích Pháp Hòa - Thuyền Tuệ Sang Sông (phần 2/6)* [Video File]. Retrieved from https://www.youtube.com/watch?v=S-9y2aCV5oo&feature=youtu.be

Truc Lam (Thích Pháp Hòa). (2011, January 16). *Thầy Thích Pháp Hòa - Thuyền Tuệ Sang Sông (phần 3/6)* [Video File]. Retrieved from https://www.youtube.com/watch?v=QMu3IUnwrEs&feature=youtu.be

Truc Lam (Thích Pháp Hòa). (2011, January 16). *Thầy Thích Pháp Hòa - Thuyền Tuệ Sang Sông (phần 4/6)* [Video File]. Retrieved from https://www.youtube.com/watch?v=gOytoq2O5us&feature=youtu.be

Truc Lam (Thích Pháp Hòa). (2011, January 16). *Thầy Thích Pháp Hòa - Thuyền Tuệ Sang Sông (phần 5/6)* [Video File]. Retrieved from https://www.youtube.com/watch?v=R2XTEnnIMBs&feature=youtu.be

Truc Lam (Thích Pháp Hòa). (2011, January 16). *Thầy Thích Pháp Hòa - Thuyền Tuệ Sang Sông (phần 6/6)* [Video File]. Retrieved from https://www.youtube.com/watch?v=7bGIwMtBa6o&feature=youtu.be

Truc Lam (Thích Pháp Hòa). (2019, February 11). *Tín Nguyện Hạnh Trong Đời Sống - Thầy Thích Pháp Hòa (Melbourne, Ngày 2.11.2018)* [Video File]. Retrieved from https://www.youtube.com/watch?v=r4fCmgGXruQ&feature=youtu.be

Truc Lam (Thích Pháp Hòa). (2019, April 19). *Tinh Tấn Đường Tu - Thầy Thích Pháp Hòa (Sydney , ngày 11.11.2018)* [Video File]. Retrieved from https://www.youtube.com/watch?v=jodoOOD9aQ4&feature=youtu.be

Truc Lam (Thích Pháp Hòa). (2015, July 9). *Trí Lực của Như Lai 1 - Thầy Thích Pháp Hòa giảng tại Chùa Hải Đức (May 23, 2015)* [Video File]. Retrieved from https://www.youtube.com/watch?v=56P7v4xTKF4&feature=youtu.be

Truc Lam (Thích Pháp Hòa). (2018, May 30). *Tu Giải Thoát - Thầy Thích Pháp Hòa (Chùa Giác Nguyên , ngày 26.11.2017)* [Video File]. Retrieved from https://www.youtube.com/watch?v=uKOm_WOJUQY&feature=youtu.be

Truc Lam (Thích Pháp Hòa). (2016, April 23). *Tu Là Sửa (vấn đáp)-Thầy. Thích Pháp Hòa (April 10, 2016)* [Video File]. Retrieved from https://www.youtube.com/watch?v=-IQYbJEUf9w&feature=youtu.be

Truc Lam (Thích Pháp Hòa). (2017, December 30). *Tu Thế Nào Cho Mau Vãng Sanh (Vấn Đáp) - Thầy Thích Pháp Hòa (11.06.2017)* [Video File]. Retrieved from https://www.youtube.com/watch?v=atnOYRr2K2M&feature=youtu.be

Truc Lam (Thích Pháp Hòa). (2017, March 24). *Tuệ Giác Qua Bờ 1 - Thầy. Thích Pháp Hòa (Dec 24, 2016)* [Video File]. Retrieved from https://www.youtube.com/watch?v=s_c_L5_L1Ms&feature=youtu.be

Truc Lam (Thích Pháp Hòa). (2017, March 27). *Tuệ Giác Qua Bờ 2 - Thầy. Thích Pháp Hòa (Jan 7, 2017)* [Video File]. Retrieved from https://www.youtube.com/watch?v=U0y4COXpfYs&feature=youtu.be

Truc Lam (Thích Pháp Hòa). (2015, January 6). *Tùy Cơ Ứng Vật - Thầy. Thích Pháp Hòa (Oct.25, 2014)* [Video File]. Retrieved from https://www.youtube.com/watch?v=Z7Yk17JSBwk&feature=youtu.be

Truc Lam (Thích Pháp Hòa). (2013, December 19). *Vạn Phước - Thầy Thích Pháp Hòa, San Diego, Jul.9 2013* [Video File]. Retrieved from https://www.youtube.com/watch?v=MYeTCyNArsA&feature=youtu.be

Truc Lam (Thích Pháp Hòa). (2012, February 27). *Vạn Sự Cát Tường - Thầy. Thích Pháp Hòa tại Regina, SK (Jan.1, 2012)* [Video File]. Retrieved from https://www.youtube.com/watch?v=k-FxixcvGsQ&feature=youtu.be

Truc Lam (Thích Pháp Hòa). (2011, March 7). *"Về Với Nguồn Tâm" - Thầy. Thích Pháp Hòa –Kinh Địa Tạng 1* [Video File]. Retrieved from https://www.youtube.com/watch?v=pyh7j37hKf4&feature=youtu.be

Truc Lam (Thích Pháp Hòa). (2017, April 5). *Viên Ngọc Pháp Hoa - Thầy. Thích Pháp Hòa (Nov 18, 2015)* [Video File]. Retrieved from https://www.youtube.com/watch?v=Ujn5CW1yKAU&feature=youtu.be

Truc Lam (Thích Pháp Hòa). (2016, May 16). *Vượt Tứ Tướng 1 - Thầy. Thích Pháp Hòa (April 21, 2016)* [Video File]. Retrieved from https://www.youtube.com/watch?v=QYCNtWNkkac&feature=youtu.be

Truc Lam (Thích Pháp Hòa). (2016, May 18). *Vượt Tứ Tướng 2 - Thầy. Thích Pháp Hòa (April 21, 2016)* [Video File]. Retrieved from https://www.youtube.com/watch?v=1zuORmfmqqQ&feature=youtu.be

Truc Lam (Thích Pháp Hòa). (2018, August 11). *Ý nghĩa Ngũ Uẩn (vấn đáp 2018 rất vui) - Thầy Thích Pháp Hòa* [Video File]. Retrieved from https://www.youtube.com/watch?v=oe7Gk6Xb1k0&feature=youtu.be

Truyền Thông Phật Giáo. (2017, August 14). *Vấn đáp Phật Pháp - Thầy Thích Pháp Hòa [quá hay]* [Video File]. Retrieved from https://www.youtube.com/watch?v=WbtjhY0-f3s&feature=youtu.be

Tự Điển Phật Học. *Thư Viện Hoa Sen.* (2016, August 9). Retrieved from https://thuvienhoasen.org/a26048/tu-dien-phat-hoc-online

Từ Ngữ Phật Học Việt -Anh. *Quảng Đức Buddhist Homepage.* (2013, August 4). Retrieved from https://quangduc.com/a4061/tu-ngu-phat-hoc-viet-anh

Tu Viện Huyền Quang. (2015, June 8). *PHÁP MÔN KHÔNG HAI (phần 1) TT Thích Pháp Hòa* [Video File]. Retrieved from https://www.youtube.com/watch?v=arqLz8BNClY&feature=youtu.be

Tu Viện Huyền Quang. (2015, June 8). *PHÁP MÔN KHÔNG HAI (phần 2) TT Thích Pháp Hòa* [Video File]. Retrieved from https://www.youtube.com/watch?v=QxUYgeM5j3Y&feature=youtu.be

Tu Viện Huyền Quang. (2015, June 8). *PHÁP MÔN KHÔNG HAI (phần 3) TT Thích Pháp Hòa* [Video File]. Retrieved from https://www.youtube.com/watch?v=orP3nzVW_YY&feature=youtu.be

Tu Viện Huyền Quang. (2016, May 18). *Vượt Tứ Tướng Phần 5 (Kinh LƯƠNG HOÀNG SÁM- Sám Pháp Khoa Nghi)* [Video File]. Retrieved from https://www.youtube.com/watch?v=-QUaULmerjA&feature=youtu.be

TuVien TrucLam. (2019, January 28). *Ân Nghĩa Hằng Ngày - Thầy. Thích Pháp Hòa (chùa Hồng An, Melbourne, Nov 3, 2018)* [Video File]. Retrieved from https://www.youtube.com/watch?v=cCSq0haPeeo&t=1s

TuVien TrucLam. (2015, August 16). *Bậc Phước Điền - Thầy. Thích Pháp Hòa (chùa Phổ Minh, June 7, 2015)* [Video File]. Retrieved from https://www.youtube.com/watch?v=VzZw4nna5z8

TuVien TrucLam. (2015, January 2). *Bàn Tay Mầu Nhiệm - Thầy. Thích Pháp Hòa (Nov.2,2014)* [Video File]. Retrieved from https://www.youtube.com/watch?v=Qu8ezflrsho

TuVien TrucLam. (2018, July 23). *Bảy Phương Pháp Chuyển Hóa (Nhứt Thiết Lậu Hoặc) –Thầy. Thích Pháp Hòa (2003)* [Video File]. Retrieved from https://www.youtube.com/watch?v=bif8OHD_5nc

TuVien TrucLam. (2016, June 26). *Biết Chướng, Vượt Chướng (vấn đáp) - Thầy. Thích Pháp Hòa (Düsseldorf Germany, Nov.3, 2013)* [Video File]. Retrieved from https://www.youtube.com/watch?v=wmTx84820UM&feature=youtu.be

TuVien TrucLam. (2018, May 4). *Biết Vô Thường để Sống Thường - Thầy. Thích Pháp Hòa (Tv.Trúc Lâm, Feb.11, 2018)* [Video File]. Retrieved from https://www.youtube.com/watch?v=GPe94yViAkQ&feature=youtu.be

TuVien TrucLam. (2017, June 2). *Bốn Pháp Sanh Phước - Thầy. Thích Pháp Hòa (Oct.17, 2010)* [Video File]. Retrieved from https://www.youtube.com/watch?v=PMxA6iTzc6M&feature=youtu.be

TuVien TrucLam. (2014, July 21). *Cách Hóa Giải Chướng Duyên 1 - Thầy. Thích Pháp Hòa (July 6, 2003)* [Video File]. Retrieved from https://www.youtube.com/watch?v=y0U33GgNNcc&feature=youtu.be

TuVien TrucLam. (2014, July 30). *Cách hóa Giải Chướng Duyên 2 - Thầy. Thích Pháp Hòa (July 13, 2003)* [Video File]. Retrieved from https://www.youtube.com/watch?v=j8tFnn_LWdc&feature=youtu.be

TuVien TrucLam. (2015, October 9). *Chí Nguyện Siêu Việt 2 - Thầy. Thích Pháp Hòa (Jan.10, 2015)* [Video File]. Retrieved from https://www.youtube.com/watch?v=LR9br4op52E&feature=youtu.be

TuVien TrucLam. (2015, May 22). *Chí Nguyện Siêu Việt 3 - Thầy Thích Pháp Hòa (january 17, 2015)* [Video File]. Retrieved from https://www.youtube.com/watch?v=4SqdKpylOFM&feature=youtu.be

TuVien TrucLam. (2015, February 22). *Chùa Đất Phật Vàng - Thầy. Thích Pháp Hòa (Dec.14, 2014)* [Video File]. Retrieved from https://www.youtube.com/watch?v=YM7PJ1Px5Sk&feature=youtu.be

TuVien TrucLam. (2015, March 3). *Chướng Ngại của Người Tu - Thầy. Thích Pháp Hòa (Dec.14, 2014)* [Video File]. Retrieved from https://www.youtube.com/watch?v=aKPLQQHCK-Y&feature=youtu.be

TuVien TrucLam. (2015, June 23). *Cúng Dường Trai Tăng - Thầy. Thích Pháp Hòa (Apr.12, 2015)* [Video File]. Retrieved from https://www.youtube.com/watch?v=tzS7DignG9o&feature=youtu.be

TuVien TrucLam. (2017, January 5). *Đời Là Một Chuyến Hành Hương - Thầy. Thích Pháp Hòa (Tv.Trúc Lâm, Dec.4, 2016)* [Video File]. Retrieved from https://www.youtube.com/watch?v=LcOTU7SceCc

TuVien TrucLam. (2016, March 4). *Được Người Thương Mến - Thầy. Thích Pháp Hòa (chùa Tâm Quang, Mar.5, 2016)* [Video File]. Retrieved from https://www.youtube.com/watch?v=fQZks7iMF3o&feature=youtu.be

TuVien TrucLam. (2016, July 14). *Gạn Đục Khơi Trong - Thầy. Thích Pháp Hòa (chùa Hải Đức, Nov.20, 2005)* [Video File]. Retrieved from https://www.youtube.com/watch?v=nJK2ZnYjFvI

TuVien TrucLam. (2016, May 10). **Hạnh** Con Khỉ *- Thầy. Thích Pháp Hòa (Busan Hàn Quốc, Apr.3, 2016)* [Video File]. Retrieved from https://www.youtube.com/watch?v=W35EroTLwzQ

TuVien TrucLam. (2016, August 2). **Hạnh** *Thương Yêu - Thầy. Thích Pháp Hòa (Jan.16, 2010)* [Video File]. Retrieved from https://www.youtube.com/watch?v=5gL5fuBA4kI&feature=youtu.be

TuVien TrucLam. (2016, February 29). *Hoằng Pháp Lợi Sanh - Thầy. Thích Pháp Hòa (chùa Hoằng Pháp, Melbourne, Nov.3, 2015)* [Video File]. Retrieved from https://www.youtube.com/watch?v=xWX7I0MWxWM&feature=youtu.be

TuVien TrucLam. (2018, October 18). *"Lửa" Của Người Tu - Thầy. Thích Pháp Hòa (Tv.TrucLam, Oct 14, 2018)* [Video File]. Retrieved from https://www.youtube.com/watch?v=gVxW8ykgRAw&feature=youtu.be

TuVien TrucLam. (2017, February 28). *Lưỡi Kiếm Văn Thù - Thầy. Thích Pháp Hòa (chùa Văn Thù, July 1, 2015)* [Video File]. Retrieved from https://www.youtube.com/watch?v=0wE-_MuaKS0&feature=youtu.be

TuVien TrucLam. (2015, June 11). *Middle Path - Thay. Thich Phap Hoa (Apr. 24,2015)* [Video File]. Retrieved from https://www.youtube.com/watch?v=7F3A-ebtGo8&feature=youtu.be

TuVien TrucLam. (2015, January 19). *Mộng - Thầy. Thích Pháp Hòa (Oct.2,2014)* [Video File]. Retrieved from https://www.youtube.com/watch?v=zexCSkgWSUs&feature=youtu.be

TuVien TrucLam. (2015, March 1). *Một Ngày Hai Việc Thiện - Thầy. Thích Pháp Hòa (Dec.28,2014)* [Video File]. Retrieved from https://www.youtube.com/watch?v=_lUNEpsSzow&feature=youtu.be

TuVien TrucLam. (2016, March 16). *Mưa Dầm Thấm Lâu - Thầy. Thích Pháp Hòa (chùa Linh Sơn, Brisbane, Nov.14, 2015)* [Video File]. Retrieved from https://www.youtube.com/watch?v=3i8TDFbQigc&feature=youtu.be

TuVien TrucLam. (2015, July 15). *Mưa Thấm Đất Tâm - Thầy. Thích Pháp Hòa (Vô Lượng Quang, June 20, 2015)* [Video File]. Retrieved from https://www.youtube.com/watch?v=h2A2rO8eIKY&feature=youtu.be

TuVien TrucLam. (2017, May 12). *Năm Tướng Của Vạn Pháp - Thầy. Thích Pháp Hòa (Tv.Huyền Quang, Apr.6, 2017)* [Video File]. Retrieved from https://www.youtube.com/watch?v=bFn52F8dxfo&feature=youtu.be

TuVien TrucLam. (2015, July 16). *Người Khó Ước Lượng - Thầy. Thích Pháp Hòa (VôLượngQuang, June 20, 2015)* [Video File]. Retrieved from https://www.youtube.com/watch?v=ZEzKz2nMwtw&feature=youtu.be

TuVien TrucLam. (2016, April 21). *Người Nào Nghiệp Nấy - Thầy. Thích Pháp Hòa (Pháp Giới Đạo Tràng Perth, Nov.12, 2015)* [Video File]. Retrieved from https://www.youtube.com/watch?v=3yG4C9PMAPs&feature=youtu.be

TuVien TrucLam. (2018, June 28). *Những Bước Thăng Trầm - Thầy. Thích Pháp Hòa (June 15, 2003)* [Video File]. Retrieved from https://www.youtube.com/watch?v=mFhXFwfJgp4&feature=youtu.be

TuVien TrucLam. (2017, April 27). *Nỗ Lực & Kiên Trì - Thầy. Thích Pháp Hòa (chùa Hải Đức, Jan.15, 2017)* [Video File]. Retrieved from https://www.youtube.com/watch?v=HcU-MZUcTyk&feature=youtu.be

TuVien TrucLam. (2017, July 11). *No Mud No Lotus - Thay. Thich Phap Hoa (Sept.19, 2008)* [Video File]. Retrieved from https://www.youtube.com/watch?v=xz-Cdp8xETg&feature=youtu.be

TuVien TrucLam. (2017, November 28). *Nuôi Dưỡng Niệm Lành - Thầy. Thích Pháp Hòa (Tv.TrucLam, July 23, 2017)* [Video File]. Retrieved from https://www.youtube.com/watch?v=h2uUpLz50CQ&feature=youtu.be

TuVien TrucLam. (2015, March 10). *Ổn Định Đời Sống - Thầy. Thích Pháp Hòa (Jan.11, 2015)* [Video File]. Retrieved from https://www.youtube.com/watch?v=6SgPot70cj0&feature=youtu.be

TuVien TrucLam. (2015, October 10). *Pháp **Hạnh** Của Phật - Thầy. Thích Pháp Hòa (chùa Lâm Tỳ Ni, June 18, 2015)* [Video File]. Retrieved from https://www.youtube.com/watch?v=Ww2-kcj5ZF0&feature=youtu.be

TuVien TrucLam. (2017, February 3). *Reflecting to live a better life - Thay. Thich Phap Hoa (Dec.18, 2016)* [Video File]. Retrieved from https://www.youtube.com/watch?reload=9&v=yNM9KgCHT6w&feature=youtu.be

TuVien TrucLam. (2015, October 23). *Ruộng Phước Nhiệm Mầu 1 - Thầy. Thích Pháp Hòa (Aug.4, 2015)* [Video File]. Retrieved from https://www.youtube.com/watch?v=Bo5ZKJJmMMs&feature=youtu.be

TuVien TrucLam. (2015, October 13). *Sống Đời Cần Thực Hiện - Thầy. Thích Pháp Hòa (chùa Lâm Tỳ Ni, June 18, 2015)* [Video File]. Retrieved from https://www.youtube.com/watch?v=wDsVcIcWaok&feature=youtu.be

TuVien TrucLam. (2016, February 22). *Sức Hấp Dẫn - Thầy. Thích Pháp Hòa (Charlotte NC,Dec.13, 2015)* [Video File]. Retrieved from https://www.youtube.com/watch?v=KfLvxBRw4zE&feature=youtu.be

TuVien TrucLam. (2017, April 15). *Tâm Không Dính Mắc 1 (vấn đáp) - Thầy. Thích Pháp Hòa (chùa Tâm Quang, May 3, 2016)* [Video File]. Retrieved from https://www.youtube.com/watch?v=WRX58_-vrLM&feature=youtu.be

TuVien TrucLam. (2017, April 16). *Tâm Không Dính Mắc 2 (vấn đáp) - Thầy. Thích Pháp Hòa (chùa Tâm Quang, May 3, 2016)* [Video File]. Retrieved from https://www.youtube.com/watch?v=CVmvTShhmIs&feature=youtu.be

TuVien TrucLam. (2019, February 10). *The Highest Wealth - Thay. Thich Phap Hoa (Jan 16, 2010)* [Video File]. Retrieved from https://www.youtube.com/watch?v=UKGETHEx_SA&feature=youtu.be

TuVien TrucLam. (2015, October 2). *Tiếng Chuông Tỉnh Thức - Thầy. Thích Pháp Hòa (July 26, 2015)* [Video File]. Retrieved from https://www.youtube.com/watch?v=mPALv6MsD10&feature=youtu.be

TuVien TrucLam. (2016, June 24). *Trong Bùn Có Sen - Thầy. Thích Pháp Hòa (chùa Hoa Sen, Augusta, May 9, 2016)* [Video File]. Retrieved from https://www.youtube.com/watch?v=sFXG7VKTkNg&feature=youtu.be

TuVien TrucLam. (2015, November 4). *Tranh Cải Để Được Gì? 1 - Thầy. Thích Pháp Hòa (Oct.3, 2015)* [Video File]. Retrieved from https://www.youtube.com/watch?v=VCxBXO8aEfo

TuVien TrucLam. (2015, November 1). *Tu Nhà - Tu Chợ - Tu Chùa - Thầy. Thích Pháp Hòa (HươngVânAm, Sep.27, 2015)* [Video File]. Retrieved from https://www.youtube.com/watch?v=BZ6vvb0LF9A&feature=youtu.be

TuVien TrucLam. (2018, February 15). *Tu Nhân Tích Đức - Thầy. Thích Pháp Hòa (chùa Bảo Đức, Oberhausen, Đức Quốc 15-6-2017)* [Video File]. Retrieved from https://www.youtube.com/watch?v=mtAl0wtCq8s&feature=youtu.be

TuVien TrucLam. (2012, April 28). *Tứ Như Ý Túc - Thầy.Thích Pháp Hòa* [Video File]. Retrieved from https://www.youtube.com/watch?v=5WYQfA-wtM4&t=1s

TuVien TrucLam. (2016, May 17). *Tùy Cơ Ứng Vật 2 - Thầy. Thích Pháp Hòa (TV.Trúc Lâm, Oct.25, 2014)* [Video File]. Retrieved from https://www.youtube.com/watch?v=LSrhqf5pg6I&feature=youtu.be

TuVien TrucLam. (2015, May 7). *Tùy Nghiệp Thọ Sanh (vấn đáp) - Thầy. Thích Pháp Hòa (March 29, 2015)* [Video File]. Retrieved from https://www.youtube.com/watch?v=jPPRU22mhkk&feature=youtu.be

TuVien TrucLam. (2019, August 3). *Using Our Three Bodies - Thay Thich Phap Hoa (12. 4. 2019)* [Video File] Retrieved from https://www.youtube.com/watch?v=YR6Bfw4BLnA

TuVien TrucLam. (2017, March 13). *View Things As They Are! - Thay. Thich Phap Hoa (Feb.3, 2017)* [Video File]. Retrieved from https://www.youtube.com/watch?v=wo28Sowi-4A&feature=youtu.be

TuVien TrucLam. (2014, December 30). *Vô Sự (vấn đáp) - Thầy. Thích Pháp Hòa (April 28, 2014)* [Video File]. Retrieved from https://www.youtube.com/watch?v=0IedE_5Q_qA&feature=youtu.be

TuVien TrucLam. (2012, May 27). *Vốn ít Lời Nhiều - Thầy.Thích Pháp Hòa* [Video File]. Retrieved from https://www.youtube.com/watch?v=5jG3_0JAyM0&feature=youtu.be

TuVien TrucLam. (2016, June 28). *Vượt Tứ Tướng 3 - Thầy. Thích Pháp Hòa (Tv.Huyền Quang, Apr.22, 2016)* [Video File]. Retrieved from https://www.youtube.com/watch?v=0TWDWAqTguA&feature=youtu.be

TuVien TrucLam. (2016, June 19). *Xuất Gia - Tại Gia - Thầy. Thích Pháp Hòa (chùa Lâm Tỳ Ni, July 4, 2014)* [Video File]. Retrieved from https://www.youtube.com/watch?v=IYP8S8EX6TE&feature=youtu.be

TuVien TrucLam. (2017, October 12). *Ý Nghĩa Mùa An Cư - Thầy. Thích Pháp Hòa (June 29, 2003)* [Video File]. Retrieved from https://www.youtube.com/watch?v=a5zvdCCJZyI&feature=youtu.be

TuVien TrucLam. (2015, October 16). *Ý Nghĩa Nhất Tâm - Thầy. Thích Pháp Hòa (TV.Từ Vân, Aug.22, 2015)* [Video File]. Retrieved from https://www.youtube.com/watch?v=cFrFCrfLOEo&feature=youtu.be

Vấn đáp Thầy Thích Pháp Hòa. (2016, February 19). *Hoa Nghiêm - Thầy. Thích Pháp Hòa (Nov 4, 2015)* [Video File]. Retrieved from https://www.youtube.com/watch?v=FPLvSDwnNLs

Vấn đáp Thầy Thích Pháp Hòa. (2018, June 30). *Thế nào là Hư Không Vô Ngã? (vấn đáp 2018) - Thầy Thích Pháp Hòa* [Video File]. Retrieved from https://www.youtube.com/watch?v=JNMSOjdq5CE&feature=youtu.be

Vinh Nguyen. (2014, July 24). *Ý Nghĩa Ngày Vía Quán Thế Âm Thích Pháp Hòa* [Video File]. Retrieved from https://www.youtube.com/watch?v=kwYwHng-MRY&feature=youtu.be

About the Author

Christine H. Huynh, M.D. has been practicing in the field of Physical Medicine and Rehabilitation since 1998. She treats the physical body but finds the treatment of mental illness equally important. Here, she shares a topic that is dear to her heart: her understanding of the philosophy and practice of Buddhism, inspired by the innumerable and delightful sermons from the Venerable Thích Pháp Hòa.

About the Illustrator

Katarina A. Lazic is from Nis, Serbia. She specializes in the field of graphic design and digital arts, from layout and package design to illustrations and all the way to branding. She is very passionate about her work and profession. Here, she demonstrates her talent and skills in bringing the inanimate objects to life by providing significant details and character to each illustration.

www.ingramcontent.com/pod-product-compliance
Lightning Source LLC
Chambersburg PA
CBHW020137130526
44591CB00030B/77